THE RIGHT THING TO DO

Kit Saunders-Nordeen and the Rise of
Women's Intercollegiate Athletics
at the University of Wisconsin and Beyond

THE RIGHT THING TO DO

Kit Saunders-Nordeen and the Rise of
Women's Intercollegiate Athletics
at the University of Wisconsin and Beyond

DOUG MOE

Henschel
HAUS
publishing, inc.

Milwaukee, Wisconsin

Other books by Doug Moe:

The World of Mike Royko

*Lords of the Ring: The Triumph and Tragedy
of College Boxing's Greatest Team*

*Uncommon Sense: The Life of Marshall Erdman
(with Alice D'Alessio)*

Surrounded by Reality: The Best of Doug Moe on Madison

Favre: His Twenty Greatest Games

*Good Men: The Lives and Philanthropy of
Irwin A. and Robert D. Goodman*

*Tommy: My Journey of a Lifetime
(with Tommy G. Thompson)*

*Stroke Runner: My Story of Stroke, Survival,
Recovery, and Advocacy (with Eric Sarno)*

To the memory of Kit and Buzz

Published by
HenschelHAUS Publishing, Inc.
Milwaukee, Wisconsin
www.henschelHAU.S.books.com

ISBN: 978159598-889-8
E-ISBN: 978159598-890-4
LCCN: 2022931048

On the cover, top to bottom:
Relay race: Pam Moore
Volleyball: Liz Tortorello
Field hockey: Karen Lunda
Track: Cindy Bremser
Badminton: Ann French

Photos courtesy of UW athletics

TABLE OF CONTENTS

"The sort of sad thing about Title IX is that most schools began to comply not because it was the right thing to do… but because they were worried about the teeth that were in it and what the federal government could do."
Kit Saunders-Nordeen, 1995,
interviewed for the University of
Wisconsin Oral History Program.

"Wasn't it fun?"
Kit Saunders-Nordeen,
from a draft of a July 2, 2011 address to a
gathering of alumni of the Wisconsin women's crew,
a reunion that included some of its earliest members.

FOREWORD

K it's story provides a history of the evolution of women's athletics specifically at Wisconsin but also parallels the experiences of female sports enthusiasts before and after Title IX became law in 1972. Doug Moe captures so effectively Kit's journey, the challenges and successes. Kit frequently said, "we have made progress but there is more to be done." As we approach the 50th anniversary of Title IX we can celebrate the positive changes that have been made but we know that there is more to be done. We must remain vigilant and ensure that our daughters have the same opportunities and support as our sons. That is one of Kit's legacies that must be honored.

I met Kit during my sophomore year at Wisconsin when I became active in the Women's Recreation Association (WRA]. I loved sports all my life, mostly enjoying playing opportunities on the Milwaukee playgrounds with my male cousins and limited high school play days through the GAA (Girls Athletics Association). After enrolling at UW, I gravitated to the WRA with its sporadic sports days and occasional badminton tournaments. I immediately was impressed with Kit's enthusiasm, energy, passion and dedication to her role as advisor to the WRA. She truly believed in the value of sports competition for girls and women. She sincerely believed in equal opportunities for all.

At Kit's urging in my junior year, I accepted the role of WRA president and national president of the ARFCW (Athletic and Recreation Federation of College Women). Both of those opportunities were life changing in setting the course for my professional career, which would not have happened without the encouragement and support from Kit. She was an inspiring mentor and wonderful role model. I know that I'm not alone in acknowledging the positive influence that Kit had on so many of us... athletes, coaches, administrators, alumni, the Madison community, the Big Ten, local and national organizations.

Not only was Kit dedicated to "the right thing to do" but she effectively did things the right way. Forever grateful.

—Judy Sweet

Judy Sweet became the first female president of the NCAA in 1991 and served as the organization's senior vice president of championships from 2001-2006.

Chapter 1

CHAMPIONS

I t was cold for a November day in Pennsylvania. The forecast in State College was for light early morning snow, a high of 34. The weather caused a short delay in the 1984 NCAA Women's Cross-Country Championship, scheduled for an 11 a.m. start.

Penn State was hosting the 5,000-meter race, Nov. 19, 1984, over its Blue Golf Course. The school's two golf courses were named for the Penn State colors and the Blue is newer and longer than the White.

Stanford University was the favorite coming into the competition. The Cardinal's best runner, Regina Jacobs, was the pick to win the individual title. Jacobs later represented the United States in three Summer Olympic Games.

One team with an upset on its mind was the University of Wisconsin Badgers, the reigning Big Ten champions. They'd arrived by plane from Madison a day earlier, jogged the course and talked strategy with their coach, Peter Tegen, a native of Germany on the cusp of a legendary career.

While it was true no Wisconsin team had won a title in any sport since the NCAA began conducting women's national championships in 1981, Tegen had convinced his runners they had a legitimate chance. He never shied away from setting a high bar of accomplishment.

Decades later, Tegen remembered that cold November morning in Pennsylvania.

"We got to the course early and saw Stanford," Tegen said. "They were the favorites. They had quite a stable."

But they weren't used to running on snow-dusted ground in near freezing temperatures.

Tegen noticed immediately that the Stanford women were "wearing coats and all bundled up."

Tegen told his team, "Take your jackets off. Get out and stretch a little bit."

More than 40 years later, Tegen's best runner, Cathy Branta, a senior from Slinger, northwest of Milwaukee, recalled Tegen's order and chuckled.

"He wanted us to act like this was really warm weather," Branta said. "Maybe play with their minds a little bit."

Checking out the course the day before, Tegen had suggested a place for Branta to make her move – increase speed in a bid for the lead. The expectation was that Jacobs would start quickly and be out front. Branta would conserve her energy at the outset,

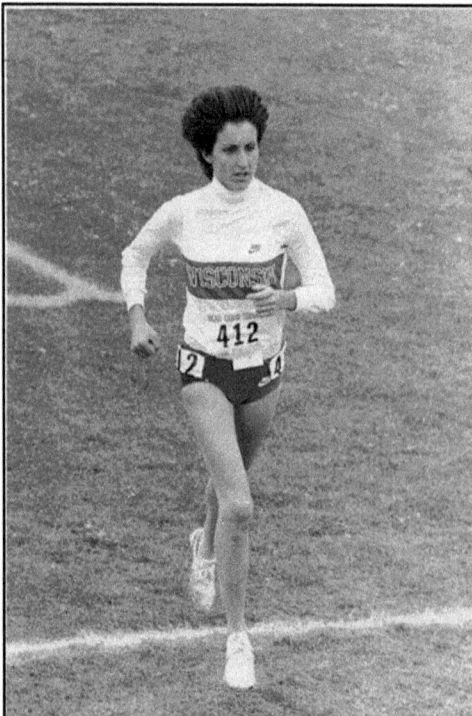

Cathy Branta (photo courtesy of UW athletics)

and then, after about two miles (the race was a little over three), shift into high gear.

"The thing about long-distance races," Tegen said, "particularly cross-country, is that you need to have some orientation as to where you are, because it's not always apparent. Typically, I would pick a spot [for a runner to accelerate] that would provide some cover. Maybe there are trees, or it's on a turn. And then – boom! – that's when you go."

"We were definitely keying on Regina Jacobs," Branta said. "She went out fast and took the lead."

"Cathy made a tactical move that was just perfectly timed," Tegen said.

Branta passed Jacobs, who eventually dropped back and finished fourth. Still, it wasn't over. Branta had the lead, but the course had a tight turn in its last half mile, and Branta, perhaps due to the snow residue on the course, momentarily lost her footing.

"It was greasy," she said. "I slipped and went down on one hand, but I bounced right back up. I was thinking, 'My God, I almost fell, right before the finish line.'"

Branta began her sprint to the finish. Behind her, several teammates also were doing well. The Wisconsin women were within reach of the school's first NCAA women's championship.

The crowd at the end included local fans, friends and family of the athletes, and coaches and administrators.

Standing near the finish line, unobtrusive but keenly interested, was a trim, athletic-looking woman of 44, five-foot, three inches tall with blue eyes and short, dark hair.

Katherine "Kit" Saunders was, in November 1984, an associate athletic director at the University of Wisconsin-Madison, supervising 22 non-revenue sports, including women's cross-country. But that title doesn't begin to measure Kit Saunders' accomplishments and impact since her arrival in Madison – for graduate school – in 1964.

Kit Saunders (photo courtesy of UW athletics)

In the ensuing 20 years, Kit, more than any other individual, was responsible for originating and building a program of competitive athletics for women on the UW-Madison campus.

It was anything but easy.

Kit battled prejudice, stereotypes, profound funding issues and a women's physical education mindset against competition that dated to the 1910s and whose greatest champion – Blanche Trilling – was the longtime director of women's physical education at UW-Madison. Yet Saunders did it – nearly always – with good humor and an optimistic spirit that won allies and would not, in the end, be denied.

"She was the right woman at the right time to seed all this, nourish it, and get it started," said Paula Bonner, who succeeded her as the leader of women's athletics in 1983 when Kit was promoted to overseeing all non-revenue sports.

"I think she had a personality that was accessible for lots of people across a wide spectrum," Bonner continued. "They felt comfortable and could talk to her."

"An extraordinary and passionate leader," said Tamara Flarup, UW's first sports information director for the women's program. "Kit's contributions to the university and the athletic department set the course for the equity and success [of] our women's sports program."

In 1974, when the University of Wisconsin athletic board approved varsity sports status for women, Kit was the manifest choice for director. Her impact extended far beyond the Madison campus. Kit was commissioner of the six-state Midwest Association for Intercollegiate Athletics for Women from 1974-1977 and served from 1979-1982 as the vice president for Division I of the Association for Intercollegiate Athletics for Women (AIAW), the preeminent governing body of women's intercollegiate athletics nationally at that time.

Yet it was at UW-Madison that Kit's influence was felt most directly. Less than a month before she stood at the finish line of the 1984 NCAA Women's Cross-Country Championship at Penn State, Kit was a charter inductee (alongside rower Carie Graves) into the newly created University of Wisconsin Women's Athletics Hall of Fame. It came during ceremonies on October 26, 1984 celebrating the 10th anniversary of women's sports gaining varsity status. The Friday night event drew 575 people to the University of Wisconsin Field House.

It was a special evening, evidence that both Kit and women's athletics had advanced a long way since Kit came to Madison to study for a master's degree in physical education in 1964.

Kit grew up in Teaneck, New Jersey, a city of just under 40,000 in Bergen County, a little more than 10 miles northwest of Manhattan. The population in 1940, the year Kit was born, was 25,275. Her father was a butcher who operated Saunders Meat Market on Cedar Avenue in Teaneck.

Kit loved sports growing up – the 1958 Teaneck High School yearbook reveals she was considered the class's "most athletic" girl – but finding any kind of organized sports activities was a problem.

In high school, she recalled later, what passed for athletics for girls were "play days" and "sports days." Play days dated to the 1920s and consisted of activities in which players from different schools were mixed so the emphasis would be on playing rather than winning. Sports days came later and were a step up, but with sports days, too, school versus school matches were not allowed. Rather – say in field hockey – one school's offense was paired with another's defense.

It wasn't much better when Kit graduated from high school and attended Trenton State College, which in 1996 changed its name to the College of New Jersey. Years after graduating Kit would get a letter from the alumni association in Trenton saying she was being considered for its athletics hall of fame. Could she recount her achievements? Kit wrote back that in her day there weren't varsity sports for women on campus.

On arriving in Madison in 1964, Kit – whose graduate study made her an historian of intercollegiate women's intercollegiate athletics – learned it was an educator at UW-Madison who arguably played the largest role in keeping college women and competitive sports separate. Her name was Blanche M. Trilling and she did it not out of malice but out of a sincere belief that for women and girls, participation was better than competition.

Trilling was a native of Syracuse, New York and worked first at the University of Missouri and then Chicago Teachers College before coming to UW-Madison in 1912 as director of physical education for women, a post she held for 34 years.

Trilling was highly regarded and much decorated for her contributions to women's physical education. In 1917, she hosted in Madison the first national meeting of the Women's Athletic Association, which had organizations overseeing women's athletics on campuses across the country.

"Blanche Trilling was a national leader in physical education," Kit said, in a 1995 interview with the UW Oral History Program. "She was an excellent speaker. She was very successful in promoting her ideas nationally. She was absolutely adamant about not putting a lot of resources into helping a small number of highly-talented women be competitive."

Kit continued, "Her whole philosophy was embodied in the motto: 'A sport for every girl, and a girl in every sport.'"

Trilling herself summed it up in a 1929 statement she made to the Wisconsin Athletic Review: "I positively do not approve of competition for women and the undue emphasis that is placed on individual accomplishment and the winning of championships."

By the time Kit came to Wisconsin, the tide was beginning to turn – more so, ironically for Kit, on the east coast, which she had just left for the heartland. It made sense that Trilling's most lasting influence would be in the Midwest, the area where she lived. Yet societal changes – the first stirrings of the feminist movement – were having a residual effect on how women's sports were perceived.

The true game-changer for women's intercollegiate athletics – though it took time to be recognized, and much longer to be fully implemented – was Title IX of the Education Amendments Act, which became law in June 1972.

Title IX stated: "No person in the United States shall on the basis of sex be excluded from participation in, denied the benefits of, or be subjected to discrimination under any activity receiving Federal financial assistance."

Women and other proponents of gender equity read that as saying universities must provide equal opportunities for female athletes on campus.

It was as if a bomb had been dropped and stuck in the ground without going off. It would detonate, but not right away, and in bits and pieces. In the meantime, Title IX was dealt with cautiously.

At UW-Madison, Chancellor Edwin Young in July 1972 appointed a committee to look at athletic facilities and opportunities for women on campus.

"Elroy Hirsch was the first chair of the committee," Kit recalled, "which seemed logical at the time, given that Elroy was director of intercollegiate athletics."

Except that Hirsch – like many athletic directors around the country – already had budget headaches and wasn't looking to create more. In eight months, the new committee met one time. A second meeting was set, then postponed.

This so irritated a number of prominent women on campus – including Muriel Sloan, head of the women's physical education department – that they complained to the chancellor, and Hirsch was removed as committee chairman, replaced by Professor Murray Fowler, who quickly began holding meetings that brought results.

Still, it was slow going, painfully slow at times. In 1979, the Wisconsin women's crew team, which had won a (pre-NCAA) national championship in 1975, staged a protest. Weary of and angry at not having locker room facilities of their own, the crew changed from street clothes to workout clothes outside the closed door of Elroy Hirsch's office. They made their point – and got their locker room – but the reaction to the protest showed not everyone was ready for equity.

"It was a traumatizing experience for me in a way," Jane Ludwig, the women's 1979 crew captain, recalled four decades later. "I had alumni calling me. Coaches telling me to stop it. My male friends on the team really weren't my friends anymore. I was so ignorant of what was going to happen. People don't like you when you stick your neck out."

That was seven years after Title IX became law.

Change is never easy. Ludwig's comments might serve as a reminder of just what Kit Saunders faced in the quarter-century she spent challenging the status quo and striving to create a strong women's athletics program at UW-Madison. It was a path fraught with peril. Missteps were magnified.

Yet Kit and her colleagues persevered, and prevailed. Tam Flarup recalled sitting with Kit high in the bleachers at the UW Field House in the late fall of 1990 while the Badgers played an

NCAA women's volleyball first-round tournament match. Nearly 11,000 fans had packed the old barn. The two women were thrilled. "We had tears in our eyes," Flarup said.

Kit was retired by then. She had also married – Madison banking executive Dale "Buzz" Nordeen – and their life together following the 1988 marriage was richly varied and joyful.

When Kit announced her retirement in 1990, she was asked in interviews to recall special moments from the past 25 years. She mentioned the women's crew winning its national title in 1975. In later interviews, she would say how she treasured being in the overflow crowd at the Field House for the women's volleyball game in 1990.

Always, Kit talked about that cold day in Pennsylvania in November 1984, standing in the snow at the finish line as the women's cross-country team tried to give Wisconsin its first NCAA women's championship.

Cathy Branta, who almost fell on the last turn, stormed across the finish line first, winning the individual title and breaking the Penn State course record by nearly 15 seconds. Three other Badgers finished in the top 30 and Wisconsin easily defeated second place Stanford for the team title.

They were NCAA champions.

That night, a crowd of some two-dozen well-wishers greeted the Wisconsin traveling party at the Dane County Regional Airport. The "Bud" song blared from a loudspeaker. Coach Peter Tegen clutched the team trophy as photographers snapped pictures. The next day, photos from the airport celebration were published with stories on the front pages of both Madison papers' sports sections.

It was another indication of how far Kit Saunders had brought the women's program. When Tam Flarup first came to Madison to work for Kit in sports information in 1977, the *Wisconsin State Journal* sports editor, Glenn Miller, told her, "I will never have women's sports in my sports section."

Miller was wrongheaded, and, as evidenced by the papers following the triumph at Penn State seven years later, just plain wrong.

Kit changed hearts and minds and when in 1990 she decided to retire, one observer who was not surprised was her accomplished track and cross-country coach, Peter Tegen.

"I thought she was probably exhausted," Tegen said.

He paused, then added, "She fought *a battle*."

For a girl who wanted to play sports growing up, the fight began early.

Chapter 2

TEANECK

"I chose her first if given the chance," noted Art Brown, who attended Emerson Elementary School in Teaneck, New Jersey with Kit. The two were classmates, graduating from sixth grade at Emerson in 1952.

"She was even then an excellent athlete," Brown continued, via email, in 2018, "and was more often than not the first person chosen for our playground games of any kind, even chosen before any of the boys. But she never lauded it over anyone. She was just a great person who loved everyone. And everyone loved her."

Teaneck produced its share of fine athletes, including three men who all played baseball at some point for the New York Yankees: catcher Elston Howard; outfielder Dave Winfield; and pitcher Jim Bouton, who authored the celebrated and controversial memoir *Ball Four*.

But Teaneck's first claim to fame came long before, in the most serious of circumstances: the Revolutionary War. In November 1776, when General George Washington withdrew his outmanned forces from Fort Lee – 5,000 British troops were approaching on the Hudson River – he marched them through Teaneck.

"Bergen County was the site of many such harrowing events," wrote Teaneck historian Robert D. Griffin in 1994, "and Teaneck was right in the thick of it. Throughout the war, both British and American forces occupied several local homesteads at various times, and Teaneck citizens played key roles on both sides of the conflict."

Teaneck's first inhabitants were Native Americans.

In 1961, the League of Women Voters of Teaneck published *This is Teaneck: A Community Handbook*, and it included this bit of history:

> "Teaneck has its roots in pre-Revolutionary War
> America. When the first Dutch settlers arrived,
> they found the land.... inhabited by the Achin-
> heschacky Indians. Their great leader, Chief
> Oratam, first of the Indian leaders to befriend the
> white men, made Teaneck his summer home…

"During this period," the handbook continued, "the Township's name evolved, although its exact derivation remains shrouded in legend. To the Indians we attribute the name 'Tekene,' their word for 'The Woods,' descriptive of the topography of this ridge of land.... Another explanation is that Teaneck comes from the Dutch words, 'Tee Neck,' meaning either 'curved piece of land bordering on a stream,' or 'neck of land where willows grow,' depending on the translation."

The Saunders family did not move to Teaneck until the 1930s. Kit's great-grandfather, Thomas Saunders, married Catharine Byrnes in Dublin, Ireland in 1882 and the couple emigrated to the United States, where Thomas died, in Manhattan, in 1892.

Kit's grandfather, Alfred Joseph Saunders, was born the year before, August 27, 1891, in Manhattan. On his World War I draft registration form, Alfred is described as tall, with a medium build, blue eyes and brown hair, with all his limbs intact. At the time he filled out the form – circa 1917 – Alfred was working as a butcher for a man named Roth at the corner of Nagle Avenue and Arden Street in the Fort George neighborhood of Manhattan.

In 1914, Alfred married Minnie Roberts in Manhattan, and the following year Minnie gave birth to Alfred Roberts Saunders, Kit's father.

The 1920 U.S. census showed them living on Arden Street but by 1925 they'd moved a block to Thayer Street, still in the Fort George neighborhood, and Alfred Sr. (though not technically a senior, given the different middle names) was still working as a butcher.

In 1930 the family was still in Manhattan but by 1935 they had moved to Teaneck. Alfred Jr. became a butcher like his father, married Katherine Krall, whom everyone called Kay, and in 1940, Kit was born. She would soon have a baby brother, Don. They were living then on Cedar Lane in Teaneck, the same street on which Kit's father operated his butcher shop.

Kit's elementary school, Emerson, was built in 1916 and named for the writer and philosopher Ralph Waldo Emerson. It is no longer in existence.

Another of Kit's Emerson classmates and friends, Peggy Van Emburgh (later Kelly), remembered Kit in a 2018 email:

"She was always so friendly and consistently had a smile on her face…. Her father owned Saunders Meat Market on Cedar Lane and my dad and I would walk to town every Saturday to

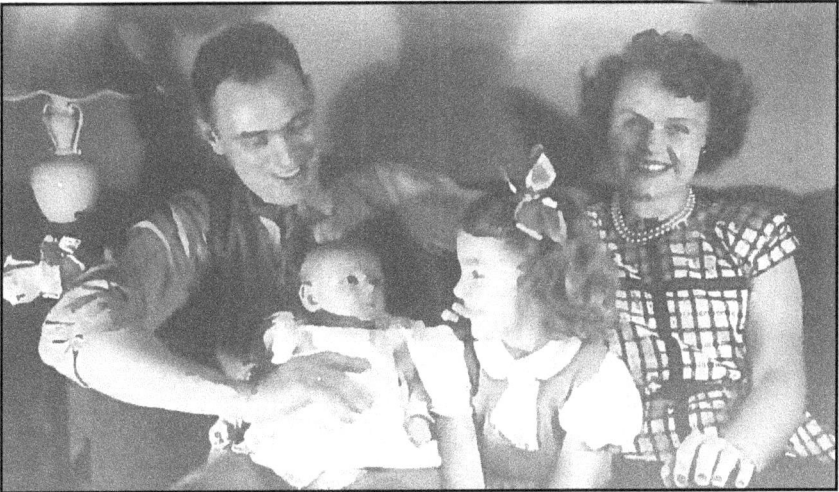

The Saunders family in Teaneck: Alfred, Kay, Kit, and baby brother, Don. (Courtesy Diana Dunn)

Kit in Teaneck (courtesy of Diana Dunn)

pick up our meat for the week. What a lovely person her dad was as well."

In 1999, one of the sixth graders in Kit's 1952 graduating class at Emerson, Dr. Earl "Skippy" Skelton, asked for recollections from his classmates and then collected them in a booklet.

Kit participated, and her contribution is notable for its humor and how it reveals Kit's willingness, even as a grade-schooler, to go against the grain, stand her ground, and speak out against perceived injustice.

Kit wrote:

> "I too have memories of Emerson days. In second grade, I believe, I had Miss Kaberle. She crunched me against the wall in the hall one day and told me that I had better 'turn over a new leaf, or else.' I believe she meant by tomorrow, and she told my parents as well!

> "I spent much of the 4th grade standing in the corner, behind the geraniums… I was unable to stand the smell of geraniums until just a few years ago!

"I remember going home one day and telling my parents a Mr. Martino story. He had created THE ROW. If you had been especially stupid in math on a particular day, you got to sit in it. (THE ROW, that is.) Can't imagine how such a creep could have gotten into teaching little children.

"Once in the fifth grade we went to a special program in the auditorium/gymnasium. Miss Collins had a projector set up and we were all told, apparently, to duck under the cord. I opted to jump over it. Not a good idea. Miss C. really read me out in front of several grades. I was scared to death of her and being notified that I would have her for my sixth grade teacher seemed like a sentence of doom.

"Actually, it turned out all right. She decided that the way to get me on the right track (she liked challenging kids, though we didn't know it) was to create softball teams and make me the captain of one of them. Maybe she determined the direction of my career, who knows?"

Kit again related the sixth-grade softball story in a 2007 interview with *Brava* magazine in Madison. In that article, she spoke with a chuckle about getting "in all kinds of trouble" as a child, usually related to her innate rambunctiousness. She recalled climbing a neighbor's maple tree in an organdy dress.

"My mother about killed me," Kit said. "She never sent me out of the house in a dress again, unless I was going to church." At other times Kit would join a group of boys practicing a variety of sports on neighborhood fields. That started in first or second grade. "I don't ever remember," Kit said, "a time when I didn't want to play."

Teaneck High School, a Tudor building that opened in 1928, is imposing enough that its nickname is "the Castle on the Hill."

The school was Kit's next stop after Emerson because, according to Bonnie Morrow, who attended school with Kit in

Teaneck – two years behind, Morrow graduated high school in 1960 – there was no middle school or junior high in Teaneck at the time. Grades seven through twelve were grouped together in the same building.

"Twelve- and thirteen-year-olds were going to the same school, at the same time, as seventeen- and eighteen-year-olds," Morrow recalled. "The hallways were choked and students were jostled as they tried to get from one class to the next."

Somewhat ironically, the crowding was due at least in part to publicity Teaneck received in the 1940s as a model community, its school system highly rated. Young families began relocating to the city in large numbers. Homes were built to accommodate them, but not a new school, at least not right away.

"I don't mean to paint a negative picture," Morrow said. "They were exciting times. Teaneck had a very high academic standing with a wonderful battery of teachers. They not only taught us how to do algebra or chemistry, they taught us good citizenship as well."

Kit makes numerous appearances in the 1958 (her senior year) Teaneck High School yearbook, named the "The Hi-Way" – the school's sports teams were called the Highwaymen.

Beneath the senior yearbook photos of all the class members are a few uncredited phrases that seek to sum up the individual. Kit's read: "An excellent athlete.... Representative to Girls State.... Bundle of energy and pep.... Wonderful sense of humor.... A college career awaits her."

Kit was selected for the National Honor Society, an honor the yearbook noted was based on "scholarship, leadership, citizenship, character and service, all weighed by the administration, faculty and student body."

She was vice-president, her senior year, of Tri-Hi-Y, a social and service club affiliated with the YMCA. In March 1958, an article in the Bergen Evening Record reported that Kit – "an honor student at Teaneck High School" – would be awarded a "good citizenship pin" at the New Jersey State Conference of the Daughters of the American Revolution.

Kit's Teaneck High School transcript reveals that she ranked 28th academically out of her class of 439. Her lowest grade across four years was a B, and that happened in only six classes – Latin and Algebra twice. Her senior year she made straight As.

Even her pre-high school years at Teaneck were filled with accomplishment. The school regularly sent a "commendation" report home to parents of students whose "effort and achievement are worthy of commendation." Kit received a thick stack of those letters from 1953 onward.

Kit was also, as noted earlier, chosen the "most athletic" girl in the 1958 class, pictured in the yearbook next to the most athletic boy, Bill Pashe, who later played one season of pro football with the New York Jets.

Being any kind of athlete as a high school girl in the 1950s – in Teaneck or elsewhere – was never going to be easy.

At Teaneck High School, Bonnie Morrow recalled, "Boys were not permitted to see girls in their gym wear. As a result, girls had to exit the locker room via a tunnel that terminated into the girls' gymnasium. The gym was enormous with a two-story high ceiling."

Morrow said one sport that girls were encouraged to play was field hockey, a stick-and-ball game played on a grass surface and somewhat like ice hockey. Kit would become a formidable field hockey player.

"Part of the year was spent playing field hockey," Morrow noted, "trying to run with massive, one-size-fits-all shin guards and wielding a hockey stick that could not be raised above the shoulder...Only a few girls could score goals on the hockey field."

The 1958 "Hi-Way" yearbook devotes a single page to "Girls' Sports."

One paragraph describes the year in girls' sports and notes "there were numerous inter-school play days. Greatly enjoyed by all who attended was the State [field] Hockey play day at Plain-field. Flavor was added when a coach from Wales spent the afternoon giving the girls pointers on hockey."

As noted briefly earlier, Kit, in high school, was not a fan of play days for aspiring female athletes.

In a later interview, she said, "You could get together with another school, but we had teams named Mickey Mouse, or Donald Duck, Snoopy or whatever. People were all mixed up so you couldn't get in a real competitive spirit against another school. You might have kids on your team from three or four different schools."

"Sports days" evolved from play days and weren't a great deal better, in Kit's estimation.

"Sports days were the next level," Kit said. "Where you could go and compete as a recognizable team. But even that, for a long time, you would go with your field hockey team and they would switch your defense to play with another team's offense. So you kind of got half an identity for your school, but not the whole thing.

"I remember," Kit continued, "in high school being so disappointed after we practiced to find out we had to split our team because we weren't supposed to have that competitive school spirit."

There certainly was no premium on winning – winning and losing being a concept judged unhealthy for girl athletes.

"Sometimes there was some little, not very intrinsically valuable thing that was given [out after a game]," Kit recalled. "Something somebody had made, or some little trophy that was made. But everybody got one. They didn't worry about winners."

In 2009, Teaneck High School established an Athletic Hall of Fame to honor the athletic accomplishments of former students and coaches. The inductees include female athletes in a wide variety of sports – basketball, golf, tennis, swimming, even fencing.

Kit Saunders is not an inductee. How could she be? In high school she never had a chance to compete. However, Teaneck High School also has an exhibit honoring the school's distinguished alumni. In 2018, a plaque for Katherine "Kit" Saunders, 1958 graduate of Teaneck High School, was added to the exhibit. It featured Kit's high school yearbook photo and a later photograph, with text highlighting her leadership role in advancing the opportunities in athletics for girls and women. Perhaps the best thing about it is that generations of new female athletes in Teaneck will know a pioneer who helped make competitive athletics possible for them walked the same halls.

If Kit's plaque might inspire young women athletes today, a fair question might be, who inspired Kit, especially considering how stacked the deck was against young women becoming athletes in the 1950s. In a later interview, Kit once listed the great track and field star and gifted golfer Babe Didrikson as an inspiration. Another likely possibility: Kit's mother, Kay. In 1977, on the acknowledgments page of her doctorate dissertation at UW-Madison, Kit thanked her mom, "who has provided

Kit's Teaneck High School plaque. (courtesy of the Nordeen family)

encouragement to 'dare to try' for thirty-some years." In a newspaper interview some years later, Kit credited her mom for urging her to pursue higher education.

"She had a scholarship to attend the Columbia University School of Journalism," Kit said. "But the Depression was on and she had to go to work. So she always wanted her children to receive educations."

For Kit in 1958, things did not get much better, from an athletic competition standpoint, when she enrolled at Trenton State College in New Jersey.

As noted, almost three decades later, in 1986, after Kit had established her considerable reputation in women's athletics, the Trenton State College Alumni Association sent Kit a letter in Madison saying they were considering her for the college's athletic hall of fame. Could she provide details of her athletic career at Trenton State?

"For most of my college career," Kit wrote back, "there were no varsity sports, although I was active in trying to get them started."

The year of Kit's enrollment – 1958 – was the year the New Jersey State Teachers College at Trenton changed its name to Trenton State College. It was founded in 1855 as New Jersey State Normal School. In 1996, the school, amid controversy, changed its name again, to the College of New Jersey. Some Trenton officials felt removing the city's name from the school was an affront; at nearby Princeton University, there was anger because for many years Princeton was known as the College of New Jersey. Nevertheless, the Trenton trustees approved the name change 8-0.

A perusal of the Trenton State College student newspaper – the State Signal – and the yearbook – the Seal – indicates that there was at least one sport during Kit's time at Trenton in which women competed on a team against teams from other schools. This wouldn't have been varsity competition but rather what was called extramural. Still, it did give the women a chance to play for their school with their own teammates. The sport was field hockey, one of Kit's best. She would also participate – against the wishes of some school administrators – in games coordinated by the New Jersey state associations of both field hockey and lacrosse.

Here is how Kit remembered it four decades later, in a draft of a 1998 speech to the Bascom Hill Society on the Madison campus:

"I started college in 1958. Still no intercollegiate sports. My friends and I got into plenty of trouble competing in field hockey and lacrosse for a state association.

"This was definitely not acceptable to our major professors," Kit continued. "We were warned. Once I got a flat tire trying to get back from a field hockey match and was late for a swim show, which I was in, and which was advised by my major professor. Not good! On the first day she came to observe my student teaching, I had a butterfly bandage over my eye where I had been hit with a lacrosse stick over the weekend. Also not good."

On another occasion – a 1990s interview for the UW Oral History Program – Kit recalled the lack of competitive opportunity on campus at Trenton, saying this:

"When I was in college the worst thing you could be found out to be doing was going off and playing basketball somewhere. We had to play field hockey or lacrosse or whatever we did outside our university, because our major advisors were adamant about our not doing it. It was really a no-no."

If her passion for athletics couldn't be fulfilled on the campus in Trenton, Kit did receive a good education – and she got it on full scholarship.

In a letter dated May 23, 1958, just as Kit was graduating high school, college president Edwin L. Martin wrote Kit the following:

"I am very happy to write you that I have been informed by the Commissioner of Education that you have been awarded a scholarship... the scholarship will pay your tuition for the four years of your college... provided your record in the college warrants its continuance."

No surprise, in and out of the classroom, Kit stood out in Trenton. The student newspapers and yearbooks from Kit's time at Trenton State College reveal she lived a busy, active life on campus.

As a freshman, Kit participated in the class cabinet (elected by classmates to plan all class events); Women's Recreation Association (WRA – the successor of the Women's Athletic Association – WAA – which coordinated women's athletics on most campuses dating to the early 1900s); modern dance group; and women's physical education club.

In March 1959, the State Signal student newspaper reported on the freshmen who had attained a "B" average or above in their first semester on campus: Kit was on the list, with her field of study listed as Health and Physical Education.

Kit's Trenton State transcript reveals that in eight semesters of college she never attained less than a 3.2 grade point average; most semesters, she was above 3.5. Kit's class schedule indicates she was interested in physical education from the outset and classes in basketball, soccer and field hockey were mixed in with math, geology and world literature.

As a sophomore – no doubt chafing at the lack of competitive sports for women on campus – Kit played on the New Jersey Women's Lacrosse Association team that in May 1959 played a "demonstration game" in Trenton against a touring team from Great Britain and Ireland. It capped a "play day" for some 350 New Jersey high school girls who had traveled to Trenton from around the state.

Kathy Riss was a classmate of Kit's at Trenton State, and like Kit a physical education major.

"I met Kit very early on, as a freshman," Riss recalled. "We participated early in field hockey and lacrosse." On field hockey alumni weekend at Trenton, Kit chaired the freshman team. Kit had a car at Trenton, Riss said, and so would drive them to the field hockey and lacrosse association matches, often held in Plainfield.

"She was a natural athlete and had a calmness and sureness about her," Riss recalled of Kit. "She was a leader. If she got involved, she really got involved and wound up in a leadership position. She knew where she was going. We got along well. We shared the same interests and came from similar backgrounds."

Riss remembered attending a Gilbert and Sullivan opera with Kit and being impressed that Kit knew the story – she'd seen it before.

"And she could be funny," Riss added. "Once we were in synchronized swimming, and I remember Kit holding up the suit by its straps." Clearly the swimsuit did not pass muster. "This is what we're wearing?" Kit said. "You've got to be kidding!"

It seems like synchronized swimming might not have topped Kit's list of favorite activities, but she participated, perhaps because the faculty advisor, Carolyn Hammond, was according to Kathy Riss a favorite of the students.

"We loved her," Riss said. "She'd invite us to her home and bake cookies. We were going to be in synchronized swimming whether we wanted to or not."

For the synchronized swimming club's performance of "Over the Rainbow," in the college pool in the spring of 1961, Kit wrote the script and participated in the water.

As a junior at Trenton State, Kit received the Mariana G. Packer Award, which included a cash benefit of $25. It was given by the Women's Health and Physical Education Club in honor of the retired head of the department to a junior student in Health and Physical Education on the basis of contribution to the department, promise of success in teaching, and perpetuation of high standards and ideals for herself and the department.

Apparently some administrators were willing to overlook Kit's participation in athletics off campus.

The 1962 class yearbook, the Seal, devoted a page to the Women's Recreation Association, which it called "a thriving organization offering such activities as archery, basketball, hockey, lacrosse, softball, volleyball, modern dance, rhythmic swimming, outing club and coeducational recreation. The dormitories have also been supplied with equipment so that every girl has an opportunity to participate in some type of recreational activity."

Competition, as Kit recalled in later interviews, was clearly not a priority. The yearbook page on the WRA ends with this quote on its purpose from the WRA constitution: "...to foster and promote a program which will initiate a desire to participate in activities, and provide opportunity for a great degree of enjoyment to every women enrolled in the college...."

Still, by Kit's senior year, Trenton State did have a women's field hockey team.

"Lillian Wright became our professor," Kathy Riss recalled, "and things changed."

The 1962 Seal yearbook noted: "This year Trenton State had a first and second school team as well as four intramural hockey teams." Kit was one of 12 women listed as playing on the first team.

The team's games were reported in the sports section of the State Signal in small boxed stories headlined "WRA."

The Nov. 17, 1961 State Signal reported the following:

"The Trenton State College field hockey team went to New Brunswick on Thursday, November 2 to play against Douglass College. Trenton's first team won 2-0. The next game will be held November 16 at Montclair State College."

The Seal yearbook reported: "Due to the superb coaching of Mrs. Lillian Wright, the teams [first and second] can boast of an undefeated season."

Kit also made the Dean's List – a scholastic achievement – as a senior and won what was called the "Book Award" from the Women's Health and Physical Education Club, presented annually "to a woman in the Health and PE Curriculum who has, by active participation and worthwhile contribution, furthered the development of the department." Kit was a member of the club all four years at Trenton State, and served as treasurer her sophomore year, vice-president as a junior, and president her last year. Finally, during her senior year, Kit served for eight weeks as a student teacher in physical education at Glen Rock Junior High School, 60 miles north of Trenton.

Every summer during her college years, Kit worked as a counselor at Camp Navarac, a camp for girls on Upper Saranac Lake in New York's Adirondack Mountains. Her first year's job description read "boating and bunk" and paid her $175 for the summer, plus $50 for teaching a small craft course on the lake. Her pay was upped each successive summer, to $500 her last season when she was head of the water-skiing unit.

Kit continued her summer work at Camp Navarac for two years even after college – her teaching job gave her summers off. And once she came to Madison to work toward a master's degree at the University of Wisconsin, Kit used the experience for her thesis, which analyzed summer camps in terms of the best activities, group living do's and don'ts, and more. In Madison in 1967, Kit even sent an article to Camping Magazine, with a tentative title, "So You Want to Be a Camp Counselor?" An editor wrote her back that while the piece was "well written and contains much useful information," the magazine had a backlog of stories and so couldn't use it.

On graduating from Trenton State with a Bachelor of Arts degree, Kit returned to Teaneck and in fall 1962 got a job at her old school, Teaneck High. Her September through June contract called for a salary of $4,800 (increased to $5,200 her second year). Kit taught physical education at Teaneck, while coaching basketball, field hockey and lacrosse. She was also sponsor for the Girls' Leaders Club, a group of 30 or so girls interested in playing sports, as well as a sponsor of the senior class cabinet.

An evaluation of Kit's performance as a teacher dated February 1964 read in part: "Miss Saunders is a capable teacher who is sincerely interested in all phases of physical education activities. She is also vitally interested in all the students with whom she works... and is recognized in the physical education field as an outstanding leader."

While teaching at Teaneck, Kit accepted a committee chairmanship for the United States Women's Lacrosse Association. She did work for the New Jersey Athletic Association for Girls. She helped bring the Danish Gymnastics Team to Teaneck for a performance in September 1963. But by late fall 1963, during her second year teaching at Teaneck, Kit had decided she wanted to return to school herself for a master's in physical education.

She applied at schools in Colorado, North Carolina, and at the University of Wisconsin-Madison, the latter having gotten on her radar from counselor colleagues at Camp Navarac who spoke highly of both the university and the city of Madison.

On January 9, 1964, Kit wrote a letter to Teaneck Superintendent of Schools Harvey Scribner outlining her graduate school plans, noting that she'd already been accepted at the University of North Carolina and was waiting to hear from Wisconsin and Colorado.

"It will he a hard thing, I know, when June arrives," Kit wrote, "to inform my students of my decision, as working with them and with the other members of my department has made the past two years most rewarding and a pleasurable way to start in teaching."

Barbara J. Houston, who ran the Health and Physical Education Department for Girls at Glen Rock Junior High – where Kit student taught in 1962 – wrote a letter of recommendation to the head of women's physical education at Wisconsin, Lolas Halverson.

"She has a keen interest in the teaching profession," Houston wrote of Kit, "a definite gift for it, and a deep-rooted philosophy of education admired by her professional peers and pupils under her guidance."

In March 1964, Halverson called Kit from Wisconsin and informed her UW had accepted her and would offer either a graduate scholarship or teaching assistant post for the 1964-65 school year. A letter following in May confirmed a teaching assistantship with a salary of $2,790.

Kit was headed west, to Madison.

Chapter 3

PIONEERS

Her first year in Madison, Kit lived in an apartment off campus on the city's south side – 620 West Badger Road, Apartment #6. The Madison city directories show that she kept the apartment for two years and then in 1966 moved to 2346 Chalet Gardens Road, Apartment #2 – an apartment complex in Fitchburg – where she stayed for several years.

It seems safe to say that Kit knew of the estimable national reputation of the women's physical education department at UW-Madison – it's likely one reason she enrolled for graduate school.

But it is also safe to say that – both before and after she began researching the history of women's athletics on college campuses, and first encountered the name Blanche Trilling – Kit was dismayed by the lack of real athletic competition for women at UW-Madison.

"The East Coast was 10 years ahead of the Midwest in developing opportunities for women," Kit said later. "When I got here [to Madison] I was just amazed. They were back where I'd been in high school."

Of course, Kit being Kit, she found a way to compete. Her first semester in Madison, Kit joined the Madison Field Hockey Club.

The Sept. 9, 1964 *Capital Times* newspaper reported the following:

> "The Madison Field Hockey Club, a group open to
> all Madison and area women, will start its 42nd
> year of play with a game against Oshkosh this

coming Sunday. As in the past, practices will be held on Saturday mornings and conference games on Sunday. The University is again allowing the club to use the Elm Drive Field on the campus for its activities."

The Madison club began in 1922, the same year the United States Field Hockey Association was founded. It was a sport highly popular with women in Great Britain and was introduced in the United States in 1901 by an Englishwoman, Constance Appleton, who was studying at Harvard.

The Madison Field Hockey Club's games were covered, at least sporadically, in the sports pages of Madison newspapers. The Nov. 8, 1931 Capital Times included a story with this headline: "Local Field Hockey Team in 9 to 0 Win," and this particularly memorable secondary headline: "Madison Fair Sex Stars Wallop Milwaukee Foes Easily."

Kit loved field hockey.

"She was passionate about it," said Claudia Pogreba, who met Kit on campus in Madison in the 1960s and became a lifelong friend. "And she was a very good player."

Kit's first mention in a Madison newspaper came less than a week after the Sept. 9, 1964 Cap Times story previewing the Madison Field Hockey Club's season.

In a story on Sept. 15, The Cap Times reported that the Madison club easily defeated Oshkosh, 9-0. The story noted that 25 players showed up for the first practice a day prior to the game.

"Eight were newcomers," The Cap Times noted, "some with considerable experience through hockey club participation in other parts of the country."

The Cap Times took note of Kit: "One of the newcomers from New Jersey, Kit Saunders, has a sectional officiating rating [able to officiate middle and high school games] and will be of great value to the team in that capacity as well [as] a player."

In early October, the Field Hockey Club joined with the UW Women's Physical Education Department to host an educational and skills clinic at La Follette High School, followed by a game pitting the Madison club against one from Milwaukee.

After the clinic, Becky Sisley, an instructor in the UW women's physical education department and field hockey club president, sent Kit a note: "Thanks so much for your assistance and services during the hockey clinic. Your dependability and willingness to help was greatly appreciated. You did a swell job with the 'advanced' at such short notice. Many thanks, Becky."

As a player, Kit quickly developed into one of the Madison club's stars. A *Wisconsin State Journal* sports page story on Monday, Oct. 19, 1964, noted that the team beat Beloit, 5-0, on Saturday and on Sunday beat Milwaukee, 1-0, while tying Iowa City, 2-2.

The paper reported: "Kit Saunders and Lucy Grant scored two goals apiece and June Breda one in the Beloit game. Jeanne Gelner had Madison's goal against Milwaukee and joined Kit Saunders to account for their team's output against Iowa City."

What may be of most enduring interest from the Madison Field Hockey Club's 1964 season is the number of team members who went on to distinguish themselves as leaders in women's athletics across their lifetimes.

Kit, of course, pioneered women's intercollegiate athletics at UW-Madison. But there were others. Becky Sisley became the first director of women's intercollegiate athletics at the University of Oregon and was an influential member of the national Association for Intercollegiate Athletics for Women. (Sisley was also, decades later in early 2020, featured in a *New York Times* story noting how the Oregon-Oregon State women's college basketball rivalry was now drawing 12,000 fans to their games.) Nancy Page played goalie for the Madison club and later became a legendary Hall of Fame women's coach at the University of Wisconsin-Stevens Point, winning 11 conference titles in field hockey, softball and tennis in 31 years of coaching. And Bobbie Konover, who played for the '64 Madison club, spent 48 years at Germantown Friends School in Pennsylvania, where, as a physical education teacher, coach and administrator she built a highly respected athletic program for girls.

All three women shared fond memories of Kit and their field hockey adventures in Madison for this narrative. But like Kit, they were often dismayed at the lack of real competitive opportunities at the university. The field hockey club was not affiliated with UW, though it played and practiced on a university field.

Lolas Halverson, who chaired the women's physical education department in the 1960s (and wrote Kit about her grad school acceptance), was cut from the Blanche Trilling – participation, not competition – cloth.

"The head of our department," Nancy Page said, "was so against any kind of competition for women. It was bleak. It really was."

Page, who grew up in Janesville and knew since grade school that she wanted to teach physical education, said the students who wanted to compete made it happen on their own.

"At noon on Fridays," Page said, "the women who wanted to play basketball gathered in the Lathrop Hall gym. Graduate students and undergrads. We just showed up and made teams. We were all pretty darn good. Kit was part of that."

Page said that before long they wanted to test themselves against off-campus competition. They reached out to Mary Bell, who coached numerous sports, including basketball, at Northern Illinois University and two decades later was inducted into that school's athletics hall of fame.

"We wrote to her," Page said, "and asked if she'd come up and play us."

Bell wrote back: "Game on."

"They rolled into Lathrop Hall in a coach bus," Page recalled. "They had uniforms and warm-ups. We had navy shorts and white blouses with numbers pinned on. We did have referees.

We had one of the faculty members open the building for us, but the head of the department didn't know about it.

"We played the game," Page continued, "and we beat them, quite soundly."

Inevitably, word of the victory began to circulate around campus. Lolas Halverson heard, and, according to Page, was highly displeased.

"The head of the department found out we had done this. We were all called into her office and read the riot act. I think she probably wanted to kick us out of the university."

That didn't happen, but it made the women continue to look beyond campus for competitive opportunities, like the field hockey club.

"Kit took me under her wing," said Page, who was a junior in 1964 while Kit was a teaching assistant in physical education studying for her master's. "She transported us, and coached us."

Page recalled that Kit played forward on the field hockey team – "because she was very fast" – and said that Kit, Becky Sisley, and Page herself were all selected to an all-star team that represented the Midwest section of the United States Field Hockey Association at a national tournament.

The women whose paths crossed in Madison in 1964 on the field hockey club would in the next decade – along with many others – begin to bring competitive sports for women and girls onto college campuses and into high schools across the country.

The vexing question of why it took so long was addressed by one of them, Becky Sisley, in an interview for this book. While the women's physical education establishment, led by Wisconsin's Blanche Trilling, played a significant role in keeping high-level competition out of the reach of women, an extraordinary event in 1928 also played a role that shouldn't be underestimated. And even though it was not directly university-related, Trilling's voice was heard.

"What happened in the 1928 Olympics limited women," Sisley said.

By 1928, and the Summer Games in Amsterdam, women had become accepted as Olympic athletes.

"It has been shown," wrote the authors of the 1974 book *American Women in Sport*, "that as early as 1900 American women competed in the Olympics for the United States and that by 1920 it could be said that they had achieved full status as team members."

Track and field and gymnastics events for women were added for the 1928 Games.

Trilling wrote an article a year later titled, "The Playtime of a Million Girls, or an Olympic Victory – Which?" It included this sentence: "Shall the spirit of wholesome play for all girls be sacrificed to developing the superior prowess of a few?"

Kit said later, "It was as if you couldn't possibly do both."

As Sisley noted, what happened in Amsterdam didn't help. In the 800-meter race, numerous women collapsed at the finish line.

"They didn't know how to pace," Sisley said. "They didn't have any training."

Criticism of the decision for women to run 800 meters in the 1928 Olympics was fierce. "Too great a call on feminine strength," the *New York Times* wrote. The *London Daily Mail* found doctors saying it would make women "become old too soon."

"They thought," Sisley said, "if they ran and jumped maybe their uteruses would fall out."

The 800-meter race was eliminated from the women's Olympics and the track and field establishment did its best to marginalize women's distance running. When Diane Leather became the first woman to run a mile in under five minutes in England in May 1954, it wasn't officially recognized.

Slowly, as the 1950s eclipsed, and the '60s began, that started to change. The 800 meters was returned to the line-up of women's events for the 1960 Summer Games in Rome.

"I think it was a natural evolution of other things that were going on in the culture," Kit said, of the evolving attitudes of athletic competition for women. "Women were beginning to get in the job market a little more. The Olympics were becoming more interesting – more sports being added for women. There were more role models out there. Women were playing tennis, women were playing golf."

At UW-Madison, as has been noted, the evolution was particularly unhurried. Into the second half of the 1960s, women's sports on the UW-Madison campus were coordinated by the Women's Recreation Association, which was essentially student run, with one faculty advisor. Whatever the virtues of the WRA, which sat in the Department of Women's Physical Education, it was ill-equipped to handle the growing drumbeat for more competition – including intercollegiate competition – for women on the Madison campus.

In her doctoral dissertation, Kit wrote, "This writer found, in 1966 and 1967, that several of the former Wisconsin State University System schools had developed the intercollegiate phase of their sports program further than had the University of Wisconsin. This could perhaps be attributed in part to the adherence of many of the faculty members of the [Madison] physical education department to the aforementioned philosophy of the 1930s. Intercollegiate type sports programs for women were not a high priority within the Department [at UW-Madison]."

Nevertheless, they were coming, helped along in no small part by the decision in 1967 to give Kit, now a faculty member, responsibility for administering the women's sports program on the Madison campus. Kit began encouraging the formation of teams in various sports which would compete with teams from other campuses.

"In the late '60s," she said, "we started extramural sports – competing against other schools."

It grew rapidly, and that became a problem.

"We were running it out of the physical education department," Kit said. "Out of the Women's Recreation Association office." There was no funding, no money to pay coaches for numerous teams – the number grew to 11.

"We did have advisors for each of our teams," Kit said. "We probably had 11 sports already. We kind of asked people who were physical education instructors, and in some cases even teaching assistants, wouldn't they like to advise this team? It's a lot of fun and it doesn't take too much time."

Kit continued: "As the sports began to develop it did take more time and the physical education department couldn't afford to give them [that] much release time from teaching classes. In fact, they didn't give them any for a long while. Then they gave them a teeny bit of release time. So it was biting into the physical education budget indirectly."

It was becoming untenable.

"Obviously this thing was starting to cost more money, even in the late '60s," Kit said. "We had to be able to get to places like Stevens Point. We had to be able to use fleet cars, which costs some money. They [the women athletes] had to wear something that made them look like a team. A lot of the time, in the beginning, it was just T-shirts and shorts, and try to get them the same color, please."

Parents of the athletes would sometimes help financially.

"We got one set of uniforms from somebody's father, who donated them," Kit said. "We had to quick wash them between sports and events and share them around."

A temporary, not completely satisfactory solution, arrived at in 1970, was to fold the women's extramural sports teams into a program of club sports, which began that year.

"The traditional concept of club sports," Kit wrote later, "is to give student organized groups an opportunity to compete and use facilities. To include women's competitive sports was stretching the club sport concept considerably. It did, however, provide a structure for the program, some priority for use of facilities, and after the first year, some funding."

Along with administrating the program, Kit coached the tennis team.

"Kit organized and fielded the first tennis team for the university, as a club sport," said Claudia Pogreba, a physical education student from La Crosse, Wisconsin, who played on one of those early club teams.

The first real tennis match between schools was in April 1969 at the new Nielsen Tennis Stadium in Madison – the University of Minnesota and Northwestern were the opponents.

Afterward, Eloise Jaeger, chairman of the physical education for women at Minnesota, wrote a letter to Kit's boss, the UW department head Lolas Halverson:

"The entire tournament was beautifully conducted," Jaeger wrote. "If you could have had a 'tape' of the comments made by University of Minnesota girls on the way home you would know how much they really enjoyed themselves."

Claudia Pogreba would turn her Badger tennis experience into a lifelong friendship with Kit.

"Somehow there was a connection with Kit and me," Pogreba said, "and I'm not even sure how that happened. Kit was a totally different personality than I am. Kit was very quiet, very humble, very sweet. She had a good sense of humor. I was probably not so serious a student at the time. More fun-loving, maybe even a little on the prankster side. I could get Kit going."

Pogreba recalled that Kit taught undergraduate courses for the physical education majors, adding that Kit introduced field hockey into the department at UW-Madison, and taught a class in it.

"In talking to Kit," Pogreba said, "and knowing her passion for field hockey, I signed up for the class. I lasted one hour."

Chuckling at the memory, Pogreba continued. "I can vividly remember going out, pads on, ready to play. But none of us had any skills in field hockey. I got hit so hard with a stick in the leg, above the pads, that I walked off the field. No one had any control. Someone just whacked me. I ran over to Kit and said, 'I'm not doing this sport.' She laughed. It became a kind of running joke between us."

Pogreba's memories of tennis trips with Kit are better, including one to play a team at the University of Illinois.

"They were a lot of fun," Pogreba said.

Looking back on those early days, she added, "Kit was instrumental, as she was her entire life, in getting women involved in athletics, at every level, recreational to competitive. She was an incredible pioneer without any of us really realizing it."

Another student on whom Kit had a significant impact was Kathy Tritschler, who came to UW-Madison in 1966 after graduating from Niles West High School in Skokie, Ill.

In an interview for this book, Tritschler recalled that she began as a pre-pharmacy major even though "I really wanted to study physical education." She'd enjoyed PE and liked sports in high school, but Tritschler said she initially succumbed to "social pressures" and the prevailing attitude that "smart girls didn't major in PE."

While she wasn't majoring in PE, Tritschler played intramural and extramural sports her first two years in Madison and spent considerable time at the WRA (Women's Recreation Association) office.

"Miss Saunders was our faculty sponsor," Tritschler recalled, "so I worked very closely with her, spending many hours in the WRA office, interacting with Kit. The WRA office is where I typically 'hung out' when not in classes. Those late 1960s were years filled with lots of social turmoil. UW did not escape the protests over the Vietnam War. I remember the tear gas lingering in the air the mornings after a protest march and the National Guard response."

"The WRA office was a safe and welcoming place," Tritschler continued, "and Miss Saunders was the calm and sage leader who knew how to make it safe and welcoming. She was always there for us with a smile and encouragement. She knew and remembered where we were from, the members of our families, the courses we were taking, etc. Miss Saunders helped us to appreciate that we were doing important work in facilitating athletic competitions for young women. UW-Madison was a large (and sometimes scary) place, but the WRA office was intimate and warm. It was a place where young women could learn and grow – from each other and from Miss Saunders."

Tritschler liked it so much she was considering changing her major. One Saturday morning in the winter of 1968-69, she was playing an intramural or extramural tennis match at the new Nielsen Tennis Stadium. Her parents had driven up from Illinois to watch. The plan was for Kathy to accompany her parents back to Skokie for the weekend.

After she finished her match, Tritschler climbed into the seats where her parents were sitting.

"The three of us watched as the other matches were finishing up," Tritschler recalled, "and then we spotted Miss Saunders, our coach, happily hitting balls with a couple of the team members on a court below us."

Tritschler turned to her mom and dad. "Wouldn't it be a great life to be a coach and PE instructor?" she said.

She recalled her parents' response: "Then why don't you do it?"

They spent the weekend considering the pros and cons of Tritschler changing course halfway through her junior year. She came back to Madison determined to try, if it was at all possible. Tritschler met with the PE transfer advisor, Dr. Marie Weber, who was highly encouraging.

"Dr. Weber figured out how to work me through the PE major (with a minor in administration) in 2½ years," Tritschler recalled. "After that morning meeting with Dr. Weber, I floated on air to my first class of the day. And when I dropped by the WRA office later that day, Miss Saunders had already heard the news that I was choosing PE. She hugged me and congratulated me."

Once she transferred to PE, Tritschler had Kit as an instructor in a few classes.

"One such course that I took from Kit was 'Methods in Teaching of Field Sports,'" Tritschler recalled, "a course that was designed to teach us the best ways to go about teaching sports such as field hockey, soccer, and lacrosse. I remember Kit being totally in her element – joyfully running up and down the grassy fields in her short navy-blue kilt, with a whistle around her neck, constantly shouting tips and suggestions to us.

"I remember," Tritschler continued, "lacrosse classes where she encouraged us to stretch ourselves to catch passes that seemed impossible. She'd say, encouragingly, 'If you can touch it, you can catch it!' Kit was never critical. If she observed something she didn't like, she merely 're-instructed,' and if she observed something good, praised. She was never stingy with her praise!"

Tritschler played for Kit on both the tennis and lacrosse teams. What she recalls most is Kit's enthusiasm and encouragement.

"I especially remember how good she was at analyzing motor skill errors and then giving cues and designing practice situations to improve those skills. Kit was what I call a 'teaching coach.' Although I didn't appreciate it at the time, I now think that it was remarkable that I don't remember any instances of intra-team conflicts. Kit must have created an environment that taught us to encourage and support our teammates.

"Perhaps," Tritschler concluded, "some of that collegiality was learned on the long automobile drives to and from athletic competitions with other Wisconsin state universities. On those long drives (Kit driving), we talked, joked, and sang. Oh, did we sing! Because it was the late 1960s, many were songs of social protest like 'Where Have All the Flowers Gone?' and 'If I Had a Hammer.' But many were old campfire songs we had grown up on. By the way, Kit didn't really sing along with us. I think she thought she didn't have a good voice. But Kit smiled. She let us know that she was happy –and we were, too."

After graduating in PE from UW-Madison in January 1972, Tritschler went on to a distinguished career in women's physical education and athletics. She acquired a master's degree at the University of Arizona and taught exercise science for three decades at Guilford College in North Carolina, authoring a book on measurement and evaluation in kinesiology and serving as chairman of the national Measurement and Evaluation Council of the American Alliance for Health, Physical Education, Recreation and Dance.

Kathy Tritschler and Kit built a long-distance friendship after Tritschler left Madison. They wrote regularly, and when Kathy visited her parents outside Chicago, she often drove up to Madison to see Kit. She recalled Kit teaching her how to cross-country ski on a frozen Lake Waubesa behind the home Kit had on the water in McFarland.

There were few sports Kit hadn't mastered before she was 30. She was also a downhill skier and taught a class that was open to male and female UW students. First semester was spent on exercises that would benefit them on the slopes; second semester, the class – 90 students in 1969, making it the most popular elective in the physical education department – spent Wednesday afternoons at Tyrol Basin outside Madison.

Before going to Tyrol Basin, however, Kit first had the students practice on campus, on famed Bascom Hill. She recalled the Bascom ski experience later in an interview with *Brava* magazine:

> "The students were just beginners, so I was just teaching them how to put their skis on and do snowplow turns. One day we went up there and there must have been a party the night before, because there were all these whiskey bottles all over. So I used them for class, making a slalom course out of them for the students to practice their turns. They thought that was great."

In 1970, the City Recreation Department asked Kit to coordinate a skiing program that was offered to adult staff members of the Madison public school system. To the astonishment of everyone, 168 people signed up. Like with the university students, Kit first took them through a series of exercises to get them in skiing shape, then they hit the slopes at Tyrol Basin.

In February 1970, the *Capital Times* caught up with a Wednesday night class, and interviewed Esther McIntosh, who worked in the office at Cherokee school.

"I don't know when I've enjoyed anything so much," she said, beaming as she finished a lesson from Kit. Nodding at Kit, McIntosh said, "She says I'm ready to traverse next!"

Along with all her teaching, coaching and administrating, Kit still had time starting in summer 1967 to work for the Madison School-Community Recreation Department, directing counselors at a camp at Olin Park in a program that included disabled kids. She received $700 for the season, though by the summer of 1969, her compensation increased to $1,400. After the 1969 camp, a group of 10 counselors and other staff sent a letter to her boss at School-Community Recreation:

"The Olin Day Camp staff wanted to let you know how very much we appreciate the job Kit does as camp director. She is deeply concerned that our camp program be exciting and challenging... She also takes a deep interest in each of us and goes out of her way to help where it is needed... Kit, in our opinion, is an excellent camp director and we are proud to serve under her."

Two years later, in 1971, Kit served as director for a new, curriculum-oriented summer camp for seventh and eighth graders – three one-week sessions at Cherokee Marsh Park. A *Cap Times* story noted: "Sand casting, folk singing, ecology science and watercolors will be taught. Outdoor activities such as cooking, archery, swimming, and canoeing also are scheduled."

Kit, of course, was accustomed to being perpetually on the go.

"My percentage of workload has always been rather difficult to figure out," Kit said in the mid-1970s. "Because half of my assignment in women's physical education is recreation, and that is always difficult, to figure out how many hours you're spending as recreation advisor. I never felt I was a good example. I knew I was overloaded when I was coaching. It's definitely an overload and it really gets tough during the competitive season."

The 1971-72 school year was the second year women's sports were under the club sports umbrella on the Madison campus.

Milt Bruhn, a former head UW football coach who took the Badgers to the 1963 Rose Bowl, was appointed director of club sports when they were founded in 1970. Kit was named coordinator of women's club sports.

There was, for the first time in 1971, money for the women's program: $2,000. For 11 sports.

"Each sport," Kit wrote later, "received $100 to $500, depending on its level of development."

"It was a struggle," said Debbie Erdman, a Madison native who played doubles on Kit's club sport tennis team from 1970-72. "There was no money for going to out of town meets, let alone out of state. We paid for ourselves. Kit occasionally came up with some help."

Erdman recalled that the tennis team took between four and six trips a year to other campuses for matches, paying for meals and hotel rooms themselves. Kit would usually drive them in a UW fleet car.

"She was more like one of us," Erdman, who entered medical school upon graduating, recalled. "She was young, maybe 10 years older than us. She always seemed more like a colleague than a coach. She was just a good person. We all liked her. There was absolutely nothing that we didn't like about Kit."

Another women's club sport was added in 1971 – women's crew. It was not new on the Madison campus – an article in the *Daily Cardinal* in 1901 noted that 60 women had joined campus rowing clubs – but it never grew into a competitive sport and had disappeared until one morning in the fall of 1971.

According to Bradley Taylor, in his 2005 history of the Badger crews, *Wisconsin Where They Row*, that fall a member of the University of Wisconsin band, Kathy Wutke, visited a friend and fellow band member, Bruce Niedermeier, at the crew boathouse – Niedermeier was also on the men's crew.

Wutke, who was a swimmer, mentioned something about how she might like to try crew.

"Rowing?" Niedermeier replied. "Women never do it."

That was all Wutke needed to summon a group of athletic female friends and approach men's crew coach Randy Jablonic about possibly getting a little time on the water.

"Some of our women students," Kit recalled later, "went and asked the men's crew coach to help them row. And [he] assigned an assistant coach to help them, assuming that it would very soon self-destruct because they'd make them work so hard they'd quit. Just the opposite happened."

The young women met with Kit, and with Milt Bruhn, and by late December 1971 women's crew was officially a club sport at UW-Madison. They received $100 in funding.

There was also, by the early 1970s, organizational movement in women's athletics, nationally and in Wisconsin. According to the 1974 book, *The American Woman in Sport*, an important development occurred in 1966 when the Division for Girls and Women's Sports (DGWS) appointed a commission to assist in the conduct of intercollegiate athletics for women.

In a 1990s interview, Kit recalled the DGWS as primarily "a rules-making body. They published rule books." The 1966 commission was eventually named the Commission on Intercollegiate Athletics for Women (CIAW) and listed among its goals: "*to encourage the holding of intercollegiate events and to assist those who are currently conducting such events.*"

It was a big step and a big deal – by 1970 the sports in which national championships were held included golf, tennis, gymnastics, badminton, volleyball, swimming and diving, and track and field. In 1971, the DGWS was replaced by an even more authoritative and comprehensive organization – the Association for Intercollegiate Athletics for Women (AIAW).

For one extraordinary pioneering female athlete at UW-Madison, those first DGWS national championships were an especially big deal. For diver D'Lynn Damron, they were about the only competition she could find. The story of how Damron became a competitive diver is itself remarkable.

Damron grew up adjacent to Madison in the village of Shorewood Hills, and like a lot of Shorewood kids, her summers were spent swimming in Lake Mendota.

"Others might have had pools, we only had the lake," Damron recalled in an interview for this book. "We had a platform that extended into the water and we would dive off that."

One summer – Damron was going to be a junior at Madison West High School – a member of the University of Wisconsin men's diving team noticed Damron diving. He was taken with her natural ability and asked if he might coach her. Damron agreed. When the young man was drafted into the military a short time later, he told the Badger men's diving coach, Jerry Darda, about Damron, suggesting that Darda take over her coaching.

"Jerry didn't want to coach girls," Damron said. "He thought they were too emotional."

But after meeting Damron, Darda agreed to help her, suggesting she come to the men's diving team practices. Damron was in her junior year at West High and would walk down to the UW Natatorium after school. There was, however, a problem. Women weren't allowed – at least by tradition – in the pool of the Natatorium, a campus facility that opened in 1966.

"When the building manager came around," Damron said, "I would have to go hide in the men's weight room, which was right behind the diving boards, until he went through. I did that for my junior and senior years of high school."

Damron enrolled at UW-Madison in fall of 1970 and continued to practice with the men's diving team. There was not even a sport club for women divers on campus. Eventually, her presence at the Nat, as it was called, came to a head.

Darda, the coach, recalled, "I had physical education guys looking at me like I was committing some kind of major immoral crime by bringing D'Lynn in there."

The men's swimming coach, John Hickman, told Darda he was getting pressure from faculty.

"They're not comfortable with this," Hickman said.

"Are you directing me to deny her this opportunity?" Darda replied.

Hickman paused for a moment. "No," he said.

Damron recalled getting on the plane to accompany the men's team to a swim and dive meet at Indiana University, where Damron would have competed against the Hoosier women divers after the men's competition.

"We screeched to a halt on the tarmac in Madison," Damron said. "They'd found out I was on the plane and I had to get off." It was something about her unofficial status and insurance, Damron was told. Darda gave her $5 for cab fare back to campus.

When you are trying to make a case for someone, it never hurts if they excel, and Damron was an exceptional diver.

The first DGWS national collegiate swimming and diving championships were in spring 1970, Damron's freshman year at UW.

Damron and a few UW women swimmers attended the national championship meet, held in Normal, Illinois.

"My mother drove us down," Damron recalled. "I swam for the relay team as well. But I was really down there to dive."

Damron took first place in the both one-meter and three-meter competitions – she was a national collegiate champion.

"She was a great role model for the guys," Darda recalled. "A good competitor. In the summer we trained at an outdoor pool and if it was chilly, the guys shivering, D'Lynn would be up there

D'Lynn Damron.
(courtesy of
UW athletics)

on the board. Lightning could strike – though we wouldn't go out then. But it could be really cold, and she wouldn't flinch."

Kit supported Damron and Darda, who eventually took over as women's diving coach when the program gained intercollegiate varsity status in 1974.

"Kit was really supportive and a big fan of any girl who was in athletics," Darda said. "She did everything she could for them. She wanted them to have the best coaching. And because we'd had D'Lynn in there [with the men's team], Kit and I had a mutual respect. It was clear I wasn't against having women in our space."

According to Damron, it was Kit who somehow found the money when, as a senior in 1973, Damron qualified for the women's national collegiate diving finals, but lacked the funds to travel to Washington state.

"Kit gave me the money to go to Spokane," Damron said.

Damron flew to the West Coast alone.

"We always stayed in people's homes, we never stayed in hotels," Damron said. But when she got to the pool in Spokane to practice, meet officials told her that because she was traveling without a chaperone, she was in violation of AIAW (the organization which had taken over from the DGWS) rules. Damron would not be allowed to dive.

"I was really upset," Damron recalled. Phone calls went back and forth into the night. Finally the AIAW relented – an exception was granted and Damron could compete.

"I dove out of my mind," she recalled, and she won the one-meter national championship.

For Kit, it was always about helping women compete. Sometimes that involved establishing conferences to encourage competition between schools.

"We started an organization in Wisconsin in 1971," Kit recalled, two decades later, "which was called the Wisconsin Women's Intercollegiate Athletic Conference (WWIAC). It was fully endorsed by each campus. It provided a state level of competition, which led to a Midwest level, which led to the AIAW."

The WWIAC grew out of an organization that formed in 1958 – the Wisconsin Athletic and Recreation Federation of College Women (WARFCW), modeled after the national ARFCW, in which governance was left to the students. It included eight Wisconsin colleges and primarily sponsored "sports days" in archery, badminton, basketball, golf, gymnastics, tennis and volleyball.

There was periodic discussion of turning it into a more competition oriented athletic conference – one such motion was defeated in 1966. By fall of 1970, the tide had turned. WARFCW member school advisors – with Kit representing UW-Madison – agreed to develop an athletic conference for women. On Jan. 31, 1971, the advisors voted unanimously to form the WWIAC.

In March 1971, a two-day meeting was held on the campus of UW-Stevens Point to solidify the WWIAC and elect officers. Kit was named secretary-treasurer.

There were a lot of positive things happening regarding the potential for competitive women's intercollegiate athletics, but an article that appeared in a Madison newspaper exactly one year after the WWIAC meeting in Stevens Point vividly demonstrated there was still a long way to go.

The Stevens Point WWIAC meeting began March 26, 1971. On March 26, 1972, the *Wisconsin State Journal* published a story on the front page of its "Family-Women" section that carried the following headline:

"U. W. Girl Athletes – They Bake Brownies."

Kit – in her role as tennis coach – was pictured beneath the headline. (It was not the first time Kit's photo appeared in a Madison paper. That happened a year earlier, in June 1971. Kit was shown paddling a canoe in the Lathrop Hall swimming pool on campus – the extended photo cutline said she would be teaching a summer class on canoeing for the Madison School-Community Recreation Department.)

The 1972 *State Journal* article began with this:

"Nancy Schmidt is a fine University of Wisconsin tennis player who may have to bake brownies to afford intercollegiate competition this year.
"In fact, her whole UW women's tennis team may have to hold a bake sale to meet expenses.

"This makes them a little bitter, knowing as they do that [Coach] Bob Johnson and his champion-ship men's hockey team didn't spend their spare time peddling chocolate chip cookies to make it through the season."

Again referencing Schmidt, the article continued two paragraphs later:

"On trips, the pretty 19-year-old from West Hartford, Conn. pays room and board out of her

own pocket, as do all her teammates. Equipment
allowance? Forget it. Facilities for practice?
They're already overcrowded."

Kit was quoted in the story, along with Muriel Sloan, chairman of
the women's physical education department at UW-Madison.
Both women lamented the lack of funding, as did Elroy Hirsch,
director of the UW men's athletic program – which in 1972 had
an annual budget of $1.6 million.

About the lack of funding for women's athletics, Hirsch
said, "It's a crime."

Hirsch was speaking figuratively, of course, and the vast
funding disparity for men's and women's athletics on college
campuses would never be criminal. Yet in June 1972, just two
months after that *State Journal* article appeared, President
Richard Nixon signed into law a piece of legislation that pro-
foundly changed the way women's athletics were treated on
campuses across the country. It took years to fully implement and
faced powerful opposition even after it became law. Still, the
legislation that amended the Higher Education Act of 1965 was a
bombshell. Kit and her colleagues had a shorthand name for it.

They called it Title IX.

Chapter 4

TITLE IX

Years later, Kit said, "If it hadn't been for Title IX, we might still be sharing uniforms and scratching the ice off the windows of the old fleet cars with our fingernails."

But while the importance of Title IX of the Education Amendments Act of 1972 to the growth of women's intercollegiate athletics cannot be overstated, it would be a mistake to regard its June 1972 adoption into law as a panacea. It took time – years – for its implications to be sorted out.

No surprise, Title IX's original route to passage was also circuitous.

Its start might be traced to 1964, when the United States Congress passed a Civil Rights Act which among its provisions included Title VI, preventing discrimination on the part of institutions receiving federal funds. But Title VI stated that discrimination on the basis of race, color and national origin would be prohibited. There was no mention of gender.

Enter United States Rep. Edith Green, a Democrat from Oregon. Green was a former teacher who in the 1960s helped pass legislation creating federal scholarships and otherwise assisting those without sufficient means to attend college.

"[Green] was passionate about making education available to everyone," wrote Karen Blumenthal, in her 2005 book, *Let Me Play: The Story of Title IX, the Law that Changed the Future of Girls in America.*

Blumenthal's book was targeted at young adults but is valuable for readers at any level. It endures as one of the most accessible accounts of how Title IX came into being.

Blumenthal shared the late-1960s story of Rep. Green quizzing a panel of American school superintendents, one of whom had extolled a program for disadvantaged boys.

"Do you mean that you had classes only for disadvantaged boys?" Green asked. "Couldn't you have classes and include both boys and girls?"

The answer came back: No. Boys needed the classes, because "they are going to be the breadwinners."

"Mrs. Green was stunned," Blumenthal wrote, and dismayed, later, to learn that there were no laws in place to prohibit sex discrimination in education. She was also positioned to do something about it: after nearly 15 years in Congress, Green chaired the higher education subcommittee of the House Education and Labor Committee.

"She had the power to initiate such legislation," wrote Bernice Resnick Sandler in a lengthy 2007 *Cleveland Law Review* article, "the legislation that became Title IX of a larger bill, the Education Amendments of 1972."

Sandler was herself a key player; indeed, the *New York Times* later called her "the godmother of Title IX." As an academic, she'd encountered discrimination firsthand.

"Let's face it," a male faculty member told Sandler when she asked why she'd missed an academic promotion, "you come on too strong for a woman."

Sandler began to cast a net, gathering stories of sex discrimination on campus. Her findings were depressingly thorough and included dozens of instances of blatant discrimination akin to this one: State colleges in Virginia, Sandler found, had turned away 21,000 women in the early 1960s, while not one man was denied entrance during the same period.

Sandler shared the research with Rep. Green, who drafted a bill and held congressional hearings on sex discrimination on college campuses. Sandler was Green's star witness.

The testimony was shocking, or might have been, had anyone been paying attention. There was no media coverage of Green's hearings. Male representatives on Green's committee left the hearings early or missed entirely. The education establishment wasn't concerned, and if anything, the college athletics power structure was even more absent.

"Because the word 'sports' appears nowhere in the bill," Sandler wrote, "... the college athletic establishment simply had no idea that Title IX existed and would affect them at their very core. In other words, Title IX was seen as a very minor bill. Hardly anyone outside of Congress was following it..."

Within a year, however, Title IX was part of the larger bill that both Congress and Richard Nixon's presidential administration were considering – a bill that would amend the Higher Education Act of 1965. Democrats were looking for more financial aid options for lower income students; Republicans, including the president, were considering ways to limit mandatory busing of students as a way of integrating schools.

Rep. Green was deeply involved, and she hadn't forgotten gender discrimination – Title IX of the bill. She just didn't make it a big deal.

Sandler recalled: "A small group of women from various women's groups met with Rep. Green. We offered to lobby for the bill and do whatever she wanted us to do. She was adamant that we not do any lobbying whatsoever. She said that if we started to lobby, people would ask questions and ask what Title IX would do."

Title IX read: *"No person shall, on the basis of sex, be excluded from participation in, be denied the benefits of, or be subjected to discrimination under any educational program receiving Federal financial assistance."*

Though there was a little harrumphing from one or two men on the committee, a majority voted to include Green's proposal. It became Title X of the new bill – later Title IX, after another section was jettisoned.

Green's low-key strategy continued once the entire House of Representatives took up the bill. But then Illinois Rep. John Erlenborn made an impassioned speech against it on the House floor in November 1971.

Erlenborn called the proposal "a dangerous precedent," adding, "… if Congress permits the Federal Government to take away from colleges their right to determine the composition of their own student bodies, it will plant the seed of destruction for our system of higher education as we know it."

He swayed enough colleagues that a weaker version of Title IX – applying only to graduate schools – was included with the financial aid and busing restrictions in the final bill that passed the House.

Meanwhile, the U.S. Senate was considering its own education bill. Eventually the House and Senate bills would have to be reconciled into a single bill that each body would vote on. If passed, that bill would go to the president for signing into law.

On the Senate side, Title IX's champion was Birch Bayh of Indiana. He told the Chicago sports journalist Melissa Isaacson in a 2005 interview that his first wife, Marvella, had been the driving force behind his sponsoring the bill. (It's worth repeating Sandler's contention that more than 20,000 women were denied entrance to Virginia's public colleges in the 1960s. Pre-1960s, one woman denied entry into the University of Virginia – despite being a 4.0 student and high school class president – was Marvella Hern, later Marvella Bayh.)

In his interview with Isaacson, Bayh quoted Marvella on Title IX: "She said we can't afford to ignore the development of 53 percent of the brainpower in this country."

It was Bayh, on the Senate side, who first put athletics on the radar of those considering Title IX. Most concentrated on equal opportunities in the classroom. But Bayh's father was a coach and high school sports administrator who once testified before Congress on the need for more funding for physical education for girls. "Little girls," he said, "need strong bodies to carry strong minds around in, just like little boys do."

During the Title IX debate, a Senate colleague of Bayh's, Peter Dominick from Colorado, suggested the proposal might require that girls play football, and that dormitories be shared by the sexes.

According to Blumenthal, Bayh replied, "I do not read this as requiring integration of dormitories between the sexes, nor do I feel it mandates the desegregation of football fields. What we are trying to do is provide equal access for women and men students to the educational process and the extracurricular activities in a school."

Bayh eventually made some concessions – the Senate bill exempted military schools – and the education bill with Title IX attached was passed by the Senate. At that point a conference committee with both House and Senate representation was convened. The House and Senate bills needed to be merged into one.

The compromise brought undergraduate schools back under the Title IX umbrella – the clause limiting it to graduate schools was eliminated – but exempted private schools. The law would pertain only to public universities. Blumenthal noted the compromise bill also weakened some financial aid provisions that the House sponsor, Edith Green, had championed. Green was distressed enough that when the final vote came, June 8, 1972, she voted against her own bill. Nevertheless, the bill passed the House and Senate, with Title IX intact.

President Richard Nixon signed the bill into law two weeks later.

It was a momentous moment that was not realized as such at the time. Other parts of the education bill – busing, financial assistance – received more attention. Title IX landed with a whisper.

Still, it was heard in Madison by Kit Saunders, who had been trying with scarce resources to get a women's athletics program going.

"I can remember," Kit recalled later, "first hearing about Title IX being passed and thinking, 'Oh, boy, somebody finally did something. This is probably going to help us.'"

And Kit, despite all her efforts, needed help. She described the landscape for women's athletics on campus, pre-Title IX, in a UW Oral History Program interview a few years after Title IX's passage.

"We were not able to pay our coaches very much at all," Kit said. "Anyone who was coaching who was also a staff member was not receiving enough release time to make it worth their while. It was practically volunteer coaching, although not quite that bad. We traveled by fleet car, not any other way. Students did have to pay some of their expenses if there were overnights. Males athletes even in non-income sports were getting their ways paid completely. Women athletes were not.

"We had no priority on facilities," Kit continued. "If a facility was available, wasn't being scheduled for something else, including intramurals and in some cases open basketball shooting, then we could get it. We were practicing in Lathrop Hall, which had no regulation-size [basketball] courts. Our swimming practices – we had one evening a week in the Natatorium. I think [in 1972] we did have a 6:00 in the morning time we could get in. Which is kind of inconvenient, especially in the middle of the winter.

"We had very limited uniforms," Kit recalled. "We had about two dozen warm-up suits, and with 11 teams going at once – it wasn't unusual to have four or five teams out on a weekend – we called it 'musical warm-ups.' We'd have to try to launder them quickly and get them to the next team. We didn't have any kind of laundry service, or laundry exchange. The coaches frequently were doing the laundry, or the athletes were doing it themselves. We had no practice uniforms. They had to use their own [clothes] to practice in."

As women's sports coordinator for the UW-Madison club sport program, Kit each year had to go in front of the intramural recreation board to request funding. The passage of Title IX in 1972 may have emboldened her – for 1972-73 the women's program received $8,000, four times the previous year's budget, if still a pittance in comparison to the men.

"These meetings were frequently harrowing experiences," Kit noted of being in front of the rec board, and indeed, for 1973-74, when she requested $25,000 to run her growing program, she was allocated only $18,000.

"The women's program," Kit noted, "was wearing out its welcome in the club sport program as it became more expensive and more closely resembled an intercollegiate program."

Kit needed about $7,000 more than the board was willing to provide.

"So I went to the chancellor and told him I was short," Kit recalled. "The chancellor came up with that for us."

Kit said that when the intramural rec board learned that she had approached Chancellor Ed Young, they threatened to withhold their original $18,000 allotment.

"They felt I had gone over their heads," she said.

Kit was incredulous. "This was unbelievable to me," she said. "That they would hold back the money they had allocated to us, just because I had gone and gotten the rest of what I needed from another source."

Later, Kit noted wryly, "This cannot be found in the intramural recreation board minutes." Eventually the board relented and allocated the original $18,000.

Presumably with Title IX on his radar, Chancellor Ed Young, in July 1972, appointed a committee to study women's athletics and make recommendations on how they might be better served on campus. But the committee included no UW women student-athletes. And Young seemingly erred in his choice of athletic director Elroy Hirsch as committee chairman. Hirsch called only two meetings between July 1972 and March 1973, and the second meeting was canceled.

This so infuriated a member of the committee, Muriel Sloan, chairman of the women's physical education department, that on March 2, 1973, she sent Hirsch a blistering letter, threatening to resign from the committee.

"For me to remain on this inactive committee," Sloan wrote, "is to continue to the illusion for women students and interested faculty groups that the problem of facilities for women is being seriously considered... You can see, therefore, that my membership on this non-functioning committee and its non-functioning status is untenable. I would prefer that the committee begin to function rather than resigning from it. If, however, you as chairman and other committee members are not equally devoted to pursuing the committee charge, then all should disband. A new committee could then be appointed by the chancellor, or existing groups concerned with equal opportunity on campus can follow up on their expressed interest in the issue."

Sloan was formidable, a New York native who came to Madison for graduate school and stayed. Sloan served as vice president of the International Association of Physical Education and Sports for Girls and Women. On leaving Madison in 1980, she went to the University of Maryland, where she became assistant vice chancellor for academic affairs.

Equally formidable on the Madison campus in 1973 was Ruth Bleier, who joined the UW's department of neurophysiology in 1967, embarking on a career that included a deep dive into gender biases in science. Bleier was a founding member of the Association of Faculty Women at UW-Madison, and it was in that role, two weeks after Sloan wrote her letter to Hirsch, that Bleier followed with one of her own.

Bleier began her March 16 letter by noting the anti-discrimination law that now existed under Title IX, and then wrote:

"Consequently, we demand immediate and equal use of all facilities: tracks, fields, courts and pools, locker rooms and showers. This means that all facilities be available to women and women's teams at times that are no more inconvenient for them than for men, such as dinner time for the tennis courts and after 5:30 p.m. for the track team, the periods currently allowed women.

"We demand adequate and equal (as needed) funding for all women's sports teams," Bleier continued, "including salaries for coaches with full time academic appointments and expenses for training and competition. Anything less than this must be negotiated with us and other women in athletics and justified to our satisfaction. We do not want to hear again about inadequacy of facilities, space and time. If they are inadequate, we will share equally with men in the inadequacy. The burden is no longer ours to wait. We have waited too long. The moral and, now, the legal burden is yours."

Hard to mistake a gauntlet being thrown down there.

One can imagine Kit finding herself in a somewhat delicate circumstance. While Kit no doubt sided with Sloan and Bleier – and Kit quoted Sloan's letter and mentioned Bleier's in a later essay – she was also operating inside the athletic administration umbrella (club sports) and would likely continue to even as change on the gender issue was initiated. Vitriol would not serve her purpose and was not her style, in any case.

In a later interview, Kit recalled, "I remember after [Title IX passed] trying to explain it to the athletic board. I'd really learned about it and what it stood for – what we were going to have to do. People had refused to act because they didn't have enough information. The women who had become versed in it were trying to tell them [various administrators] what it was. And they were saying, 'This can't be.'"

Kit later wrote that on March 21, five days after Bleier's letter to Elroy Hirsch "demanding" equal funding and facilities for women's sports, "Assistant Chancellor Cyrena Pondrom offered use of a shower facility in the memorial shell (today, the Camp Randall Memorial Sports Center), and the athletic department offered to provide soap and towels to women joggers."

Whether this would have been enough to appease Bleier and the Association of Faculty Women is unlikely, but, as Kit noted, "through some quirk in communication, perhaps, the faculty women were not aware of this offer."

In any case, on April 3, 1973, a complaint against the University of Wisconsin was filed with the United States Department of Health, Education and Welfare's (HEW) Office of Civil Rights.

> "The University of Wisconsin, Madison campus, is in flagrant violation of Executive Order 11246 [a 1965 non-discrimination order issued by President Lyndon Johnson] and of Title IX… in its continued provision of unequal facilities and funding for athletics programs for women students and employees and unequal compensation for the coaching of its women's teams."

HEW, led by Secretary Caspar Weinberger, was tasked with interpreting and implementing Title IX as it related to high school and intercollegiate athletics. They went slowly, in part because it was a sea change. Were university athletics departments really going to have to treat men and women's sports equally?

"The male athletic establishment was close to hysteria," Sandler wrote. "We're talking big money – where would the money come from to fund athletics for women?"

"HEW was in no hurry," wrote author Karen Blumenthal, who interviewed Weinberger. But she felt Weinberger did come to sense the inherent unfairness of the way the system had worked, and his department proceeded with implementation.

In Madison, Kit and her colleagues were grateful for signals from Washington that Title IX would be enforced.

"The sort of sad thing about Title IX," Kit said, "is that most schools began to comply not because it was the right thing to do and had gotten started anyway, but because they were worried about the teeth that were in it and what the federal government could do. Like take away their federal funding and lots of other types of programs."

According to Kit, if things weren't moving quickly enough, the women sometimes took matters into their own hands.

"The Red Gym was the pool on campus where men traditionally swam without swim trunks," Kit said. "There was a group of women on campus who were out to open up everything for women and I think they appeared at the swimming pool at the Red Gym – more to the embarrassment of the men than them. And they also hit the showers in the [Memorial] shell, one weekend. Which had been just open to men."

Kit recalled, "The administration at the time denied that any such actions moved them along any faster than they were planning on moving. In essence, I think it probably did."

On April 19, 1973 – 16 days after the Title IX complaint on the Madison campus was filed with HEW – UW Chancellor Ed Young stepped in and replaced Elroy Hirsch as chairman of the Committee on Women's Athletic Programs and Facilities – the committee that had met once in eight months.

"The chancellor appointed a new chair," Kit said. "Murray Fowler, from the department of linguistics. Just a wonderful person."

Young wrote a letter to Fowler stating his hopes for the committee.

"This committee," Young wrote, "is charged with advising me of the most appropriate ways to achieve equity in men's and women's recreational, intercollegiate and intramural athletic and physical education programs and facilities on the Madison campus.

"This committee," Young continued, "should offer both a short-run and long-range report. For our immediate purposes, I should like to receive recommendations from the committee by or before July 1 concerning remodeling, rescheduling, or other changes which will enable us to achieve a great degree of equity for women staff and students in athletic programs and facilities for the coming academic year.

"Following that," Young concluded, "as rapidly as is consonant with a full and careful review of needs, problems and alternatives, I should like to receive recommendations concerning the best way fully to achieve equity in athletic programs and facilities."

Of Murray Fowler, Kit said, "He got the committee going. It met 18 times over a period of a year."

The first the general public knew of this new mission came near the end of the month, at an April 27 meeting of the University of Wisconsin athletic board.

Young did not appear, but Assistant Chancellor Cyrena Pondrom – who was also UW's director of affirmative action – did. Pondrom shared Young's letter, as well as three equity initiatives that were already underway.

As reported in the next day's *Wisconsin State Journal* sports section, those steps included:

1) Remodeling the women's toilets in the Camp Randall Memorial building to allow for six shower heads and 30 lockers. There previously were no shower or dressing facilities for women.

2) The visiting team's locker room in the Field House was now being used for women's shower and dressing facilities.

3) A towel facility for women was being set up at the University Natatorium.

That the campus administration was taking the Title IX complaint filed earlier that month seriously could be seen in a comment from athletic board chairman Fred Haberman: "I'm sure this committee is going to move things along quickly. It is imperative that we be able to prove to the federal government that we are moving on this."

The *State Journal* article – written by sports editor Glenn Miller, who to that point hadn't tried to disguise his antipathy toward women's sports – never mentioned the Title IX lawsuit, and indeed Miller may not have known about it. His story ran on page four of the sports section.

The chancellor's committee moved quickly. By May, according to Kit in a later essay, the committee had passed a recommendation requiring that "all physical recreation facilities administered by the University of Wisconsin should be made available for use by both men and women."

As for competition and taking the women's program from club sport to intercollegiate varsity status, Kit presented a proposal to the executive committee of the department of physical education for women that would have had the department administering women's intercollegiate athletics. It wasn't likely to happen – after all, the women's physical education department had been a leader nationally for decades in discouraging competition (as opposed to participation) for women.

Kit recalled that while some in the department were agreeable to the idea, it was not approved by the executive committee. The bias against competition for women athletes played a role, as did funding concerns – the school of education, where the department sat, was not prepared to finance a competitive athletic program.

The most likely home for an intercollegiate women's program was inside the UW athletic department. The athletic board took a step in that direction in September 1973 during a meeting that the *State Journal* reported "opened the door to women's intercollegiate athletic competition within the framework of the Department of Intercollegiate Athletics."

"The board did not immediately invite the ladies inside," wrote Glenn Miller in his inimitable way. "Still, it was an historic step."

What the board did was insert the following into its policy book:

> "It is the policy of the athletic board to make intercollegiate athletic competition, facilities, finances, administrative resources, coaching and ancillary personnel available to all qualified undergraduate students without regard to race, creed, religion, national origin or sex."

The Fowler committee – the chancellor's committee on women's athletics – was meanwhile formulating its own recommendations. The women members of the committee – who included Kit and Muriel Sloan, chairman of the women's physical education department and a newly seated member of the UW athletic board – presented a proposal to the full committee in December 1973.

The committee accepted the proposal in its entirety, with the chairman, Fowler, saying that it would then be up to Chancellor Ed Young to act on it. The headliner among the committee's recommendations was this:

> "We believe that combining athletic programs [men's and women's] will be beneficial from the outset for women's athletics and in the long run also for men's athletics in the educational setting of the university."

And this:

> "That a woman whose title shall be director of intercollegiate athletics for women shall be responsible directly to the director of intercolle- giate athletics."

Other provisions included:

"In as expedient a manner as possible, more women shall be included in the membership of the athletic board."

"Separate teams by sex shall be supported and the separate coaches for men's and women's teams shall be hired whenever this is feasible."

"As soon as possible provision shall be made for the inclusion of more women in the division of intercollegiate athletics. [Including sports information and an athletic trainer.]

"In order to meet the HEW guidelines effectuating Title IX of the Educational Amendments Act of 1972, provision must be made for funding of women's athletics."

It was this last – how to pay for making women's athletics equitable – that caused the most confusion and controversy.

In a *Capital Times* story headlined "Hirsch Cries 'Foul!' on Women's Sports Plan," the UW athletic director said, "I hate to see our existing program torn down to put another into effect."

Chancellor Young, meanwhile, took the Fowler committee's recommendations and handed them to the athletic board, telling board chairman Fred Haberman to develop a "plan of action," which some saw as the chancellor punting the issue, to use a sports metaphor. Haberman responded by appointing a committee to study it.

It was contentious, and Kit, as ever, was a voice of calm. She gave an interview to *State Journal* sports columnist Tom Butler stressing how well she got along with Otto Breitenbach, Hirsch's top assistant.

"Our philosophies are similar," Kit said.

The uncertain status of Title IX nationally couldn't have helped. They had taken months to wake up, but the male college sports establishment – exemplified by the executives who ran the National Collegiate Athletic Association (NCAA) – was sounding a five-alarm alert. In numerous interviews they predicted doom if the Title IX regulations were enforced.

The NCAA got a friendly U.S. senator, John Tower of Texas, to introduce an amendment to a 1974 education bill that would have exempted men's football and basketball from Title IX requirements, essentially gutting the law. While that ultimately failed, HEW rules were amended so that cost differences between sports could be taken into consideration. Powerful male voices – including the male football coaches at top university programs – continued to predict disaster if Title IX was implemented.

Back in Madison, on March 11, 1974, an extraordinary panel discussion took place at the Wisconsin Center on campus. Its stated purpose was to discuss the progress of women's athletics at UW and the program's direction going forward.

Members of the panel included Kit; Elroy Hirsch; Murray Fowler; assistant to the chancellor Cyrena Pondrum; Muriel Sloan, from women's physical education and the athletic board; and four women student-athletes.

That the evening would be lively was assured by the moderator: Ruth Bleier, chair of the Association of Faculty Women, whose letter to Hirsch a year earlier, in April 1973, had demanded equity for women's athletics now. The audience gathered for the panel discussion apparently agreed with that sentiment.

Fred Milverstedt, a young sports columnist for *The Capital Times*, was in attendance and didn't mince words when it came to the audience reaction to Elroy Hirsch's comments: "Most everything he said subsequently was greeted with hissing, boos, some subdued cursing, and occasional angry shouts," Milverstedt wrote.

Somehow – quite possibly owing to the unflappable, behind the scenes work of Kit – the campus went from that raucous scene to another, vastly different gathering less than two months later.

On May 3, 1974, a news conference was held in which athletic director Elroy Hirsch and athletic board chairman Fred

Haberman announced the first director of women's intercollegiate athletics at the University of Wisconsin.

It was Kit Saunders.

That it could hardly have been anyone else did not lessen the excitement and anticipation accompanying the announcement, although Kit later told *Brava* magazine that her getting the women's athletic director job was not the slam dunk it might have appeared.

"When I was first trying to get the [director] job," she said, "there were women in the physical education department who didn't really want me to get it."

It was the holdover from the old "participation vs. competition" days that dated to Blanche Trilling and the middle decades of the 20th century.

"They really didn't want [women's] athletics to happen at all," Kit said.

The magazine writer asked why that mindset endured, even in the post-Title IX 1970s.

Kit sighed and threw up her hands. "I don't know," she said. "I didn't get it."

At the press conference where her new position was announced, Kit was flanked by Hirsch and Haberman, and told reporters that while there was "a great deal of work to be done," women's athletics at UW had "an exciting future."

As usual, Kit wasn't wrong. She officially started in her new job on July 1, 1974. Within a year, she had a national championship.

Chapter 5

DIRECTOR OF WOMEN'S ATHLETICS

E ven Glenn Miller, the *Wisconsin State Journal* sports editor who found little to embrace about women's intercollegiate athletics, acknowledged that if the program had to have a director, there was no one better than Kit Saunders, who was given a first-year salary of $16,000 and a first-year budget of $118,000 to administer 11 sports.

Decades later, in a magazine interview, Kit recalled that immediately after the press conference announcing her new position, she found herself walking down a hallway in the company of Miller.

"I've got one word of advice for you," Miller said.

"What would that be?" Kit replied.

Miller responded: "Don't be a bitch."

All those years later, Kit laughed at the memory. "He knew that wasn't my approach, anyway."

The sports editor, just a few days after the press conference announcing Kit's new position, wrote a column headlined, "An Excellent Decision."

"It wasn't a difficult choice," Miller opined, adding that the athletic board was "lucky to have Kit waiting for the job."

To be fair to Miller, the sports editor was right on the button in his assessment of why Kit was the best choice.

"I have heard Kit Saunders speak – and argue – at many athletic board meetings," Miller wrote. "I have argued with her on a telephone. But I declare her to be the voice of reason that is needed at this point in the development of women's athletics at

Wisconsin. She is fair, temperate, and reasonable. She fights like the devil for what she believes in – and she should. But she listens as much as she talks, and she senses the difference between what is possible and what is not immediately possible."

All the state's biggest newspapers covered the announcement of Kit's new position. In the first week of May 1974 there were stories in the *State Journal*, *The Capital Times*, and the *Milwaukee Journal*. *The Milwaukee Sentinel* had two – one on May 4, the day after the press conference, and another a week later, in its "world of women" section.

Not surprisingly, there was another round of stories in July, when Kit officially assumed her athletic director's role.

An Associated Press story that ran in several papers focused, as did most, on the $118,000 budget for 1974-75, up substantially from $18,000 a year earlier.

Reporter Lisa C. Berman wrote: "The new budget, however, does not mean dramatic new programs, Katherine Saunders, director of women's intercollegiate athletics said.

"She likens its effect to that of polishing silver tarnished from lack of attention. The bigger budget will bring out the shine in women's sports, she says.

"Instead of a spanking new sports program, young ladies returning to campus this fall will find that coaches have more time to spend with them, they have better equipment, and the university supplies all uniforms.

"Right now Miss Saunders is busy arranging for coaching staff, uniforms, equipment and facilities. She said the biggest expense and the biggest problem will be hiring coaches."

A campus newspaper, the *Daily Cardinal*, included in its fall registration issue a long story headlined "UW women's sports enter new era." It noted that "head coaches hired so far include Nancy Kristof, field hockey; Jane Eastham, golf; Carol Eastgate, badminton; and Marion Snowden, gymnastics." Eastgate was a native of England and Snowden a native of New Zealand.

Kit in 1974.
(courtesy of
UW athletics)

For an interview with Margo Huston of the *Milwaukee Journal*, the state's largest newspaper, Kit invited the reporter into the air-conditioned lounge of the W Club in Camp Randall Stadium, better digs than would have been available a year earlier in Lathrop Hall. "I have to start taking advantage of all the opportunities of my position," Kit said, and revealed her W Club unfamiliarity by struggling with the key to open the door.

"As far as the men around here are concerned," Kit told Huston, "we've seen a lot of attitudes change in the last three years. Attitudes, you know, are the hardest thing to change."

That was Kit being a diplomat for a story that would appear within a few days. She was more forthright regarding the attitudes of her male athletic department colleagues in an interview she gave 40 years later to *Brava* magazine.

"I can name," Kit said, "maybe three men in that department who would talk to me when I first got in."

One of them who would, it should be noted, was associate athletic director Otto Breitenbach. When Breitenbach died in 2007, Kit recalled how she visited Breitenbach often in his office, seeking advice and counsel. "There weren't too many men in the department when I first walked in there who talked to me very much," Kit told the *State Journal*. "I had the feeling he had to go to bat for me a lot of times."

In her July 1974 interview with the *Milwaukee Journal*, Kit talked about facilities. Even with intercollegiate status and a new budget, they were a mixed bag.

Volleyball was a positive.

"Two years ago," Kit said, "we were allowed to use the regulation volleyball courts [at the Natatorium] for matches only. Last year, we could use them for matches and only big practice sessions before matches. This year, we'll get the regulation courts for all matches and all practices."

Less positive was the situation with the women's crew. "The crew house," Kit said. "That's one place they still don't have [women's] showers."

A month prior to the interview, in June 1974, the women's crew had gone to Oakland, California for the National Women's Rowing Championship – the biggest prize in women's rowing, with university and club teams allowed to participate. (The NCAA didn't establish a rowing championship until 1997.)

Few may have realized it, but as they made that trip to Oakland, the Badger women's crew was on the cusp of greatness. It would take a year to fully flower, but the seed was there.

They had a new coach, Jay Mimier, who had rowed for the UW men's crew in the 1960s, graduating in 1971. Mimier then enrolled in law school in Madison. In spring 1973, the women's crew coaching job opened when Doug Neil, the men's freshman coach who had also been coaching the women, stepped down.

"A bunch of people turned it down," Mimier recalled, in an interview for this book. "It got down to me and I said sure. I was flattered – and 500 bucks is 500 bucks."

Jay Mimier.
(courtesy of
UW athletics)

That was the stipend – $500 – for coaching the women's crew, which when Mimier took over in 1973 was part of the club sport program Kit administered. Intercollegiate varsity status was still a year away.

"I was hoping to find kids from farms," Mimier said of his early efforts at recruiting athletes. "You didn't find high school [female] athletes. If they did anything, it was intramural. But kids who grew up on farms knew what hard work was. That's what I was looking for, and I got a decent number."

One of those Wisconsin farm girls – from the village of Rochester, in Racine County – was Sue Ela.

In an interview for this book, Ela recalled that a group of women who lived in the lakeshore dorms originally began talking about initiating a women's crew team.

Ela noted that they knew some of the guys on the men's team.

"We all gravitated to the top of the boathouse to watch [the men's practice on Lake Mendota]," Ela said. "I'll never forget the first time I saw the shells from above. It's really a unique, artistic perspective. I think I was drawn to that as much as anything. The movement and symmetry. I came from a farm and had never heard of rowing."

One of the young women, Kathy Wutke, put up a flyer. "It said, 'Anyone interested in starting a girls' rowing team,'" Ela recalled. "There was a poster and sign-up sheet. Maybe 15 or 20 girls signed up."

Wutke talked to the men's coach, Randy Jablonic, who got the women rowing in an indoor tank. They were not, it should be noted, widely welcomed.

"One of the first days we showed up for the tank," Ela recalled, "a bunch of the guys were standing right there. There was no bathroom or locker room for women – you just walked into the tank. One of the guys, under his breath, said, 'What are you women doing here? This is a man's sport.' That went on for a fairly long time."

In spring 1972, Jablonic asked Neil, the men's freshman coach, to take over, and Neil got the women out on the water.

"We didn't go very far," Ela said. "We had old clunkers. But we got on the water and actually raced once that spring and won our race. That started us on our way."

Ela said that the women had corn roasts and sock hops and raked leaves to raise money for expenses. In fall 1972, the team traveled to Boston for a race on the Charles River. They paid their own way. For uniforms, Ela drew the assignment to go to Lathrop Hall and get whatever she could find.

"That's when I met Kit Saunders," Ela said. Kit was able to provide used men's rowing shirts and what Ela believes were women's basketball shorts. "Nylon," she recalled. "Not appropriate for rowing."

One needs to remember at that point (1972-73) Kit's budget for around a dozen club sports was $8,000. But what she couldn't provide in material assistance she made up for in spirit.

"She had a smile on her face, always," Ela said. "She was so upbeat and effervescent with enthusiasm for sports, and especially for us, it seemed, getting going. It rubbed off on us. We didn't really know what we were getting into except that we loved it and knew how to work hard."

Mimier, when he took over coaching the women in 1973, knew there was a challenge regarding resources.

"Oh, God, yes," he said. "We didn't have our own equipment. We were using men's equipment. It wasn't designed for women. Fortunately, most of the programs in the country were in the same position. When you went to regattas, you used men's equipment. Nobody had enough money to ship their own boat out to a race. The host crew would set up the boats and you would row whatever kind of – frankly – junk they could find. But everybody was stuck equally."

Pending intercollegiate varsity status for the women's program – officially set to kick off in July 1974 – didn't solve the resource issue when the women's crew wanted to attend the National Women's Rowing Association (NWRA) national championship in Oakland that June.

By 1973-74, the club sports budget had grown to $18,000. Still, what the women's crew received – $1,850 – was not going to finance West Coast travel. The women crew members supplemented it by working concessions at Badger sporting events; they sold rowing T-shirts and posters; they did lawn work, and cleaned ovens. In the end, they were $500 short of being able to go to California. At which point three women's service clubs in Madison – Altrusa, Soroptimist, and Zonta – got together and advanced them the money. In return, the women's crew agreed to act as ushers at a showing of *Mame* – a new movie starring Lucille Ball – sponsored by the service clubs at the Hilldale Theater in Madison. Proceeds from that screening – on June 26, 10 days after the team returned from the Oakland regatta – would also benefit UW women's athletics.

Kit was quoted in the *State Journal*: "It's just great that the three women's service clubs are getting together to support other women in sports. A whole lot of work by a whole lot of people has gone into this. The students really appreciate it."

It would have been nice if the women's crew had excelled in Oakland, but they did not. They were still a year away.

"We were still using borrowed equipment," Ela recalled of the Oakland meet, held on Lake Merritt. "The homemade coxswain amplifier system that was in the boat was made by Jabo's [men's coach Randy Jablonic] manager. When we got out on the lake, it was pulling in radio stations. It was crazy."

"We drew a very tough heat," Mimier, still relatively new as coach, recalled, and the Badgers didn't make the finals.

"That may have been the thing that put a fire in us for the next year," Ela said.

And for that next year – 1975 – there was, at long last, at least some money for the women's crew. The budget for 11 varsity intercollegiate women's sports for 1974-75 was $118,000.

Mimier recalled, "We were going to get a race out east before we had to go to the nationals."

That race "out east" was the Eastern Sprints, the championship of the Eastern Association of Women's Rowing Colleges, a prestigious race held each May to which the Badger women were invited.

The Badgers – led by their star rower, Spring Green native and future Olympian Carie Graves – enjoyed a successful early season but weren't really on the national radar prior to heading to Connecticut for the Sprints. The rangy Graves was seated in the "stroke" position in the Badgers' boat – the seat closest to the boat's stern usually reserved for the strongest rower.

The boat the Badgers would utilize at the Sprints was new, another example of the improved finances for women's athletics (though Graves' father, Spring Green businessman Robert Graves, himself a former Badger rower, had helped finance the new boat). The new boat was a Schoenbrod – named for boat-

Carie Graves. (courtesy of UW athletics)

builder Helmut Schoenbrod – made of light glass fiber and utilizing adjustable riggers.

It was an excellent boat, but it was new to the Badger rowers and new to Mimier, their coach, who looked on in dismay when it was delivered, in sections, to Connecticut prior to the race. Mimier was accustomed to wood boats with nonadjustable rigging.

Sue Ela recalled that while they were taking this in, the Yale coach's dog walked over and peed on one of the Wisconsin rigger bags.

Maybe that gave Mimier the excuse to approach the Yale coach, Nat Case, and introduce himself.

Somewhat sheepishly, Mimier pointed to his new boat and said, "I don't know how to rig this thing. I don't know what I'm doing."

Yale had a similar boat, fully assembled, with the oarlocks set.

"I'm just going to ask you flat out," Mimier continued. "Can I copy your rigging?"

Mimier recalled that Case – who subsequently became a good friend – gave him a look that implied, "What the hell, let's make this a fair race." And Case said, "Sure, go ahead."

The Badger varsity won its heat – beating Yale and Princeton – but in the finals lost to Radcliffe. What really impressed Mimier was the performance of his freshman boat. They won their race by two lengths of open water.

"The freshmen won by so much it wasn't funny," Mimier said. The coach recalled that the freshmen's time registered as fourth or fifth best of the entire regatta, which included three heats of varsity crews.

Back in Madison, preparing for the NWRA national championship, at Princeton in New Jersey in June, Mimier decided to move three freshman women – Peggy McCarthy, Jackie Zoch, and Mary Grace Knight – up to the varsity boat.

The new varsity eight meshed well and began to record some impressive practice times on Lake Mendota. During a phone conversation with the Princeton coach, primarily confirming travel and lodging plans for the June nationals, Mimier asked about the favorite, Vesper Boat Club out of Philadelphia. What kind of times had they been posting?

As mentioned, the NWRA national championship was open to both college and university teams and women's rowing clubs, of which Vesper was the most venerable. So good was Vesper that when it was announced there would be a camp following the NWRA title race, the first step toward selecting the 1976 United States women's Olympic rowing team – women's rowing debuted in those Montreal Games – Vesper filed a lawsuit claiming that if it won the NWRA championship, the Vesper team as a whole should be allowed to represent the United States.

(In the past, the winning national team had gone intact to compete in the world championship. But with the Olympics now in play, the camp was designed to make certain the top American women made the team. In fairness, since many of the Vesper athletes were no longer students and had jobs, attending the selection camp could be problematic. The suit was still pending that spring.)

On the phone with Mimier, Princeton coach Al Piranian ticked off some recent Vesper performances at 1,000 meters.

"Really?" Mimier said. "That's it?" His newly formed varsity eight had bettered those times practicing on Lake Mendota. He was quietly confident heading to Princeton for the NWRA championship on Lake Carnegie in June.

And his rowers?

"I think we didn't know," Sue Ela recalled.

In an interview for this book, Carie Graves made the same point. "We didn't know," Graves said. "But I do remember we weren't supposed to win. It was going to be Vesper. They were older, really established. We were farm kids."

With an eye on the budget, Kit Saunders did not accompany the team to New Jersey. Ela recalled that when they arrived at Lake Carnegie in Princeton, what really impressed them were the facilities.

"They had a boathouse with a women's locker room," Ela said. "For some reason, we started weighing ourselves on their scale."

The semi-final heats were on Saturday, June 21. The top three teams in two heats would advance to the finals. The Badgers were in the faster heat, and finished third, behind Vesper and another club team, the Eastern Development Camp. Yale, Princeton and California-Berkeley qualified in the other heat. And heat was the operative word. "It was hot and humid," Ela said, the temperature approaching 90 degrees.

The next day was the final, six boats, the national championship on the line. Minutes before the race, Mimier gathered his team under a large beech tree on the bank of the dammed river that was Lake Carnegie.

"It's a speech we all remember," Ela said.

Ela – she and Mimier would later marry – recalled the coach's remarks with a mix of humor and affection.

"Jay, when he would talk to the team, always looked at his feet," Ela said. "He has these great big feet. When he ran behind us, you could hear him flopping around. We always joked about him staring at his feet."

His words, however, caught the moment.

"He was talking about how hard we had trained," Ela recalled, "and how we were better than we showed in the heat."

And in closing, Mimier said, "Now it's time to go piss with the big dogs."

As rallying cries go, it may have lacked poetry, but the message was clear. They were the right team at the right place at the right time.

Ela recalled, "As we were leaving our little gathering under the tree, and headed in to get the boat, one of my teammates next to me said, 'I don't know. Do you think we can do this?'"

"You remember how hard we trained?" Ela replied. "There's no way we're not ready for this."

As the women carried their boat to the water, Ela glanced over at Mimier and saw him in conversation with Harry Parker, the legendary Harvard men's crew coach who would coach the first U.S. women's crew in the '76 Montreal Olympics. Later, she asked Mimier what Parker had said.

"They're really quiet," Parker had observed. "That's good."

"Once our hands were on the boat, we were all business," Ela said. "We were determined. We knew we had speed. We'd gotten over the fear of a big national race."

Mimier made his way 1,000 meters to the finish line as the teams settled into their boats. In his brief talk to the team, he'd reminded them not to try to row at more than 36 strokes per minute. Anything faster was an all-out sprint and inviting trouble, a pace hard to maintain in unison, the key to gliding most efficiently on the water. They'd seen it in the semi-final heat, when Carie Graves, in the stroke position in the boat, increased the pace to 38 after they fell behind early. The Badgers never found their rhythm.

"The race plan [for the final] was to start and settle at maybe 35," Ela said.

Carie Graves, however, wasn't big on settling. Physically and psychologically, she was constructed for all-out effort. Even if she had intended to try to follow her coach's instructions – and that's anything but certain – it didn't happen.

The Wisconsin boat came off the starting line full tilt. Somehow – helped by a tailwind – her teammates kept up.

"We never settled," Ela said. "We kind of raced the whole way at 39."

Mimier, ensconced at the finish line, couldn't see it, but the race was being broadcast, and he heard:

"Wisconsin's out to a quarter to a half-length lead! They're not really settling! They're maintaining their lead!"

The coach – his prerace comments notwithstanding – began talking urgently under his breath: "Keep doing what you're doing. Don't settle. Just don't settle!"

The boats came into view. Mimier was standing near a woman named Joanne Iverson, cofounder of the NWRA. Because of the lawsuit filed by the Vesper Boat Club – related to representation on the national team at the world championship, and, eventually, at the Olympics – Iverson's life would be made easier if someone other than Vesper won the championship.

"She was really invested in having someone beat Vesper," Mimier recalled. "She wanted the selection camp to succeed."

As the boats came into view, it was hard for Mimier, with an angled view from the finish line, to tell which boat was ahead. He could see Joanne Iverson begin to jump up and down.

In the boat, Sue Ela wasn't certain either. "I remember I could see boats," she said. If you can see a boat, you're ahead of it. Ela thought the finish line was near but couldn't be sure. She heard coxswain Beth Traut call the last 20 meters. The Badgers kept digging. And then – potential disaster.

"Somebody caught a crab," Ela said. "A big crab."

"Crab" is crew-speak for catching an oar in the water, and it rocked the Badgers' boat.

Ela couldn't see it, but her future husband, Mimier, standing at the finish line on shore, was being rocked himself – gleefully mugged by NWRA administrator Joanne Iverson.

"She came running over and tackled me to the ground," Mimier said. "She was screaming, 'You did it! You did it!'"

In the water, Ela recalled, "We were all trying to recover from the crab, and it turned out we were over the finish line."

Ela heard Traut, the coxswain, shouting, "I think we won! I think we won!"

Ela recalled: "I remember just falling back into the lap of Debbie Oetzel, totally obliterated from the effort."

They had indeed won, beating second-place Vesper by 3.3 seconds.

Less than a year after Kit Saunders officially took over as director of women's athletics at the University of Wisconsin, the program had its first national championship.

Jay Mimier remembered the dockside celebration.

"I promised them if they won, I'd get them a case of beer," he said. He had a case of Pabst Blue Ribbon ready.

"They threw themselves in the water," Mimier said. "They threw me in the water. They were as happy as they should have been."

"The Princeton women gave us a bottle of champagne," Ela said. "We all had a swig of champagne."

Carie Graves' clearest memory?

"What it felt like on the podium," she said. They were national champions. "I just couldn't believe it. It was wonderful."

Ela recalled that for her, Carie Graves, Peggy McCarthy, and Jackie Zoch, the celebration was muted because they were leaving early the next day for tryouts at the national camp. Eventually, Graves, McCarthy, and Zoch would row on the first U.S. women's crew team to participate in the Olympics, winning a bronze medal, a stirring story very well told in Daniel J. Boyne's 2000 book, *The Red Rose Crew*.

Back in Madison, the Badgers' national title was front-page news on the sports section of *The Capital Times* the following day. Kit wrote a letter of congratulations to each of the rowers. A few months later, in October, the Wisconsin state Legislature presented the women's crew with a special legislative citation, marking their national championship.

State Rep. Midge Miller from Madison and State Sen. Dale McKenna from Jefferson co-sponsored the resolution, which was the first such award ever presented to UW women athletes.

"Congratulations to the women's crew and their coach for athletic achievement," it read in part, "and the contribution they have made to excellence and quality in the University's athletic program."

Miller and McKenna presented the resolution in a small ceremony at the W Club. Kit was there, along with coach Jay Mimier, and rowers Peggy McCarthy and Beth Traut, now Beth Bosio – the women's coxswain had married John Bosio, the coxswain of the UW men's crew.

Beth gave a quote to *The Capital Times*: "It is nice they took the time to come here and do this," she said. "Crew is an unusual sport – not everyone knows about it. So it is nice to get this recognition."

Mimier, her coach, echoed those sentiments: "It is good that these athletes are receiving recognition. When you turn on the radio or television, all you hear about is football and its stars – never about women," Mimier said. "This citation shows that our accomplishments are recognized by people in leading positions in society. People will start to understand that these women are very serious about what they are doing."

Sen. McKenna said, "Hopefully this will give women's athletics a boost – a shot in the arm."

Two other women's sports at Wisconsin garnering attention in 1975, thanks largely to their coach, Peter Tegen, and a relatively inexperienced but highly promising athlete, Cindy Bremser, were track and field and cross-country.

It was Tegen who coached the Badgers' cross-country team to the women's program's first NCAA championship, in the snow in Pennsylvania in 1984, recounted here in the first chapter.

Tegen had been on the Madison campus for a decade by then. He would eventually become a coaching legend, but in 1973, when he landed in Madison, the native of Germany was just looking to get a doctorate in biomechanics.

"It was not yet a field in German sports science," Tegen said, in an interview for this book.

He had coached track in Peru prior to coming to Madison, with enough success that some of his Peruvian athletes competed in the 1972 Olympics in Munich. In a sense, the timing of Tegen's arrival in Madison was fortuitous.

"I saw a note on the board in Lathrop Hall," Tegan recalled. "They were looking for help in starting a women's track team."

The note directed him to Kit's Lathrop office.

"When I walked in, she looked kind of baffled," Tegen said, even more so when Tegen related his credentials, his success with the Peruvian national team.

"But I can't pay you," Kit said. "At least not very much."

"That's OK," Tegen said.

The truth was, he was missing coaching. "She seemed perplexed that a student – which I was at the time – had quite a bit of coaching experience."

Tegen recalled, "But Kit and I hit it off beautifully. She told me, 'This is not going to be easy.' I said I understood. Kit was very warm. She tried to be fair to all the teams [in her program], no matter where they stood on the totem pole."

An early athlete who came under Tegen's tutelage – and who became one of his very best – also saw a sign in Lathrop Hall. Tegen tacked it up. "Interested in track or cross-country?"

Cindy Bremser wasn't sure. Born in Milwaukee, Bremser attended high school in Mishicot. There were no competitive sports for girls at Mishicot High School but in an interview for this book, Bremser recalled that the school had a first-rate physical education teacher who encouraged her.

There came a time when the girls were required to run 600 yards, essentially two laps around the school's football field.

"I thought that didn't seem like that much," Bremser recalled, in an interview for this book. "Everyone took off, and pretty soon I was passing people. When I finished, my teacher said, 'You just ran the fastest time ever by a female at Mishicot High School.' Then I knew I was sort of fast. I hadn't had a clue."

In Madison in 1974, living in the Chadbourne dormitory, Bremser went to Lathrop Hall to exercise, saw Tegen's sign, and met the coach. "I remember Peter telling me his paycheck was $750 a year," she said.

"Peter made me a distance runner pretty early," Bremser continued. Before long, Bremser finished sixth in a national cross-country invitational, and third in the 1975 mile at the Association for Intercollegiate Athletics for Women (AIAW) –

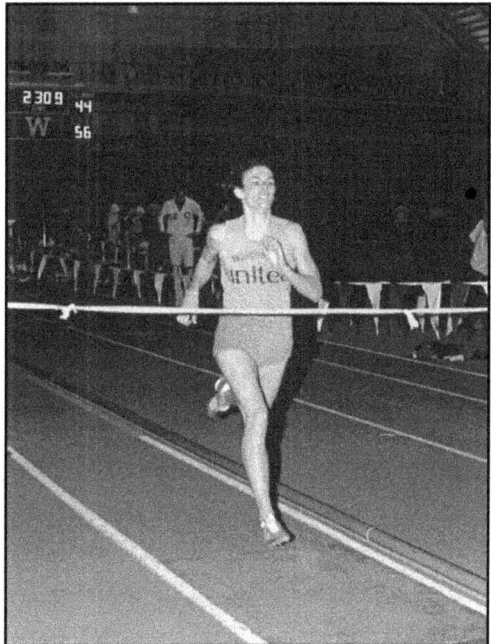

Cindy Bremser.
(courtesy of
UW athletics)

which administered women's athletics prior to the NCAA – national championship, becoming the women Badgers' first All-American runner. (Bremser's career included six Drake Relays 1,500-meter titles and she finished fourth in the 3,000 meters at the 1984 Olympics in Los Angeles.)

"I met Kit around [1974-75]," Bremser said. "I most remember her being a real champion for women's sports. She came to meets and watched us. She talked to me afterward. She was down to earth. She told it like it was. She had it pretty rough sometimes because not everybody was for all the women's advances. But she never alienated them, because of the way she was."

Money continued to be an issue for the women's program.

"My first national invitational championship in cross-country," Bremser said, "I wore [Coach] Peter's [Tegen] shoes. They were the best I could get, and they fit. Kids today don't have a clue."

Money wasn't the only issue. At an athletic board meeting in December 1974 – five months after Kit became women's athletic director – the board slow-walked Kit's proposal, backed by other women's athletic directors in the Big Ten, to have the women's programs established under the conference umbrella. Rather than make that resolution, the UW athletic board passed a resolution saying it "approves moves by the women's athletic directors of the Big Ten to explore methods of establishing a viable program of women's sports within the Big Ten."

Still, money – for coaches, travel, facilities and more – was Kit's primary concern. A February 1975 *Milwaukee Journal* article on women's collegiate sports was headlined, "Women's Officials Enthusiastic but Broke."

Kit told the reporter, Tom Flaherty, "Being sure of adequate funding is most important. Our budget is $118,000 for this year, but we only have $92,000 of it."

Flaherty explained: "The $92,000 was secured when the NCAA cut football scholarships from 120 to 104. The money that would have been used for the 16 extra scholarships was diverted to women's sports."

Kit continued: "The university acted in good faith getting us the money we needed. Of course, we're still $26,000 short, and we've started a fund-raising drive to make up the difference."

Spearheading the fund drive, which women's athletics conducted in association with the University of Wisconsin Foundation, was a letter that went out to some 11,000 members of the Wisconsin Alumni Association, mostly those in Wisconsin and the Chicago area.

The letter, signed by Kit and Betty Vaughn, an alumni member of the athletic board, began by acknowledging the "giant step" the women's program had made in gaining intercollegiate varsity status within the athletic department. It highlighted the early achievements of the Badger women athletes.

Then – as Kit did in her *Milwaukee Journal* interview – it presented the hard facts.

"Our budget is $118,000. We have $92,000. We need $26,000.

"For the first time," the letter continued, "we are asking that your verbal support be transferred into dollars. We want the men's program to remain strong. We want the women's program to be self-supporting. You can make this step possible with a gift of $1,000, $100, $10 or $1."

Glenn Miller, the *State Journal* sports editor, wrote a column in March 1975 saying he'd gotten the letter and made a contribution. It's possible Miller's portrayal in these pages has been too harsh. As time went on, he seemed to grudgingly realize women's athletics was here to stay. Miller interviewed Kit for a column after getting the fund-raising letter. Kit pointed out that they were working to keep expenses in line, but that it was difficult, especially if it affected her student-athletes.

"We are trying awfully hard," Kit said. "For example, we qualified 10 swimmers for the nationals – and we sent only three to the meet. That's tough."

In September 1975, an important new fund-raising tool was established: the Women's Intercollegiate Sports Club – WIS-Club for short.

"We followed the men's model of the booster club," Doreen Adamany, who served as WIS-Club president in 1975-76, said in an interview for this book. "We felt like we needed a women's athletics booster club."

Adamany is a Green Bay native and competed in the limited sports available to girls during high school. She studied history at UW–Madison and when Kit was hiring someone to handle women's sports information in 1975 – though it was not yet a fulltime position – Adamany applied for the job.

"It was a long shot on my part," Adamany recalled, almost 45 years later. "I applied for the job without having great credentials, other than a love of sports."

The sports information job went to Phyllis Krutsch.

"I'd met with Kit," Adamany said, "and as always, she was very gracious. When she called back to tell me she had hired someone else, she did offer me something."

That "something" was to write a weekly piece on UW women's athletics for the *Badger Report*, a publication devoted to Badger sports. The women's program was allowed one story each week. Adamany got $10 per article. She also became the first president of WIS-Club, and there was a photo of her in the *Wisconsin State Journal* baking bran muffins in advance of the first WIS-Club meeting, Sept. 25, 1975 – by coincidence, Kit's 35th birthday.

Kit and Betty Vaughn, the second female member of the UW athletic board (after Muriel Sloan), served as co-chairs of the event, which was held at 2 p.m. at the Wisconsin Alumni House, overlooking Lake Mendota at the north end of Lake Street.

When Vaughn joined the athletic board as an alumni member in the early 1970s – she was an Iowa native who came to UW-Madison for graduate school – she said she stayed quiet for the first few meetings until a question was raised about how the men's and women's programs should be treated on the issue of academic standards.

"I spoke right up," Vaughn recalled, in a 1977 magazine interview, "and said they should be the same. After that I didn't have a chance to stay quiet because I was appointed to the student affairs committee, the ad hoc committee on athletic tenders, and the executive committee. I see women's rights as simply a matter of justice and fairness."

The event Vaughn and Kit co-chaired in September 1975 – which introduced WIS-Club – was a rousing success, befitting the first meeting of the first women's athletics booster club for any Big Ten school.

The attendees were a *Who's Who* of campus and athletic luminaries, including athletic director Elroy Hirsch and his top assistant, Otto Breitenbach; athletic board chair Fred Haberman; head football coach John Jardine; Ruberta Weaver, wife of UW System President John Weaver; Joyce Erdman, a member of the UW Board of Regents; and Phyllis Young, wife of UW Chancellor Ed Young; along with, of course, co-chairs Kit and Betty Vaughn.

One hundred fifty were present all told. Along with cranberry juice and bran muffins, they were given a fencing demonstration and crew exhibition, the latter featuring star rower Carie Graves, fresh off the national championship performance the previous spring.

Fencers Liz Shier and Karen Beidel were also on hand, along with Tony Gillham, a native of England and a highly respected fencing instructor who coached both the men's and women's teams at UW.

The women were equipped with electric scoring equipment programmed to beep when either fencer scored a hit – the tip of the foil contacting the opponent's body. Naturally, the equipment malfunctioned – beeping indiscriminately – leading Gillham to disable it. "Wouldn't you know," he said. "We've never had this problem before."

Still, the demonstration captivated the audience, as Gillham described the intricacies of the sport.

"We start out by teaching the fencers how to lunge and hit the opponent," Gillham said. "Then we teach them how to defend themselves against an attack. This is where it gets interesting.

"An attack may start in six or seven different ways while the defender has three or four ways to combat it," Gillham continued. "There are several hundred combinations of movements a fencer may assume to defend herself or counterattack. These movements are further complicated by variations of distance and speed.

"Fencing is physically very demanding," Gillham concluded, "so we emphasize physical fitness through calisthenics and running. It is important for a fencer to develop strength and endurance because one five-minute match can be excruciating, both mentally and physically."

In 2019 – 44 years after she participated in the fencing event at the first WIS-Club meeting – Karen Beidel was living in Columbia, South Carolina and in an interview, said that while she didn't specifically recall that Alumni House demonstration, her memories of fencing at UW were good ones.

Beidel came to Madison as a freshman in 1974 to study Norwegian and wound up a dual major in Scandinavian Studies and Geography.

"I got into fencing because I saw a mimeographed flyer someone had posted," Beidel recalled. "What I remember most about it is it was attached to the wall with two band-aids."

Rudimentary as that was, Beidel was intrigued. A popular recent Hollywood movie, *The Three Musketeers*, starring Michael York and Oliver Reed, had featured considerable sword play and put the sport on the radar of young people. Beidel's four years of high school French had also introduced her to the original *Musketeers* novel by Alexander Dumas. She was ready to try fencing.

"We practiced at the Natatorium," she said, adding that the men and women practiced together, so there was no question of the women having inferior facilities.

"We got exactly what the men were getting," Beidel said. "Tony [Gillham] was very good at working with each of us individually, but at the beginning of every practice, we did a team thing in which we'd go through drills all together.

"Tony was very keen on us running laps," she continued. "He'd have us go to the Shell and run several times a week. He was a wonderful coach. He explained things clearly, but more than that, he was a really good body mimic. A lot of times you can be told to do things in a certain way and you think you're doing it, but you're not. Tony could show you what you were doing and then adjust himself to show how you should be doing it."

Beidel's memories of Kit are likewise appreciative.

"We would speak of her as our hero because it was clear she was fighting for women's athletics," Beidel said. "We were very conscious of the fact that what we were doing really hadn't been done by other people. There hadn't been a chance for women before us. There might have been club teams but there hadn't been a chance to fence competitively with any sort of organization.

"I was struck," Beidel concluded, "by how Kit made an effort to spread money and attention to all of the women's sports."

Beidel said she was saddened by the decision of UW athletics to drop men's and women's fencing from the roster of varsity sports in 1991. Tony Gillham had retired one year earlier after a distinguished two-decade run as coach. The women finished tenth in the nation in 1977-78, Beidel's last season, but the program was just hitting its stride. In a 1987 newspaper interview, a few years before he retired, Gillham noted, "Our men's teams have won the Big Ten championship six times in the past 11 years," and added, "Our women's team has won the Big

Ten championship for the past two years. They have never failed to make the nationals and have placed in the top 12 in the country every year since 1978."

Interviewed 40 years later for this book, Gillham smiled recalling his arrival in Madison. Educated as an engineer, Gillham was working in Janesville for the Hough Corporation when the Badgers' men's fencing coach, an attorney named Archie Simonson, was elected to a Dane County circuit judgeship.

"They were looking for someone to take over the fencing program," Gillham said. "They approached me. I thought, 'Well, it might be fun for a year.'"

Gillham, who eventually moved to Madison, was well known in Midwest fencing circles. He won a state individual championship in 1972. The sport was relatively obscure and the list of qualified coaches not lengthy. Gillham's father had taught him in England, and then seeing the swashbuckling movie *Scaramouche* had further piqued his interest.

Gillham was hired in 1972 as the Badgers' men's coach.

"At the time they had a women's club team," he recalled. "Kit Saunders was in charge of the club sports and she asked if I would take over the club."

Gillham agreed to do it. "I really liked Kit. She was very easy to talk to and really passionate about women's sports."

In 1974, when women's sports gained varsity status at UW-Madison and Kit was named director, she spoke with Gillham again.

"Kit begged me to start a women's varsity fencing team. Which of course I decided to do because it doubled my pay."

Regardless, the pay wasn't much, and fencing would always struggle for resources.

"When we started, we practiced at the Natatorium," Gillham recalled. "They had us behind the bleachers overlooking the swimming pool. They kept the temperature at 84 down by the pool. It was often at 90 degrees when we were fencing, on a tile floor where they'd had a meet the previous weekend. When we pushed the bleachers back, the floor was covered with chocolate milk and other spillage. It was the most dreadful place you could think of."

Gillham was able to appropriate a section of the gym that was used by the university golf teams to hit balls into nets. There was an artificial turf putting green that worked as floor space for the fencers.

Madison hosted the men's and women's Big Ten fencing championships at the Natatorium in 1976 (although the women weren't yet officially under the Big Ten umbrella). It was March, and the week of the tournament, Madison had one of its most significant weather events of the past 50 years: an ice storm that nearly shut down the city.

"I was having the coaches meeting at my house," Gillham recalled. "My street looked like a bomb zone. Branches every-where. The power was out. For the coaches who made it to my house, we ordered out for food and had our meeting in the dark."

There was a happy ending: The women Badgers did well, and the men won the Big Ten championship.

"They threw me in the pool," Gillham said.

Things just seemed to happen around Gillham, who had multiple talents. He made the uniforms for the fencing team and they were popular enough that in 1980, athletic department officials asked if he might be able to fix the suit of famed mascot Bucky Badger. It included a paper maché head that hung on wires, rendered Bucky's head virtually unmovable, and kept breaking.

"I fixed it three times," Gillham said, "and then I told them I could make a better one." He did. "Now [Bucky's] head is made of fiberglass on steel braces and it moves freely."

In April 1982, with his university teams finished for the season, Gillham boarded a plane from Chicago to Miami, where he would join the U.S. team for the junior world fencing champi-onships, to be held in Buenos Aries, Argentina. Gillham fell asleep during the flight to Miami. When he woke, he smelled gas and heard someone mention Havana. Gillham asked the woman next to him what was going on.

"We're all doing to die," she said.

A Cuban man and his two sons had hijacked the plane. The men had thrown gasoline around the cabin and threatened to blow up the aircraft if they weren't taken to Havana. The pilot put on the "No Smoking" sign and announced on the speakers they were flying to Havana, where they landed without incident. The men deplaned and the aircraft flew to Miami. Later, the pilot told Gillham, "I liked it better when those guys used guns."

Gillham retired as men's and women's fencing coach in 1990. "I wanted to do some other things," he said. "I wanted to go sailing." A year later, citing budget issues, UW dropped the sport from its varsity roster. "A sad time," Gillham said.

Back in 1975, when Gillham and his fencers finished their demonstration at the first WIS-Club meeting in 1975, women's crew members Carie Graves and Beth Brenzel – the team's coxswain – took over. They'd brought a 20-foot rowing shell into Alumni House for a demonstration; meanwhile, out the window on Lake Mendota, their teammates rowed past. Graves spoke poignantly about the sacrifices required to be successful in crew, the hours of practice that push athletes to the limit of their endurance. And yet, she added, "The rewards are the greatest I've ever known. Being a member of the crew team has been an invaluable experience for me."

Kit spoke last that day, thanking everyone for coming, and expressing the goals of WIS-Club.

"Through fundraising," she said, "we hope the overall effect of WIS-Club will be to provide additional supportive services for the women athletes. Some of our funds will be used to sponsor a dinner for our athletes at the end of the year. We'd also like to be able to cover costs for those women who may be invited to participate in national sports events.

"Two hundred fifty women are participating in 11 sports at the UW this year," Kit continued. "In addition, our members will continually encourage the community to support and attend various women's athletic events that are held on the Madison campus throughout the year."

By the time of the second WIS-Club kickoff event a year later, in September 1976, the club had 180 members, 30 of them men, including three on the board of directors.

"Some men feel they can't support both men's and women's athletics," Kit said. "We want to get away from that type of thinking – from the feeling you are a Benedict Arnold if you support women. So we not only encourage men to join, but also to take part in all the activities the club sponsors.

"We not only want to support women's sports financially," Kit continued, "we want to get people in the community involved and interested. To get them more aware of our program. People in this city with young daughters are excited about what we are doing – they see that their children will have more opportunities than they had. They think [WIS-Club] is a great idea and that it is about time women had one."

The following year, WIS-Club announced an ambitious departure from its usual fundraising. In February 1977, the women's tennis star Billie Jean King – still riding high from her 1973 trouncing of Bobby Riggs in a celebrated exhibition – would come to Madison for an afternoon lecture-demonstration at Nielsen Tennis Stadium and a singles and mixed doubles match that night at the UW Field House, proceeds to benefit UW women's athletics.

In an interview with *The Capital Times* a week prior to the Feb. 22 event, new WIS-Club president Jackie Vastola – having taken the baton from Doreen Adamany – said King would play the young star Dianne Fromholtz in singles and then the women would mix it up with former UW men's basketball coach John Powless and current UW men's tennis star Rich Silverthorn in doubles. "Patron" tickets allowing access to both the Nielsen and Field House events were $25.

The event did generate considerable publicity, but in the end, not all of it was good. Kit later told reporters that two weeks before the event, they'd received word from King's agent that knee surgery the previous fall might prevent King from playing singles in Madison, though the afternoon demonstration and evening doubles were still doable.

It left Kit and the other organizers in a tough spot – do you issue a release saying King might not play singles?

"I couldn't see making an announcement that she might not play because we didn't know for sure," Kit said.

In hindsight, it seems fair to say WIS-Club made the best of a series of bad breaks and miscommunication. Just before Kit left for the airport early on the afternoon of Feb. 22 to pick up King, she got a calling saying Fromholtz had the chicken pox and couldn't play. Then, at the airport, King said she was out of both singles and doubles but would attend the evening matches and do the Nielsen demonstration that afternoon. King's representatives had apparently already reached out to two other touring pros, Rosie Casals and Francoise Durr, to serve as substitutes that night. To everyone's credit, Casals and Durr made it to the Field House in time to play a singles match. King, for her part, was engaging and charmed the crowd during the Nielsen portion of the event, where she demonstrated serving, volleying, and the best way to warm up. In mixed doubles at the Field House, Powless and Casals defeated Durr and Silverthorn, 6-3. It was Powless who noted that while King's absence from the evening matches was regrettable, the night served a larger purpose.

"I have been an advocate of women's sports long before Title IX came on the scene," Powless said. Unknown to anyone at the time, he was, in 1977, on the cusp of a senior playing career that would make him the most decorated player in senior tennis history. "I have felt," Powless continued that night, "that men have benefited through the years and now women should have the same chances."

Marketing and publicity were as much a part of the learning curve as any other aspect of women's intercollegiate athletics. In 1977 Kit would hire a fulltime sports information director – Tamara Flarup – and by the 1980s WIS-Club would have its own weekly radio program, "The Badger Women's Sports Show," broadcast out of the Brat and Brau restaurant on Regent Street, not far from Camp Randall Stadium. The show was hosted by Paula Bonner and Barbara Wegner. Bonner and Flarup especially would each play significant roles in the growth of women's athletics at UW.

In 1975, it was Doreen Adamany's weekly features in the *Badger Report* that kept readers up on the happenings of UW women athletes. In a September 25, 1975 article, Adamany profiled UW women's track and cross-country coach Peter Tegen. A decade on, of course, Tegen would pilot the cross-country team to Wisconsin's first women's NCAA championship in the snow at Penn State. The program was nascent in 1975; Cindy Bremser, who had come out of nowhere to star for the track team, had moved on to international competition.

"On a crisp, early September day," Adamany wrote, "Tegen rounded up his cross-country runners for a preliminary three-mile time trial. One athlete showed up with holes in her shoes, obviously after a hard summer of working out. Tegen, who has petite feet of his own, thought she needed better support so he traded shoes with her. Another girl started out for the track that day on her bicycle when the sun was shining but by the time she reached her destination, the sky was overcast and the wind from Lake Mendota was stirring up. Clad in her track shorts and T-shirt, she arrived at practice with shivering teeth. Tegen gave her his jacket. He then instructed the group to warm-up for 30 minutes before the three-mile run. It was just the beginning of a new season."

From that fitful start – the athletes borrowing shoes and jackets – it didn't take long for Tegen's tutelage to bear fruit. The following fall – in November 1976 – UW hosted its first national women's championship: the second annual Association for

Intercollegiate Athletics for Women (AIAW) cross-country meet. The site was Yahara Hills Golf Course. Five hundred people turned out to watch on a chilly 32-degree day. They weren't disappointed. The Badgers finished third, a "fantastic" performance in Tegen's estimation, led by a freshman, Prairie du Chien native Ann Mulrooney, who finished fifth individually. They were on their way.

Full-time coaches, premium facilities, travel budgets, scholarships – the wish list for UW women's athletics was long. Goals were achieved in increments. In 1975, Kit reached one she had long deemed important – she hired a full-time athletic trainer. Gail Hirn's experience in that job demonstrated that while women were indisputably making gains, their male counterparts were sometimes slow to accept it.

Chapter 6

BONNER AND FLARUP

U W women's athletics' first full-time trainer was a Green Bay girl who would have played more sports in high school had they been available.

"I played every chance I could get," Gail Hirn said, in an interview for this book. "At Green Bay West, we played Tuesday nights. I always looked forward to it. We never got coached. We were always on our own, but we managed to have a good time."

Hirn came to UW–Madison to study physical therapy in the late 1960s, and after graduating, worked briefly for a time in West Virginia. But she missed Madison, and soon took a physical therapist job at Methodist Hospital.

Hirn still had campus contacts, women with whom she hung out and played sports. One day not long after she came back to town, the group got talking about how it wasn't fair that the Red Gym on Langdon Street was open to men for basketball and swimming, but not to women.

"We really were not welcome," Hirn said.

It wasn't an official policy, but it might just as well have been. The men were widely known to swim naked in the small pool and there was a men's locker room but nothing for women.

"A group of us wanted to liberate the Red Gym," Hirn recalled. "We walked in on a Sunday. There were probably six or eight of us. We took our clothes off. I'm incredibly modest, but I did it. We dove in the pool nude."

Regrettably, there was no social media to record the scene.

"The men didn't care," Hirn said. "But the facility supervisors could not believe it. They called the university police. We got out of there before they showed up."

They did it again the following Sunday. The police were called and once more the women decamped prior to their arrival. On the third Sunday, there was no official word of any change, but when the women showed up, there was a partition behind which they could change into swimsuits.

"Every week, there was a little bit more," Hirn said. "Finally, they gave us a locker room and a shower." (Though the shower was only a curtained off portion of the men's shower. Hirn would occasionally see men peeking through.)

Working in physical therapy at Methodist Hospital in 1975, Hirn had a female patient, a graduating high school gymnast, who had broken her leg. The young woman was headed to UW and wanted to know what facilities might be available for training and rehabilitation. Hirn phoned UW athletics on behalf of her patient and eventually connected with Kit. Their conversation led to a discussion about Kit's wish to hire a full-time trainer. Hirn had some sports medicine experience. She'd worked with members of the semi-pro Madison Mustangs football team at Methodist. When Kit offered the job, Hirn took it.

"Kit had advocated for there to be an athletic trainer for women," Hirn said. "That she did it within a year of being hired [as athletic director] was an amazing feat."

Hirn stayed in the job three years. Of Kit, she said, "Kit was very warm, likable, humble, easy to be with. I don't know how she managed all those sports and also had a presence on the national stage. She was great behind the scenes. She did a lot without people even knowing. She did not exaggerate her skills as an administrator, but we all felt it. All the women felt it."

Then Hirn added this: "The men felt it, too. They thought they were losing something by this. It was their domain."

When Hirn started, the training room in Camp Randall Stadium – the best equipped facility on campus – was open to women in the morning but not the afternoon. In addition, the office of the top UW sports medical doctor, William Clancy, was located just off the men's shower, so, as Hirn put it at the time, "a woman may be ushered into his office only when the coast is clear."

In a 1975 interview with Doreen Adamany for *Badger Report*, Hirn said with the stadium training room off limits to women in the afternoon, she found space at the Natatorium.

"Every day," Hirn said, "we do preventative taping here before the volleyball, field hockey, and cross-country practices. The athletes also come here for whirlpools and various other treatments.

"I actually act as a go-between for the athletes, sports medical staff, the coaching staff and the administration," Hirn continued. "If something is bothering an athlete, it usually shows up in his or her performance. Often, the coaches or student trainers will direct the athlete to me for an evaluation.

"An athlete is more susceptible to injury if he or she is distracted by fatigue, worry, or depression. By concerning ourselves with the athletes emotional and physical well-being before, during, and after practices and games, we can prevent injuries."

One frightening moment came during a basketball game in Green Bay. Hirn, traveling with the team and seated on the bench, noticed one of the Badger players laboring for breath. At the next dead ball, Hirn called her over, but as the woman walked toward the sideline, she slumped over, gasping. Hirn rushed onto the court, got the player on her back, and did mouth-to-mouth resuscitation.

"We ended up in the emergency room," Hirn recalled, and fortunately the woman made a full recovery.

That was scary, but most of the time, Hirn enjoyed working with the athletes. While the disparity in facilities for women bothered her, they could, and would, be improved. More troubling was the reaction of men in the department to her presence.

There were notable exceptions – assistant (later associate) athletic director Otto Breitenbach was one – but Hirn recalled that in general, "I was not warmly welcomed."

Hirn elaborated: "That was hard. That had an impact on my length of tenure. I was cold-shouldered by the men's athletic training staff. I don't think I shared it much with Kit. I thought she had bigger battles. And I thought it was kind of my weakness. Why couldn't I cope better with it? Was I being namby-pamby about it? But they were very dismissive of me. It was micro-aggressive. No eye contact. I'd say good morning and get nothing back."

Hirn stayed for as long as she did because working with the athletes, going to games and matches – all that was exciting. There was a feeling in the air, times were changing, slowly in some cases, but it was happening.

"The excitement drove a lot of our ability to work within an inequitable situation," Hirn said.

She stayed, too, because of her admiration for Kit. "She traveled with the teams, especially during tournament time," Hirn recalled. "She was so accessible to the athletes and coaches. She was so encouraging. It was just awesome. She was an educator, an athlete, an administrator, she put out fires – and she was good at all those things."

One vexing issue for Kit in the first few years after she was named women's athletics director was scholarships. The implementation of Title IX gender-equity requirements was progressing slowly due in part to legal challenges to its interpretation. In 1974, Texas Sen. John Tower's amendment that would have exempted men's income sports (with their dozens of scholarships) from Title IX requirements failed to pass the House of Representatives.

In July of the following year, the Department of Health, Education and Welfare issued regulations regarding Title IX enforcement in athletics – but schools were given three years to comply. Just seven months later, the NCAA filed a lawsuit challenging Title IX's legality, suggesting that since athletic departments don't receive federal funds directly, they should be exempt. The suit was eventually dismissed.

UW was doing better than many universities and athletic programs on its path to equity, but it was a thorny process, and that certainly included athletic scholarships. What was equitable?

"Right now," Kit said in her 1976 UW Oral History Program interview, "it looks very much like the interpretation of Title IX is going to be that if there are scholarships given for men in any institution, then you have to do it for women also."

Kit wanted scholarships for the Badger women athletes. Not everyone agreed. In a July 1976 *Capital Times* story headlined, "UW women make large gains with help from federal edict," two women from the department of women's physical education expressed doubts about athletic scholarships for women.

"I am afraid to think where it can be headed," said Dr. Frances Cumbee, who had been with the department since the 1940s. "I am worried that we will get into recruiting activities now that we are offering financial aid. We will neglect the women who came here for an education.

"We know where men's athletics have gone," Cumbee continued. "We have fellows on this campus that are here to be professional athletes, not scholars. I don't want women to head that way. Sports is big business, and when money changes hands in the form of scholarships, all kinds of funny things start to happen."

Her view was shared by UW physical education historian Mary Lou Remley, who told *The Cap Times*: "I believe that financial aid is the biggest problem in men's athletics and can result in problems for the women. If we can move away from that, then the money can be used for expansion – to provide opportunities for many women rather than using it to support a few talented athletes."

It was the old Blanche Trilling argument again: Participation vs. competition. Isn't it better to serve the many than be concerned with the elite few? Kit's answer was always that it was possible – indeed, necessary – to do both.

To *The Cap Times*, Kit said she was in favor of athletic scholarships for women. They'd awarded 20 in 1975, the first year that was done in Madison.

"We have 40 grants-in-aids for the coming school year [1976]," Kit said. "We are doing it not only to keep up with the other schools or get the best athletes here. We have some student athletes who are really putting out a lot. They don't have time to hold down the job they need, and they are up to their ears in loans. They try to work, study and train, and don't eat or sleep enough. These are the women we want to help."

Still, around the same time, in her Oral History Program interview, Kit conceded that the athletes themselves were not really on board with the idea of scholarships. It seems remarkable in retrospect.

Kit said that if she fought for scholarships equal to the number of men's – at least in men's non-income sports – she would do it without the support of her student athletes.

"They have made it very clear," Kit said, "that they do not want scholarships. I met with them last year… They said at that point they do not want scholarships… I interpreted Title IX for them and explained the legalities of it. And they still don't want scholarships. They don't want to see their sports changed. They don't want to feel women athletes are being paid to play.

"They have a one-sided view of it," Kit continued. "But they're embroiled in the middle of it and it's hard to see things broadly when you're right in the middle of it. They don't like the idea that half a team may be on scholarship and the other half that's out there working just as hard, just as many hours, is having to hold down jobs to get through school."

Kit said she respected their position, but in the end felt that out of overall fairness, the future should include athletic scholarships for women.

"It's really tough for me," she said, "to talk to a high school recruit or her parents who can't get any help, and maybe she has a brother who is getting help. It happens all the time."

Kit's conclusion: "As long as the men have them, there's no way for me not to ask for them."

By 1976, Kit was an important figure on the Madison landscape. That July, the *Wisconsin State Journal* profiled her in its Sunday "Know Your Madisonian" feature, a kind of unofficial benediction of "prominent citizen" status. More concretely, July 1976 also brought a five-year contract extension for Kit. In announcing it, athletic board chairman Fred Haberman said,

> "Kit has been a driving force behind the develop-
> ment of women's athletics at Wisconsin. She has
> not only managed the program with great efficien-
> cy but has also achieved a position of national
> leadership in establishing a philosophy and method
> of operation for women's athletics."

Among her attributes: an eye for, and ability to attract, talented colleagues. No single hire of Kit's would prove more important than Paula Bonner. Bonner came to Madison in 1976 for graduate school and within two years had gained Kit's trust to the extent Bonner was offered a position as assistant director of women's athletics.

Paula Bonner was originally from South Carolina, and she came from a family where women valued both education and sports. Her paternal grandmother attended the Women's College of South Carolina (later Winthrop College), where she played field hockey and tennis. Paula's dad was superintendent of the Berkeley County schools in South Carolina. They lived in the small town of Moncks Corner.

"The tomboy in me started coming out early in my life," Bonner wrote later. "I was the only girl on Pinewood Drive in Moncks Corner that would tackle big Jimmy Goodyear in our neighborhood football games. Actually, I think I was the only girl on the street who played."

Kit and Paula Bonner. (courtesy of UW athletics)

Bonner liked Moncks Corner but wanted to go away for college, and she ended up at the University of North Carolina at Greensboro (UNCG), starting as a freshman in the fall of 1971. Bonner later recalled the excitement on campus when Title IX passed the following year.

"Many of our professors at UNCG were involved in testifying in Congress about the importance and value of sports for girls and women," Bonner wrote. "The women's movement was in high gear and the Title IX legislation was set to break down another inequity in educational opportunities."

UNCG had a strong women's physical education program and that became Bonner's major. Her class advisor, starting freshman year, was a woman named Pat Hielscher. Wisconsin had a strong reputation for its women's physical education program dating to the days of Blanche Trilling, and a pipeline of sorts had developed with undergrads from one school going to the other for graduate study. With Hielscher, it went one step further. In 1975 Kit hired her to be the first full-time women's volleyball coach.

"How Kit Saunders was able to lure Coach Pat Hielscher away from the sunny South and her alma mater, the University of North Carolina at Greensboro, is still somewhat of an enigma," Doreen Adamany wrote in *Badger Report.* "The Wisconsin weather was certainly not an incentive for the Florida native but a full-time coaching position without teaching responsibilities for the first semester was."

Hielscher said, "Very few such opportunities are available today to women's coaches."

After Bonner got her undergrad degree from Greensboro, she taught and coached for a year in a small South Carolina town, then decided to follow her former advisor, Hielscher, to Madison. Bonner drove up in late summer 1976 with a friend whom Hielscher had hired as a graduate assistant volleyball coach.

Bonner got a research assistant position in the physical education department.

"I was going to be getting a master's in physical education," she recalled in an interview for this book, "with a specialization in higher ed administration. My goal was intercollegiate athletics administration."

Bonner met Kit soon after landing in Madison.

"I remember her being very warm, very active and fit," Bonner said. "She loved to play tennis. At that point when I first met her, it was going into fall and it turned out to be one of the coldest winters on record in the state of Wisconsin. By my birthday – December 4 – all the lakes were frozen. There was snow on the ground. For my birthday, Kit, who lived on Lake Kegonsa in Stoughton, had a big party and we were all cross-country skiing – or I was trying to, anyway."

By then Bonner was helping around women's athletics.

"Kit was just very welcoming and supportive," Bonner said. "She kept introducing me to people. I got involved pretty quickly. Even though I had [a research assistant position] I was doing officiating of basketball and volleyball. And volunteering – running around and doing stuff for events and games. I remember running to McDonald's and filling these big, old-fashioned coolers with orange soda and bringing them to the Natatorium for volleyball tournaments – then wiping up the spilled soda off the floor afterward."

Decades later, Bonner would recall – winter weather aside – how welcoming Madison seemed and how comfortable she felt in the city.

"To this day," she wrote, "I can still remember that first year here in Madison. At some point early on, I realized that I had a deep sense of 'having come home.' This town and this university and the people I was getting to know and the atmosphere, culture, attitudes, politics and openness all felt so right, so good. I felt as if I could spread my wings and be all that I wanted or could be. I could breathe and I could be a little more relaxed. There were more women in the professions than I had seen before. More women in politics, business, in government, in various kinds of leadership roles – and compared to what I had experienced 'down South,' the working relationships and friendships between men and women seemed more genuine, more real."

After Bonner's first year in Madison, while she was still working on her master's degree, Kit hired her as an administrative assistant, a half-time position.

"I had a pretty cool office up in Camp Randall Stadium," Bonner recalled. "Kit was there, too. We were up in the area where there had been some men's non-income sports offices."

The move of the women's athletics offices from Lathrop Hall to Camp Randall Stadium brought a circumstance that made Kit laugh – at least in retrospect.

In a 1995 UW Oral History Program interview she did in company with longtime sports information director Tamara Flarup, Kit recalled:

"It was an interesting attitude when we first arrived in the stadium, because if we ran into any of the men's coaches or staff, they thought we were goofing off because we weren't at our desks. The only women in the stadium [previously] were secretaries and had been for a hundred years. If they were away from their desks, it was suspect. I had to explain that parts of my job weren't at my desk. I had to be on campus seeing people."

Kit once said her first office in Camp Randall Stadium had been the mimeograph room for men's sports information.

In 1978 – two years after Bonner arrived in Madison – she successfully defended her master's thesis, at which point Kit took her aside.

"We want you," Kit said, "to stay on as full-time assistant women's athletic director."

"Great!" Bonner said.

"I was very, very fortunate," Bonner noted much later, reflecting on a decade-long run with Kit, which ended in 1989 when Bonner moved over to the Wisconsin Alumni Association.

The announcement of Bonner's hiring as assistant women's athletic director, effective July 1, 1978, ran in the *Wisconsin State Journal* in late June that year. A brief story was accompanied by a photo of Bonner. That might not seem like much, but one needs to remember that it wasn't too long prior when what little news coverage of women's athletics there was could only be found on the "society" or "women's" pages.

In July 1977, Kit hired a full-time sports information director, a woman who would stay in the position for nearly four decades.

Tam Flarup attended Iowa State University and double-majored in journalism and physical education. In 1976 she got a job in women's sports information at the University of Kansas. It was a full-time position, extremely rare for women's athletics at the time, and decades later Flarup still remembered the annual salary: $6,000.

After a year or so, Flarup heard from her old Iowa State advisor that the University of Wisconsin was looking for a full-time women's sports information director. When Flarup applied, her Kansas experience made her more qualified than most.

Tamara Flarup. (courtesy of UW athletics)

"At the time [1977]," Flarup recalled, in an interview for this book, "Kit lived on Lake Kegonsa. We did my interview in a canoe going across the lake to a friend's house where there was a barbecue taking place. I was in the front of the canoe. Kit was in the back. It was the funniest interview I'd ever done."

Of first meeting Kit, Flarup recalled, "She was very easy to talk to. Her reputation preceded her, even at that time. I was a golfer at Iowa State and had some knowledge of the AIAW and other things. Kit had been a part of all of it, starting in the 1960s here, with the Women's Recreation Association. She was very impressive and very well spoken."

Flarup got the job and went back to Kansas to get ready to move.

"Kit wrote me a letter and asked what I needed for my office," Flarup recalled. "I asked her for an electric typewriter. And if possible, could it have a dual pitch and a carbon ribbon. She got it for me."

Tam Flarup wanted an electric typewriter – Jackie Hayes wanted a van. Hayes in 1976 was the newly minted UW women's golf coach. She was a Madison girl, daughter of Frank "Moon" Molinaro, an avid golfer and UW supporter who served a term as president of the National W Club. He was a member of Nakoma Golf Club and that's where Jackie began to play. She played her first city tournament at age 12 and became a formidable competitive golfer. Jackie won the Wisconsin Women's Amateur championship in 1975 and was named Madison Sportswoman of the Year in 1976, the year she took over as the Badgers' head women's golf coach. (When Moon died, in 1979, a scholarship fund to benefit UW women's golf was established in his name.)

In an interview for this book, Hayes recalled that the young women she competed against in summer tournaments – a number of whom were on the UW team – had asked her to consider coaching. The first women's coach – Jane Eastham – stepped down, and Hayes met with Kit to talk about the job.

"It was pretty casual," Hayes recalled. "It was a conversation. I don't even recall that salary was discussed. Kit knew my background and basically asked, 'Do you want the job?' I did."

There was a question of whether Hayes would relinquish her amateur status as a golfer if she took any salary at all, but she got around that by always having her players see a local PGA professional when it came to working on their games.

Hayes' duties included everything else, including fundraising. "I got into it because we didn't have any [funds]," she recalled. One goal was a van for travel, and Hayes helped organize both a raffle and a golf outing to make that happen.

"My dad was always playing in W Club golf outings," she remembered. "I thought, 'Why can't we do that?' So I started an outing [to benefit women's athletics] at Nakoma. I went around town and got all kinds of donations. We had a great prize table.

"It was a Monday at Nakoma," Hayes continued. "Nakoma donated the course. My husband, Hugh, was at the grill making hamburgers. People came from all over and had a great time, but I

Jackie Hayes. (courtesy of UW athletics)

remember that first year it was pouring rain when I got there at like 6:00 in the morning. I was crying and saying I hadn't made any provision for rain. What was I going to do? I called our greenskeeper, and he said, 'Delay it 45 minutes. It's going to clear.' And it did!"

Eventually they got their van – "a beautiful red and white one," in Hayes' recollection.

Hayes coached for a little under a decade. Forty years on, her car license plate still read "UW GOLF." She recalled Kit as "very easy to talk to, always. As years go on, you are going to have issues. Her door was always open. She always stood behind me."

There was a problem, early, with a scholarship athlete who once securing her scholarship, basically stopped practicing. Hayes engaged her in multiple discussions, but when no progress was made, the scholarship was withdrawn.

"Her father wrote a letter," Hayes recalled. "My husband, who is a lawyer, wrote a letter in response. I took it into Kit. She said, 'I can't do any better.' She stood behind me."

A happier memory for Hayes came about midway through her coaching tenure when she answered her phone at home and a young woman's voice said she was in Madison from Bogota, Colombia, visiting a relative. The young woman's name was Monica Tamayo and she was a golfer. In fact, she was calling Hayes from Odana Hills Golf Course.

"I think I might be able to play on your golf team," she said.

"What's your handicap?" Hayes asked.

"Four."

"I'll be right there."

Hayes laughed at the memory. "She was a delightful young lady. She had relatives here... She just put a post on Facebook saying one of the best times of her life was playing golf for the University of Wisconsin."

Tamayo subsequently assumed leadership positions in golf teaching and administration in Latin America – in 2021, she was head coach with the Golf Federation of Peru.

Kit made another significant coaching hire in 1976. Edwina Qualls, an African American native of New Haven, Connecticut, was picked in April to be head women's basketball coach. She would stay a decade, and enjoy some success, including taking the Badgers to the Sweet Sixteen round of the last AIAW women's national basketball championship in 1982. Yet Qualls would also be controversial, perhaps the most contentious hire of Kit's career.

Qualls attended Southern Connecticut State College, where she was an outstanding athlete, playing basketball, volleyball, track, and field hockey – in the latter, Qualls was twice named to the United States national team. She taught physical education and coached basketball for seven years at Richard C. Lee High School in New Haven. Her coaching record over seven seasons was a remarkable 82-15. Over the last four, the won-loss total was even more extraordinary: 63-4.

When Qualls' coach at Southern Connecticut, Louise O'Neal, took the head coaching job at Yale, Qualls signed on as an assistant. It was there that Kit – who was friendly with O'Neal – found her.

"Edwina was a good coach," said longtime UW women's sports information director Tam Flarup. "She knew her stuff. She was an especially good preparation coach."

A *Wisconsin State Journal* article in December 1976, previewing both the new coach and the UW women's basketball season, reported that Qualls "chose Wisconsin after considering openings at Indiana, Stanford, Arizona, and Miami Dade, as well as others."

Qualls was bullish on the Badgers, the paper noted. "She said Wisconsin was the 'ideal' school because of the well-organized athletic program, good practice facilities, the availability of trainers and the presence of an athlete's physician."

The article quoted Qualls: "Right now the Midwest area is less developed than other parts of the country in basketball. But since Wisconsin is nationally ranked academically and has such a diversified offering of majors, it shouldn't be too hard to attract talented players."

One player who arrived a few years into Qualls' tenure and who 40 years on retains fond memories of her time as a basketball Badger was three-year letter-winner Debbie Ambruso.

Growing up in Kenosha, Wisconsin, Ambruso played a lot of playground sports with her dad and brother. Entering seventh grade, she discovered there was a boys' basketball team, but no team for girls. Ambruso went out for the boys' team.

"I made it," Ambruso recalled. "There was a lot of pushback. Not that I was that good, but maybe some of the boys were that bad that I played more than they did. The parents were upset. So the next year we got a girls team."

When Ambruso got to St. Joseph's High School, it was the first year the school had a girls' varsity basketball team.

"We didn't even have softball at my high school until I was a junior," Ambruso said. "In basketball, myself and two other freshmen were the only ones who had any experience, so we played varsity right away."

By the time she was a senior, Ambruso had the attention of Qualls and her staff in Madison. It was interesting how they recruited state players. A one-day tryout was held at the UW Field House, with 20 or 25 players from around the state.

"Coach Qualls was running it," Ambruso recalled. "They had us there doing different drills and playing pick-up games. They mixed us up with some of the players on the team and we played some games."

Ambruso played well that day. A week or two later – it was Easter Sunday, 1979 – Ambruso was outside in her driveway shooting baskets. Her dad came out and told her there was a phone call for her inside.

"He had a scowl on his face," she said. "I was like, 'Oh, my God, what did I do?' Then he smiled and said, 'It's the coach from Wisconsin.'"

Edwina Qualls offered her a scholarship to come play for the Badgers.

"It was exciting," Ambruso said. "All told, a great experience. I appreciated getting the scholarship. I met some great women, some great people in general. I went from being a big fish in a small pond to a smaller fish in a bigger pond. That taught me a lot. The traveling and meeting people and learning how to deal with people from different walks of life – it's important."

Of Kit Saunders, Ambruso recalled, "We'd see her all the time in the Field House. She was at all the games. What she did and how she fought for the women's teams – I'm sure it wasn't easy. It's rough to this day. It's still not an even playing field."

And Coach Edwina Qualls?

"She was tiny," Ambruso said. "But she ran a practice. She expected a lot out of us, but nothing that was unrealistic."

It soon became clear that Qualls expected a lot – or at least equity – out of the UW administration as well. She touched briefly on it in the December 1976 *State Journal* article that effectively introduced her to the city.

"One added challenge for Qualls," the *State Journal* noted, "has been coping with limited facilities" during a renovation of the Field House. Qualls said her team was practicing in a gym with only two baskets. "If our shooting isn't right on at first, you'll know why," she said.

Within a year, Qualls would up the ante considerably on the issue of facilities and gender equity.

Chapter 7

A BASKETBALL COACH MAKES WAVES AND THE WOMEN'S CREW DISROBES

In 1977, Kit moved from her small home on Lake Kegonsa into an apartment at Chalet Gardens, off Verona Road on Madison's west side. She described the move in a letter that December to her college friend, Kathy Riss, back in New Jersey.

"Really needed a bit more space," Kit wrote. "And I do have lots of space in my new apartment. At present, my living room has two bean bags, a TV, record player and a Christmas tree. But I'll enjoy shaping it up slowly."

Kit wrote the letter Dec. 23 after skiing all day with her brother, Don, during a holiday visit to Don's home in the mountains of New Hampshire.

"Don's house," Kit wrote, "is a 200-year-old farmhouse which he heats with a wood stove and blower. It feels like an old-fashioned Christmas. Yesterday cut down a Christmas tree from the wood lot behind the house and we have the whole family here."

Kit noted that in Madison she had "gotten back to playing more tennis and intend to do as much skiing – cross-country and downhill – as possible this winter."

She had some additional free time, having completed in May her doctoral thesis, titled, "The Governance of Intercollegiate Athletics."

"It feels really good to have the Ph.D. behind me," she wrote Riss. "It's nice to be able to enjoy weekends without a typewriter. I'm almost used to it."

In the acknowledgments section of the thesis – which is an impressive document and indeed has been quoted more than once in this narrative – Kit thanked Lanore A. Netzer, a professor of education administration who supervised Kit's work. Netzer assumed emeritus status shortly after signing off on Kit's thesis.

Kit wrote: "Appreciation is expressed to Professor Lanore A. Netzer, who stood by her last official graduate student and provided the guidance and advice which made it possible to reach the goal of a completed degree."

Finally – in her December 1977 letter to Riss – Kit addressed her working life as women's athletic director.

"Still like my job in spite of a bit of pressure," Kit wrote. "The challenges of breaking down the jock mentality still are fun for me." Referencing the recent hiring of Paula Bonner, Tam Flarup and others, Kit noted, "We have a super staff and lots of support from the Madison community and the university."

Say this for Kit: She did not take that community support, be it in Madison, or Wisconsin, or even at Badger outposts across the country, for granted. She was the face of UW women's athletics and she worked hard to nurture relationships and generate enthusiasm to keep the program moving forward.

To illustrate, consider a few weeks in spring 1978. Spring is always a busy time for "Founders Day" events that celebrate the opening on the University of Wisconsin on Feb. 5, 1849. The celebratory gatherings stretch from February to May.

On April 4, 1978, Kit was the featured speaker at the Sheboygan County Founders Day Dinner. Two weeks later, she was in Jefferson. Following the Jefferson event, Wisconsin Alumni Association executive director Arlie Mucks sent Kit the following note:

"Thank you for taking time from a hectic schedule
to journey to Jefferson. You did a good job and
certainly had much enthusiasm. I wish some of the
people there were just half as enthusiastic."

On April 24, Kit was in Hudson, speaking at Hudson High
School's second annual girls' athletic banquet. In the second
week of May, she was in Shawano, speaking at a high school
awards dinner. That speech brought an appreciative letter from
Tom Lyon of Shawano, who launched a cattle breeders' association and would later serve on the UW Board of Regents.

"I want to take this opportunity to personally
thank you for taking the time and putting forth the
effort to come to Shawano and speak at the
Awards Dinner," Lyon wrote. "We are making an
attempt to revitalize the sports program in the
school system and your contribution was much
appreciated."

In between Hudson and Shawano, Kit accepted an invitation from
the University of Wisconsin Alumni Club of New York to present
at their Founders Day celebration in New York City.

Club member Richard C. John wrote Kit afterward, "I
thought your presentation was marvelous, and that was confirmed
by everyone with whom I talked."

Even better was the note Mary Brown, who worked in the
office of UW System President Edwin Young, and whose
daughter was secretary of the UW Alumni Club of New York,
sent to UW-Madison Chancellor Irving Shain.

"My daughter called me from New York last week
with news of their Annual Alumni Club meeting.
Kit Saunders was the main speaker for the evening. And, according to Kathy, did an excellent job
– one of the best speakers they have ever had.
They were all very pleased with her and quite
impressed with the progress of Women's Athletics
on the Madison campus. So much so, that after the
program their Man of the Year – President of Con-

Ed, sorry his name escapes me for the moment –
asked for brochures and other literature Kit had
brought with her."

Brown concluded by telling Shain, "President Young asked me to pass this information on to you – that it might be useful."

Shain forwarded the note to Elroy Hirsch, Kit's boss, who in turn forwarded it to Kit, with this: "Kit – Good going!"

Competitively, too, it was a good season for the Badger women. Though the women's programs were not yet officially under the Big Ten Conference umbrella, they held the first Big Ten Women's Indoor Track and Field Championship at the Camp Randall Memorial Center – the Shell – in March 1978. Every conference school except Indiana and Minnesota participated, and the Badgers took the team title.

In an unusual editorial – in that it appeared on the Op-Ed pages rather than the sports pages – *The Capital Times* saluted the victory and the event's larger statement about women's athletics and women's evolving role in American life.

"What the few hundreds who attended the wom-
en's track and field contest saw," the paper noted,
"in addition to some exciting action, was the
happy culmination of one gratifying aspect of the
changing status of women in our society… And
when the final totals were announced, the
[Wisconsin] women, like their male counterparts,
joyously hoisted their male coach, Peter Tegen, to
their shoulders. The women's movement got a
strong push forward here last weekend."

By fall 1978, much was going right with Kit's program, as she noted in an October 22 letter to college friend Kathy Riss.

"Our school year got off to a smooth start," Kit wrote. "I have a full time assistant [Paula Bonner] and a sports info director [Tam Flarup] with a couple of years' experience under her belt. Two new coaches, volleyball [Kristi Conklin] and gymnastics [Jenny Hoffman-Convisor] were no problem, either. A terrific staff and so far the best competitive season yet.

"We also did some fancy negotiating over the summer," Kit continued, "and upgraded scholarships, salaries and program budget."

But then Kit mentioned to Riss what she called "the only fly in the ointment." It involved women's basketball coach Edwina Qualls, about to start her third season. "Unbeknownst to me," Kit wrote Riss, Qualls had filed a Title IX complaint against the university.

The complaint had only come to light that month – October 1978. But in fact Qualls had filed it with the Department of Health, Education and Welfare 10 months earlier – in December 1977 – as Qualls' second season as coach was getting underway.

The clues were there that month – unheeded – for readers of the *Wisconsin State Journal* sports pages. On Dec. 1, 1977, the paper carried a sports page headline that read: "Badger women cagers intent on building." The story talked about Qualls' efforts to mount a successful team, noting that for the first time she had four players on full scholarship and four more on tuition-only scholarship.

But it was a short sidebar, inserted in the main story, that portended what was to come. The short piece was headlined, "Equality lagging." The story read as follows:

> "Women's basketball may be gaining in recogni-
> tion and popularity at the University of Wisconsin,
> but all is not rosy yet for head coach Edwina
> Qualls.
> "For one thing, the women don't get equal
> treatment, she said. "It appears the men's team has
> priority on practicing in the Field House.
> "But that's not the worst…, Qualls said.
> "What's worse is the visiting men's teams have
> priority over us,' she said.
> "That should be changed.'
> "In the meantime, the UW women often have to
> practice at the Natatorium."

THE RIGHT THING TO DO

Eleven days later, on Dec. 12, Qualls filed her Title IX complaint with HEW.

When news of the suit was officially announced – 10 months later! – it was the first Kit or anybody else at UW knew about it. University attorney Michael Liethen told the *State Journal* that a member of his staff had been at HEW's regional office in Chicago a week earlier where it had been suggested there were no outstanding complaints against UW.

Qualls' complaint was not a page-one story in Madison, but it was on the front of the *State Journal* sports section (below the fold) with this headline: "Complaint filed against UW claims sports discrimination."

Sportswriter Randy Lenz sifted through the document, then wrote: "Qualls' complaint specified four major areas: athletic scholarships, team travel, facilities, and coaching staffs."

Lenz addressed each in his Oct. 11 story, starting with travel:

> "Qualls claims that while the men's basketball
> team uses buses or planes to go to away games, the
> women's basketball team is forced to use vans.
> Qualls, in her complaint, states that when asked for
> university cars or buses for transportation to away
> games, she was told that there wasn't enough
> money in the athletic budget."

On facilities:
> "Qualls claims the UW men's basketball team and
> all visiting men's teams are given practice priority
> in the Fieldhouse over the practice time for the
> UW women's team."

On scholarships and coaching staffs, it was more of the same: Qualls claimed that considerably more resources were afforded men's basketball than the women's team.

Kit was quoted after the story jumped to an inside page, and she was uncharacteristically equivocal about the matter, perhaps reflecting frustration that Qualls had not alerted her to the complaint when it was filed in December 1977.

"Since December we have spent quite a bit of time working on the areas that Edwina listed in her complaint," Kit said. "A lot of changes have occurred since the charges were filed."

And this, again seemingly out of character for Kit: "How do you tell an income sport, which in this case is men's basketball, that they have to give up time or practice somewhere else so that a non-income sport, in this case women's basketball, can use their facility? It's a very hard problem to deal with."

Forty years on, Tam Flarup said, "Edwina did that [filed the Title IX complaint] on behalf of all the [women's] coaches. And yet she [alone] had to bear the resentment for that for the rest of her tenure."

Not for the first or last time, Kit was in a tough spot. No one fought harder for resources for the women's program than she did, but she also went to work each day with men whose attitudes and deportment concerning women's athletics ran the gamut from collegial to hostile. In that atmosphere her reasoned and nonconfrontational style had produced results. One suspects Kit might not have tried to dissuade Qualls from filing a Title IX complaint, but she must have been hurt to not even have been told about it.

In her letter to college chum Kathy Riss two weeks after the news broke, Kit wrote:

> "Now that the smoke has begun to clear, I think
> that everyone is just trying to look at what positive
> things might come out of it all for our program –
> the athletic department will have to put some
> policies in writing, which they would not other-
> wise have done, like travel policies and talent
> assessment funds for income/non-income sports. I
> have a feeling HEW will find some of them quite
> unacceptable. We shall see – never a dull moment.
> God forbid that I should get bored!"

A month earlier, Kit had celebrated her 38th birthday. Her letter to Riss revealed Kit's philosophical side as they approached middle age.

"I remember," Kit wrote, "that you always had a leaning toward psych fields – you even took one more course than I did – I think it was clinical psych. About this time in our lives, we seem to examine what we are doing and contemplate making some changes.

"There are even some federally funded programs coming up to help identify women who could move up in education admin-istration and other conferences are being held in many states to help women assess what qualifications they have to move up in ed admin or to find good positions in government or private business.

"I went to one a few weekends ago and it was really stimu-lating – leaves me confused, but more aware of options and able to assess what else we may be able to do.

"Right now I enjoy what I'm doing," Kit concluded, "and I like the flexibility and the salary and the feeling of being in on the ground floor of developing something exciting. However I don't know that I'll always want to fight quite so hard or knock heads with some of these establishment jocks!"

For college athletic departments in late 1978, Title IX remained the elephant in the room. Since 1972, just what those 37 words that make up Title IX meant for college athletics had been studied, challenged and championed on many fronts. HEW in 1975 had announced a three-year transitional period for schools to comply with the gender equity requirements. Those three years were running out. And so, on December 7, 1978, the top line headline of the State Journal sports section announced this: "HEW exempts football from rules."

The wire service story noted that HEW was "proposing" Title IX guidelines for universities that would require equitable treatment of men's and women's programs while exempting football and possibly men's basketball. From the women's standpoint, this would not make things equitable at all. The story noted that an attorney for the AIAW – the governing body of women's intercollegiate athletics – "said they appear to accept a status quo in which intercollegiate athletics are dominated by men."

Indeed, the proposal echoed the infamous – to gender equity proponents – amendment advanced by Texas Sen. John Tower in 1974, two years after Title IX passed. As referenced earlier in this narrative, Tower's amendment – which would have exempted sports that earned money from ticket sales from Title IX – failed to pass.

Now it appeared again in slightly different language in the proposed HEW guidelines, which were set to go into effect in fall 1979 after public comment was solicited.

Kit's "never a dull moment" remark to Kathy Riss in her October letter had never rung truer. In late January 1979 – soon after the tentative HEW guidelines announcement – the *State Journal* top line sports headline read: "Money crunch hits women's athletics."

In the story, Kit and her boss, Elroy Hirsch, agreed that it was unfortunate that increases in the women's athletics budget were coming at least partly from the existing men's sports budget. But they disagreed on the issue of exempting the men's income sports – with Hirsch in favor of exempting, and Kit not – from Title IX.

Progress on equity was being made, Kit said, while adding a statement that would seem highly prescient before the year was out.

"We still have some problems in some of the areas," Kit said. "Like the crew house. Since we only have one crew house and we have a men's and women's team, that kind of tells you that an addition is the only answer. And that's going to cost a lot of money."

That same month – January 1979 – Kit flew to Los Angeles for the annual Delegate Assembly of the AIAW, an organization she was increasingly committed to. It was an important meeting for the group in that it restructured its divisions and championships from a small college-large college scheme to three divisions, which would hold national championships in basketball, softball, gymnastics, cross-country, field hockey, volleyball, tennis, and swimming and diving. Schools could choose which division to compete in for each sport, with the divisions separated by the number of scholarships allowed. Division I allowed the most scholarships and Wisconsin women's sports were all declared Division I.

The change also affected Kit personally, as she had been considering – with encouragement from AIAW colleagues – running for vice president of the large college division. With the change, she decided to run in Division I.

Word arrived in the spring: Kit had been elected AIAW Division I vice president.

Chancellor Irving Shain wrote Kit a congratulatory letter on May 8: "Congratulations on being elected vice president of AIAW. It is a recognition both of you and the University, and of the leadership you can bring to the organization."

It was a high honor, but it fit directly into Kit's description of her professional life never having a dull moment. In spring 1979 the AIAW was involved in a fight for its very existence.

Ever since the passage of Title IX in 1972, the NCAA had held discussions about the possibility of bringing women's college athletics under the NCAA umbrella. Since the NCAA was concurrently mounting legal challenges to Title IX and trying to subvert its gender equity requirements, women athletics administrators could be forgiven for being leery of the NCAA's intentions with its discussions of a merger.

In his 2015 book, *Changing the Playbook: How Power, Profit and Politics Transformed College Sports*, Brown University Professor Howard P. Chudacoff wrote:

> "In 1974, an NCAA report recommended that the
> association sponsor championship competition for

women just as it did for men, and it proposed a
pilot program to begin in 1975. The NCAA's
membership balked at the swift and secret way the
proposal had been drafted and defeated it at the
NCAA convention in January 1975. But members
left the door ajar for further discussion."

In the November-December 1978 issue of *Athletic Business* magazine, John Toner, the athletic director at the University of Connecticut, made the case for a merger of the AIAW into the NCAA. Two AIAW executives, Kaye Hart and Carol Oglesby, wrote a biting response to Toner in the March-April 1979 issue.

"The 'Toner Solution' is quite a perfect exemplification of why the merger of NCAA and AIAW is presently unacceptable to the great majority of women in college athletics," they wrote. The chief concern among several was that while the AIAW was largely governed and administered by women, the NCAA executive roster was predominantly, if not exclusively, male.

"What women would surrender," Hart and Oglesby wrote, "in this proposed merger is having a significant and equitable voice and vote in the governance of university sport, both nationally and internationally."

They concluded,

"At the present time, the AIAW memberships
remains united in their common belief in the
essential justice of Title IX and in the mandate for
AIAW to continued to act as the sole governing
body for women's intercollegiate athletics… In
any future merger with the NCAA, the 'trust
factor' would have to be carefully weighed, since
the AIAW was created out of the void which
existed through the failure of the men's governing
bodies to provide full and equitable programs for
women."

Kit, as one might guess from her position of prominence in the AIAW by spring 1979, was in no hurry to see a merger.

"Kit and Wisconsin were really strong about AIAW and staying in AIAW," Paula Bonner recalled. "Part of that was the [potential] loss of leadership roles and that kind of thing [that might result from a merger].

"The Midwest bloc [of women's athletics administrators] was totally against merging," Tam Flarup said.

That wasn't the case nationally. "There was," Bonner said, "a category of women directors who felt we couldn't be separate and equal."

Then, too, a merger with the NCAA held a big financial carrot: the NCAA paid the expenses for teams to travel to its championships. For women's programs that were constantly strapped for funds, that was enticing. Talks continued through the rest of 1979.

While Kit's job came with pressure and controversies, she was buoyed by the knowledge that the work of her team was having a positive impact where it mattered most: on the women athletes themselves.

In fall 1979, Kit's office received a letter addressed to "Kit, Tam and Paula" from a graduating member of the women's tennis team.

> "I want to thank you for your efforts to improve women's athletics," the letter began. "In writing my essay for my medical school application, I find that my experiences on the tennis team have been an invaluable part of my education at Wisconsin. Although I was fairly certain that I would not make tennis my life, either as a teaching pro or tournament player, I valued the opportunity to improve my tennis, but more important, I value the people I've met and the personal growth that I have experienced because of them... Thank you again for contributing to a very positive experience."

A few months earlier, Kit had received a heartfelt letter from the mother of a Badger volleyball player. The woman's husband had suffered a heart attack, leaving the family unable to fully fund their daughter's school expenses. Kit was able to find some scholarship money to help. Referring to her daughter, the mother wrote:

> "[She] would not have been able to return to
> school last year without your assistance, and my
> husband and I want you to know that we truly
> appreciate all you have done for us. [She] loves the
> school and enjoys playing volleyball very much."

Perhaps no Badger athlete had a more interesting backstory – and sincere appreciation of Kit's help – than track star Rose Chepyator-Thomson, who arrived in Madison in September 1979 from Kenya.

"Kit was absolutely outstanding," Chepyator-Thomson said, in an interview for this book. "You could not have asked for a better women's athletics director. She really worked hard and made sure we had enough resources."

Chepyator-Thomson began running early in her Kenyan hometown of Iten, a town famous for producing exceptional distance runners.

"It was the lifestyle," she said. "We had to run to school. We had to run to school because the teachers were very strict. Classes started at 8:00 and the bell rang at five minutes to 8:00. Whatever you did, you had to get your legs moving."

Eventually Rose met a young Peace Corps volunteer who was teaching at St. Patrick's High School, a boys' school, whose alumni include many Olympic gold-medal-winning distance runners. Norm Thomson, the Peace Corps volunteer, was from Wisconsin. They fell in love, married, and had two children.

Rose taught primary school in Kenya and competed as a distance runner even after having children, which was "unthinkable" to many Kenyans, Chepyator-Thomson said – a woman leaving her two little children to compete.

In 1979, at Norm's urging, the family moved back to his native Wisconsin, to Madison, where he would pursue graduate

Rose Chepyator-Thomson.
(courtesy of UW athletics)

degrees in education and Rose would do the same – along with competing for the Badgers.

Rose was 25 – and, as noted, twice a mother – when she showed up, two weeks into the fall semester, to run for Peter Tegen's track team.

"I didn't get the full ride [scholarship] the first semester," Chepyator-Thomson recalled. "I think for Tegen I was a surprise. He didn't know my background and all of a sudden I did very well."

Very well indeed. A *Wisconsin State Journal* article from November 1979 noted that Thomson (she competed as Rose Thomson at UW) had run track in Kenya but not cross-country – it's not a sport there. She had no trouble adapting.

"Since arriving here," the *State Journal* noted, "Thomson has won three individual championships, set two course records and a meet mark."

If Thomson had any issues, it was the Midwest's fall weather. "In Kenya," she said, "we think 63 degrees is really cold. So you imagine how cold 36 feels to me."

How well did Chepyator-Thomson acclimate? In the course of her career as a Badger, she was an 11-time All-American; a national AIAW champion outdoors in the 1,500 meters; a three-time Big Ten cross-country champion; a member of the 1983 NCAA champion two-mile relay UW team; and was inducted into the UW Athletic Hall of Fame in 1994.

She was, too, a brilliant student, earning the Big Ten Medal of Honor in 1983 for proficiency in academics and athletics, and that year received an NCAA post-graduate scholarship. Chepyator-Thomson eventually earned two master's degrees and a doctorate at UW–Madison. She taught at the University of Georgia on kinesiology, gender and public policy and sport.

Rose called her time at UW "as all around one of the best experiences I ever had," again referencing Kit, as well as the UW faculty and in particular a Professor Michael Apple.

Interviewed in early 2021, Chepyator-Thomson said she still runs every day. "Two miles a day and five on Saturday," she said. "I really enjoy it. It's fun."

December 1979 – three months after Chepyator-Thomson arrived in Madison – brought one of the most infamous controversies of Kit's career. The women's crew team had enjoyed considerable success on the water, culminating in a 1975 national championship. Yet their facilities – sharing the men's locker room, with no showers of their own – were among the poorest on campus.

"The boathouse was built in 1968 for a men's-only program of about 75 men," said Sue Ela, the 1979 women's coach, who had been on the earliest women's club sport crew in 1972. "We tippy-toed and felt very out of place," Ela said of the 1970s facilities. "We had no shower rooms. We would work out then go out into the cold and walk to our dorms or apartments."

Sue Ela, who rowed with the women's crew and then later coached them. (courtesy of UW athletics)

Kit targeted the "crew house" problem in an interview with the *State Journal* in early 1979. She was working to fix it, but the athletes felt the time had come, and had an idea of their own.

On the night of Dec. 3, 1979, crew coach Sue Ela got a call from one of her athletes, saying the team would be late for practice the following day. There was a running workout scheduled and they were to meet in the Natatorium.

The athlete said, "Not to worry, Sue, we'll be there. We're just going to be late."

The women's crew captain in 1979 was Jane Ludwig, and Ludwig had been doing some research on Title IX. Edwina Qualls' Title IX lawsuit was on her radar. But the biggest inspiration for the captain and her teammates – Ludwig recalled in an interview 40 years later – was the women's crew at Yale, which in 1976 had disrobed in the office of the director of women's athletics in protest of poor locker room facilities and an overall lack of equity with the men's program.

Jane Ludwig.
(courtesy of
UW athletics)

"We totally copied Yale," Ludwig said, interviewed for this book four decades on.

On the afternoon of Dec. 4, 1979, a group of around two dozen women rowers walked into the outer office of UW athletic director Elroy Hirsch – who happened to be out of town – and changed from their civilian clothes to the sweats they would be wearing to practice. They'd alerted the local TV stations and cameras were present.

Beyond the call to the TV stations, Ludwig said, "There wasn't a lot of thought that went into it. We were saying we're going to use your office as a locker room because we don't have one. We basically just changed our clothes and walked out."

A member of the crew, Barb Bradley, told *The Capital Times*: "We're tired of all the promises we've heard in the last few years. They keep telling us to be patient but we think the situation is appalling. We're hoping this draws attention to our problem."

Tam Flarup, women's sports information director, recalled being at her desk in the rear of the suite of athletics' offices at the time of the protest.

"Kit came in and said, 'Tam, go see what they're doing.' I went and looked, came back and said, 'Kit, they're changing clothes.'"

Kit recalled it differently. In an interview in 2004 on the 30th anniversary of varsity women's athletics at UW, she said this:

> "One day I came back from a Big Ten meeting,
> and I walked into the parking lot and there were all
> these television vans out there. I thought, 'What on
> earth are they here for?' I walked up the stairs, and
> there the crew women were changing their clothes
> in front of Elroy's office with cameras rolling. I
> tried to get back to my office. I made a beeline for
> it. I couldn't get by [Hirsch's assistant athletic
> director] Otto Breitenbach's office because there
> were a whole bunch of athletic board people there.
> They ordered me to go out and stop [the women
> from disrobing]. I declined the offer."

In fact, Kit had been working – with limited funds – to find at least a temporary resolution for the women's crew. She was quoted in the next day's *Capital Times*: "We're working on a solution that should be ready by spring."

The basement of Humphrey Hall, near the boathouse, was being converted into locker room and shower space for the women's crew. That happened in March 1980, three months after the protest.

Ironically, at the same time – December 1979 – the women's crew was changing clothes outside Hirsch's office, HEW formally announced its guidelines – which had been teased a year earlier – for schools to comply with Title IX.

The Dec. 5 headline of the *State Journal* sports section read: "Title IX ruling rocks NCAA."

The guidelines gave schools what became known as a "three-part test" to determine Title IX compliance. To comply, they must be able to do one of the following:

1) Demonstrate that the percentage of its female athletes is nearly the same as the percentage of female undergraduate students.

2) Show that it is steadily increasing opportunities for women.

3) Prove that it is meeting the athletic interests and abilities of female students.

In the *State Journal* story – which was from the Associated Press – what "rocked" the NCAA was the stipulation that sports scholarship funds be distributed in proportion to the number of male and female athletes enrolled.

"If 40 percent of a school's athletes are women," the story noted, "female athletes must receive 40 percent of the money a college allots for scholarships."

The new HEW secretary, Patricia Roberts Harris, was quoted:

> "It is important to note that HEW is not requiring that benefits – such as locker rooms or coaching staffs – be identical. We will, however, compare programs to determine whether policies and practices provide equivalent opportunities throughout men's and women's sports programs."

The NCAA immediately came out against the guidelines, with executive director Walter Byers stating:

> "Unfortunately, the new [HEW secretary] places a sex-dictated quota system on scholarships, instead of letting such money properly be awarded on the basis of merit."

In a short sidebar *State Journal* reaction story, Kit said of the guidelines, "I think it will be a positive influence for women's athletics."

What HEW did not provide along with its guidelines, of course, was instruction on how bringing gender equity to university athletics programs would be funded. By the following summer, the Madison sports pages included a series of articles that illustrated that Kit was doing her part.

An August 20, 1980 article in *The Capital Times* was headlined, "Saunders initiates money hunt."

Columnist Mike Lucas visited Kit in her office and remarked on a hardcover book, *Fund Raising* by Thomas E. Broce, that sat in a prominent position on her desk.

"I'm not used to asking people for things," Kit told Lucas. "It's a whole different way of thinking. I don't know anything about it. That's why I've been reading a lot.

"I came up through education," Kit continued, "and I don't have a business background. But I'm learning quickly. In the last couple of weeks, I've learned that fund-raising takes a lot of effort and work. And that it takes more than one visit [to a prospective donor]."

But in this and other interviews, Kit was steadfast in noting that while her 11-sport program did not include any sports that produced income, the men's program included 10 sports that likewise were not income-producing. Only men's football, basketball and hockey brought dollars in.

"It always looks like it's the women's program that causes the budget deficits, and that bothers me and my staff," Kit said. "You look at the money spent on the 11 women's non-income sports and the 10 men's non-income sports, and we're [the women's program] spending less."

Kit continued, "I'm not saying, 'Don't blame us, blame them.' I'm saying the program for both men and women is expensive. All the non-income makers have to share the burden. You just can't pin it on the women's half. We have to stop pointing the finger of blame and start looking at what we can do."

Five months on from that *Capital Times* story, Kit was interviewed – along with two of her coaches, Peter Tegen (track

Kit in the Camp Randall Press Box, late 1970s. (courtesy UW athletics)

and cross-country) and Sue Ela (crew) – for a lengthy article in *Isthmus*, a Madison weekly. "UW Women Caught in a Crunch," the headline read, with a secondary headline: "Budget Deficit Signals Cutbacks."

The article traced the history of women's athletics on the Madison campus, and quoted Ela saying acceptance sometimes remained a struggle:

"I think that women in athletics are a little frustrated sometimes by the lack of acceptance," Ela said, "and how much work you have to do to prove that you're in it for the sports – that you really know what you're doing. It's really frustrating some-times in daily associations, when you feel like you've constantly got to prove yourself."

Tegen noted that the ongoing battle for funding might be taking a toll on Kit.

"I think," Tegen said, "that the struggle – really, the load – has obviously been on Kit Saunders. All I could do was complain to Kit, and then I guess somehow she has managed to increase our budgets and so forth. But just speaking generally, yes, I think it has been quite a struggle to come up to the level where we are now."

Isthmus reported that the women's program budget for the year was $600,000, while noting the overall UW athletic department had a budget deficit of $475,000. Athletic director Elroy Hirsch warned of cuts.

"The last thing we want to do is drop a sport," Hirsch said. "That's the worst thing. But there's definitely got to be cutbacks."

Just a month later, in January 1981, it was announced at a UW athletic board meeting that women's field hockey was being terminated. There was a silver lining: women's soccer would be added.

Still, it must have been difficult for Kit, who dearly loved the sport of field hockey. Wearing her administrator's cap, she saw little choice. At a Jan. 30, 1981 athletic board meeting, Kit told the board it was becoming "increasingly difficult to field a viable field hockey team." Few Wisconsin high schools had field hockey teams, meaning most of the Badger players needed to be recruited from out of state. That begat a slippery slope where coaches were also hard to find. It was hard to envision a way forward that could stimulate growth.

Speaking to the board, Kit contrasted that with soccer. The WIAA – the governing body of Wisconsin high school sports – had announced it would sanction girls' soccer and begin a state tournament in 1982. On the national level, the AIAW also planned a championship tournament, likewise to begin in 1982.

It was hard to argue the logic, but it was also difficult to ignore the passionate plea of a field hockey player, Melissa Ernest, a team captain from Cranbury, New Jersey (50 miles from Kit's hometown of Teaneck).

Ernest, a field hockey captain, said she and her teammates didn't question the validity of adding women's soccer. But why must it come at the expense of field hockey?

The board voted 9-2 to discontinue field hockey, though, significantly, all athletes receiving scholarship assistance would continue to while they remained enrolled at UW.

The woman who likely had the clearest lens on the field hockey-soccer issue – both in 1981 and nearly four decades later – was Karen Lunda, a Madison native who played three years of field hockey on scholarship at UW and then, when the sports were effectively swapped out, starred for the women's soccer team in fall 1981, her senior year, earning All-American recognition.

"It was bittersweet," Lunda said, of the switch from field hockey to soccer, speaking in an interview for this book. "On one hand it was distressing. I felt bad for my field hockey teammates. But on the other hand, I was unbelievably excited to get to play a year of college soccer."

Lunda grew up in an athletic family in the shadow of Camp Randall Stadium, on West Lawn Avenue. Her older sister, Kay,

Karen Lunda.
(courtesy of
UW athletics)

was a member of the 1972 United States Olympic speedskating team.

Following in her sister's footsteps, Karen started speedskating while in elementary school. Off-season, they played soccer, and Lunda was athletic enough that by sixth grade, she was as good or better than the boys. She played on a local boys' club soccer team.

"I was laughed at, as the only girl, until they saw I could play," Lunda said. "I got pointed out by the other teams as well. I can still remember vividly a game we played up in Green Bay. This redheaded kid was pointing at me and laughing. What it took was me stealing the ball, or dribbling past a boy, or scoring a goal, and that behavior stopped. It flipped a switch, and instead of ridiculing me, they had some respect for me."

Lunda's senior year at Madison West High School, they began an intramural program for girls' soccer. She'd already played four years of tennis and softball, helping the softball Regents win a state championship her sophomore year and making the state tennis tournament in doubles as a senior.

As a UW freshman, Lunda was looking for a sport to play. Neither softball nor soccer was on the varsity roster for women. During high school a friend had loaned her a field hockey stick and ball, and her dad had rigged up a net into which Lunda would fire shots. She had enough of a feel for the game to go out for the varsity at UW.

"My goal was to make the traveling team," Lunda said. "I ended up being leading scorer and getting a scholarship."

At the same time, she and some friends started a campus soccer team, as a club sport. It gave Lunda a view – early in her college career – of the contrasting arcs of the two sports. While they had trouble finding women for the field hockey team – a varsity sport – by Lunda's sophomore year they had enough participants for two club soccer teams.

Of course, the club teams lacked funds. Lunda recalled that her soccer team was hoping to play in a club tournament in

Indianapolis but had no way to get there. An assistant women's track coach, Loren Seagrave, lived a block from Lunda's parents' house, and she knew he had a van. Might they borrow it for the trip?

"Sure, but there's a problem," Seagrave said. "The battery's dead."

Lunda's dad took the van to a repair shop on Monroe Street and got a new battery. But it developed that the van was also missing a front seat.

"So we literally duct-taped a lawn chair to the front of the van and we all piled in." Lunda paused, thinking back across nearly four decades.

"We just wanted to play," she said.

As noted, in Lunda's senior year, the opportunity to play varsity soccer arrived with UW adding a women's program.

"It was thrilling to have a chance to play collegiate soccer at a varsity level," she said.

Over the previous summer, a Madison men's club team had made a trip to Europe to play a series of games, and they took a women's team, too, that included Lunda and a half dozen other members of what would be the first UW women's soccer team. They played games in England and Belgium, building a camaraderie that carried over back in Madison.

"I have a vivid memory of the first day of practice," Lunda said. "We played on the field behind Camp Randall, on Breese Terrace. We were walking out onto the practice field and we were just giddy. This was our first varsity practice! One of the women who had been on the trip, Linda Soucek, jumped into Theresa Senn's arms. Everybody was just excited."

The first-year coach, Craig Webb, had been a member of one of the boys' teams Lunda played on in junior high school.

The Badgers did well enough that first season, finishing 12th in the AIAW national championship tournament. Lunda herself truly shined, leading the team in goals scored (22), assists (18) and points (62).

After college, Lunda moved to Arizona, where she runs Lunda and Associates, a work injury evaluation and prevention firm.

In Tucson in 2012, she got a voicemail asking her to call Barry Alvarez in Madison. The UW athletic director told Lunda she had been selected for the UW Athletic Hall of Fame.

"It was shocking," she said, and thrilling, too.

Of Kit, Lunda recalled, "I thought she was a tremendous woman. She was very supportive of us. She and Paula Bonner came to the games. When Kit came, it was kind of a big deal."

In summer 2019, Lunda watched on television with a friend as the United States women's soccer team played for the World Cup title in the final against the Netherlands. Lunda had not been following the tournament closely, and when Rose Lavelle scored a goal late to seal the 2-0 win for the Americans, Lunda's friend did a Google search on Lavelle. That's how Lunda learned the World Cup star was a University of Wisconsin Badger, playing the sport Lunda and her teammates initiated in Madison 38 years earlier.

"That was tremendous," Karen Lunda said.

Chapter 8
AIAW vs. NCAA

T he extraordinary success of Rose Lavelle and the U.S. Women's National Soccer Team led journalists and others, in summer 2019, to the history books, and a lesson in just how far women's athletics had come.

In 1972, the year Title IX passed, 700 girls in the United States played high school soccer. By 2018 – according to the National Federation of State High School Associations – that number was 390,482.

Yet in 1981, the year soccer become a varsity sport for women on the Madison campus and Karen Lunda became an All-American, the best path forward for intercollegiate women's athletics was still a subject of some controversy.

It involved the decade-old Association for Intercollegiate Athletics for Women – Kit was the organization's Division I vice-president – and whether it could, or should, survive. The NCAA had its eye on the AIAW, and as noted earlier in this narrative, the notion of a merger was viewed with skepticism by some women administrators within the AIAW. That shouldn't have surprised anyone.

Recent history did not reveal an NCAA magnanimous toward women's athletics. The organization had resisted the athletics component of Title IX since it first became law in 1972. In 1980, according to Howard Chudacoff's book, *Changing the Playbook*, the NCAA sued the U.S. Department of Health, Education and Welfare claiming Title IX and its requirements were "arbitrary and capricious." The lawsuit went nowhere, but that it was filed spoke to the NCAA's mindset.

"While trying to topple Title IX," Chudacoff wrote, "the NCAA simultaneously launched an effort to overpower AIAW and absorb women's college sports."

The key time period for that was 1981-82.

In January 1981, Kit attended the annual AIAW convention. On one hand, the organization had never been stronger, with 960 member colleges and universities. But during that first week of 1981, the AIAW's convention was overshadowed by a gathering being held in Florida the following week: the NCAA's annual convention, during which the NCAA was expected to announce it would hold women's championships in nine Division I sports. (At its 1980 convention, the NCAA had authorized women's championships for five sports in Divisions II and III.) If the NCAA brought Division I women's programs under its umbrella, it was difficult to see a future for the AIAW.

A Jan. 7, 1981, *New York Times* article began: "The AIAW is 10 years old and fighting to stay alive."

In a second *New York Times* story six days later, the AIAW president, Donna Lopiano, women's athletic director at the University of Texas, had harsh words for Ruth Berkey, a former women's athletic director who had taken a job as director of NCAA women's championships.

Lopiano called her a turncoat. "She forgets where she came from," Lopiano said. "She forgets what Title IX did for her and women's sports. Yes, I guess you can say she's a turncoat."

Berkey said she didn't believe adding Division I women's championships in the NCAA would necessarily doom the AIAW. "There is room for both," she said, "and I think there should be both so there is a choice for the college and athletes as to which tournaments they go to."

At the NCAA meeting in Miami Beach Jan. 13-14, the discussion about expanding women's athletics to Division I was contentious at times. "Not all NCAA interests bought into the venture," Chudacoff wrote in *Changing the Playbook*, "because it would require the NCAA to finance women's tournaments, something that male sports interests, especially football and basketball coaches, opposed."

It came to a vote. Should the NCAA sponsor Division I women's championships?

Chudacoff wrote: "The first vote on the measure ended in a 124-124 tie. A second vote narrowly defeated it, 128-127. After a half hour of rancorous debate, a third ballot overturned the second."

Chudacoff concluded: "The AIAW was doomed."

They didn't give up immediately. Schools could choose whether to join the NCAA or remain with AIAW. An AIAW attorney was quoted in the next day's *New York Times*: "They've bought women's athletics but they haven't bought the women of the AIAW."

Kit was among many AIAW officers and members who still felt loyal to the organization and were leery of life under the NCAA umbrella.

At a UW athletic board meeting in April 1981, Kit urged the board to allow the UW women's program to remain in the AIAW – which would continue to run championships, at least in the short term – rather than jump to the NCAA.

"AIAW has done a good job for us," Kit told the board. She pointed out that the NCAA was not yet offering women's championships in badminton, soccer or crew, adding that she could see "no advantage" to forsaking the AIAW. The board agreed. UW would remain with the AIAW – at least for one more year.

One woman with a unique perspective on the NCAA-AIAW controversy, as well as the struggle and growth of women's intercollegiate athletics across four decades, is Judy Sweet.

Sweet, from Milwaukee, was a UW-Madison undergraduate in the late 1960s and recalled cutting down and selling trees at Christmas to raise money for the nascent Women's Recreation Association (WRA) on the Madison campus.

Sweet was interested in athletics administration and in spring 1968 became the national president of the student-run Athletic Recreation Federation of College Women, which served as national coordinator for the WRAs on campuses across the country. In March 1968, Sweet and Kit attended the ARFCW national conference at the University of Arizona in Tucson.

For decades, Kit hung onto the spring 1968 edition of *Sportlight*, published three times a year by the ARFCW. It included a photo and essay by Sweet:

"My name is Judy Sweet and I have been selected to succeed Barbara Nieman as president of the ARFCW. I am a junior at the University of Wisconsin and am majoring in physical education.... I believe in the platform adopted by the ARFCW.... It is our responsibility to stimulate interest and participation in recreation, as well as to provide opportunities for experiences that

Judy Sweet (L) and Kit, 1969.

contribute to social and leadership development during the college years."

On returning from the Tucson conference, Kit in April received a note from an ARFCW executive: "It was a pleasure being with you in Tucson again. Judy Sweet makes a very fine president which compliments a very capable adviser!"

As Sweet's career in intercollegiate athletics administration ascended – and it would go all the way to the top – Kit frequently cited her as a prized pupil.

Sweet, in an interview for this book, said of Kit: "I respected her, I idolized her, I often thought of her as the Energizer Bunny, as she was always go-go-go. I have great respect for Kit and appreciation for all that she did at Wisconsin and on the national level."

Addressing the NCAA-AIAW controversy of the early 1980s, Sweet said she thought some sort of merger was inevitable.

"But I don't think it happened in the professional way it should have," she said. "My understanding is that leaders inside the AIAW had asked the NCAA to meet with them to try to identify the strategy that would work. And that never happened."

By 1981, Sweet was director of both men's and women's athletics at the University of California, San Diego, one of few women presiding over both a women's and men's program. She landed in San Diego in 1973 as an assistant athletic director, having previously taught physical education at Tulane University and the University of Arizona.

In 1975, Sweet was promoted to director of men's and women's athletics at UC-San Diego.

"It immediately jumped out at me that the men were getting 10 times [the resources] as the women," she said.

That was literally true in basketball: the women's team had a total budget of $1,000 compared with $10,000 for the men. Sweet was fortunate to be in a position – backed by Title IX – to more fairly allocate the resources. She made practice schedules more equitable and put more money into the women's sports.

Sweet also realized that halfway across the country, Kit was swimming upstream trying to accomplish the same thing.

"Kit was in a very challenging position," Sweet said. "Trying to build up the women's program – make sure there was equity – while at the same time there were other people who wanted to hold the program down. Unfortunately, there was this attitude that if we gave resources to the women's program it would hurt the men."

Sweet didn't buy it. "If you really looked into how money was being spent in the men's program [at UC-San Diego], there were things that really weren't going to hurt the men if we reallocated the money to the women."

In 1981, amid the brewing AIAW-NCAA controversy, Sweet was nominated to serve on the NCAA communications committee. Her position supervising both the men's and women's programs in San Diego led to the nomination. She'd serve on some 20 additional NCAA committees through the 1980s, and in 1991, Judy Sweet was named the first female president of the NCAA, while continuing her role at UC-San Diego.

It was a proud moment, but along with congratulations, Sweet experienced a more sobering reaction.

"I'm glad there was no Internet when I became [UC-San Diego] athletic director or NCAA president," she said. "I frankly was stunned by how many people took the time to hand-write letters, and they weren't necessarily positive ones. There were a lot of critical letters that I received, claiming I was taking this job from a man, and I should go back to the kitchen. That happened both when I became athletic director and when I became NCAA president in 1991."

Atlanta sports columnist Furman Bisher called her NCAA appointment "pure tokenism. Like having a debutante as head of the National Mule Skinners Association."

Back in 1981, Sweet, as noted, felt an alignment between the AIAW and NCAA was inescapable. But she believes the way it transpired – a power play by the NCAA – left many with a sour taste.

"You have to go all the way back to the late '60s and early '70s," Sweet said. "When the NCAA was adamant that they were not interested in women's athletics. As a result, the AIAW was born, with separate men's and women's athletics department at almost every university. UC-San Diego was unique in having a combined program almost from the beginning. It was one of the things that attracted me to the university.

"AIAW served a great function," Sweet continued, "in supporting and promoting competition for women at the collegiate level. When some individuals in the NCAA saw that women's athletics was growing and generating interest, there became a different attitude about sponsoring women's athletics under the NCAA umbrella."

Sweet concluded:

> "It really was an insult to the AIAW that the NCAA went about it the way they did. It really wasn't a merger. It was a sub-merger. And the most detrimental thing was that programs throughout the country then started to combine their men's and women's athletics programs, and where you'd had a director of men's athletics and women's athletics, now it was a director of athletics, and in almost every situation, that went to the male. The concern about women losing decision making authority was a real one, both in terms of governance of women's athletics, as well as the oversight of university programs."

Nearly four decades on, more women were in the top athletics director role on campuses across the country, though it's still uncommon, especially among larger institutions. A *New York Times* article from September 2019 stated that in the so-called Power 5 conferences, which includes the Big Ten and a total of

65 universities, only four athletics departments were headed by women. (The same article noted that a longtime UW-Madison female associate athletics director, Terry Gawlik, had recently been named to the top job at the University of Idaho.) Beyond there being few women directors of athletics, in 2021 the NCAA found itself issuing a highly publicized and embarrassing apology to participants in the 2021 basketball tournament after it was revealed training facilities for women were vastly inferior to those provided men.

Although UW women's athletics retained its affiliation with the AIAW after the early 1981 NCAA decision to begin holding Division I women's championships, many other schools did not. A later court filing noted in the 1981-82 sports season, "AIAW suffered a significant drop in membership and participation in its events. AIAW's loss in membership dues totaled $124,000, which represented approximately 22 percent of the dues collected the previous year. Forty-nine percent of those institutions leaving AIAW elected to place their women's sports programs under NCAA's governance."

NBC, which had broadcast the AIAW basketball champion-ship, opted out for the next tournament, citing the loss of prestigious schools.

On Oct. 9, 1981, AIAW filed an antitrust lawsuit seeking to prevent the NCAA from holding championships in women's sports.

In the *New York Times*, AIAW president Donna Lopiano called the NCAA "predatory" and "blatantly unfair," adding, "It became increasingly apparent that this [negative financial] impact was not the result of fair competition, but the result of a massive effort to buy women's athletics to add to the NCAA's conglomer-ate interests."

While the controversy boiled, competition continued, and one standout UW athlete had a career defining race in the AIAW indoor track and field championship in 1981.

Pam Moore grew up in Milwaukee and moved to Madison her junior year of high school, where she competed in basketball, volleyball, and track for Madison Memorial. She was offered scholarships to UW–Madison in both track and basketball, and played both sports her freshman year, though basketball caused her to miss the indoor track season that first year.

"I wanted to try basketball on the college level," Moore said, in an interview for this book. "My high school team wasn't very good. I wasn't sure how good I could be."

She liked the idea, too, of playing for Edwina Qualls. "I thought it would be great to play for a black women's coach. I wanted to give it a shot."

Moore was good enough to set school freshman records for both scoring and rebounding. But in the end, she left basketball behind after one season (although years later, she was the proud basketball mom of NBA star Wesley Matthews).

"Track ended up being more my love," Moore said. "I decided to focus on it."

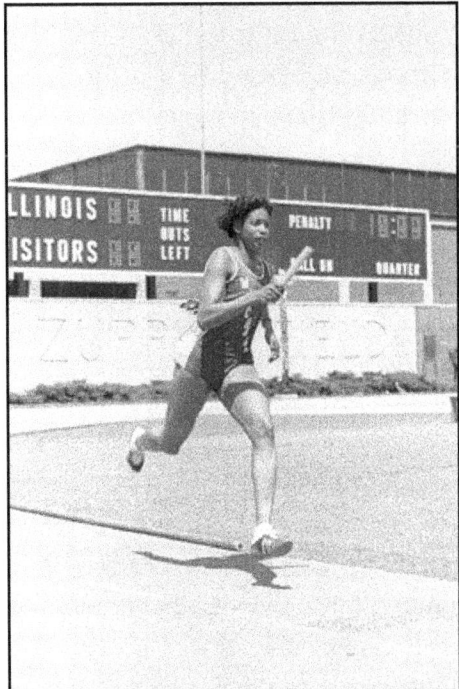

Pam Moore.
(courtesy of
UW athletics)

That focus produced an astonishing record of excellence. From 1978-1981 Moore won 11 Big Ten titles including four straight victories in the outdoor 400 meters for coach Peter Tegen.

"I loved Peter," Moore said. "Everybody didn't always agree with his philosophies, but I loved him. I was a worker. I worked hard."

Her specialty – the 400 meters – was a grueling distance that while not really a sprint, asked competitors to go full out in the manner of a sprint. "You try to do the best you can without dying," Moore said, wryly.

In March 1981, Moore's senior year, the Badgers competed in the AIAW National Indoor Track and Field Championships in Pocatello, Idaho, finishing a respectable fifth. Moore led the way, though she had only qualified for the field in the 400 meters a week earlier.

"You needed a 55.5 [second] qualifying time and I didn't get it until a week before nationals," Moore said in an interview later that year.

In Idaho, she ran the race of her life, waiting until the final turn on the track to pass Lisa Garrett of Virginia and Charmaine Crooks of Texas-El Paso for the victory. Moore's time was 53.8 seconds. She'd never run faster.

"After trying so hard to qualify," she said, "I ran the race of my life. I was ecstatic, When I heard the time, I applauded."

Four decades on, Moore recalled the Idaho race as "one of my pride and joys. One of the best times I ever ran."

Moore was inducted into the UW Athletic Hall of Fame in 2006. Her memory of Kit?

"She was awesome," Moore said. "All about the women. I didn't get to spend a lot of time with her, but she was always welcoming and always made us feel important."

On Sept. 10, 1981, Kit and her colleagues in women's athletics at UW set the AIAW-NCAA controversy aside and threw themselves a seventh anniversary party. It was 1974 when women became varsity athletes at UW-Madison. As their struggle for equity continued, it was important to step back and see just how much had been accomplished.

The event was sponsored by WIS-Club and marked the five-year anniversary of the founding of the women's athletics booster group.

The dinner – "A Celebration of Excellence" – was held at the UW Field House and drew more than 500 people who paid $12 a ticket.

"I'm excited," Kit told the *Wisconsin State Journal*, "so many people went out of their way for us. This is the biggest event we've ever had for women's athletics."

Twenty-two of UW's 27 All-American women athletes and Olympians made it to Madison for the event.

Husband and wife John and Polly Erickson shared keynote speaking duties. John was a former UW men's basketball coach and general manager of the Milwaukee Bucks. Polly was a much-decorated amateur golf champion.

"I'm thrilled to be part of this celebration," John Erickson said. "Excellence" – he was referencing the title for the night – "does not mean perfection. True excellence provides for maturity and growth. True excellence has lasting results. We are here because we believe in the virtues of true excellence."

Polly said, "I know what it can do for women to compete. It's exciting to see what Wisconsin is doing for women athletes."

The first years of the 1980s were also instrumental for the women's athletics programs gaining inclusion into the Big Ten Conference.

In an extended personal essay reflecting on the growth of women's athletics from 1977-1990 (an essay that appears not to have been published, but was written as a sequel to Kit's contribution to a 1970s book of essays about women at UW titled *Women Emerge in the Seventies)*, Kit noted the women sports administrators from Big Ten Conference schools had in fact been meeting since the late 1960s to discuss the shared concerns of their developing programs.

"Before their programs officially became intercollegiate," Kit observed. "Before there were national governance organizations for women or national championships. This unofficial organization, camaraderie and avenue for communication proved to be most helpful as more official meetings began to mark the transition to the intercollegiate conference competition which would have the full blessing of our institutions."

The governing body of the Big Ten Conference in the early 1980s was called the Council of 10, and it consisted of the president or chancellor from each member institution. (In 1990, with the addition of Penn State to the conference, the name was changed to the Council of Presidents and Chancellors.)

According to Kit, the women athletic administrators at the conference schools had made a proposal for inclusion prior to 1980 and the Council of 10 had expressed interest in exploring it further. The UW athletic board went on the record three times between 1975 and 1980 in support of adding the women's programs to the conference.

"Finally in July of 1980," Kit wrote, "the Council of 10 established a task force to prepare a plan for incorporating women into the conference."

The task force's report was completed the following year and endorsed by the Council of 10, and by October 1981, according to Kit, all 10 schools had voted to affiliate their women's programs with the conference. (In their book on the history of Badger athletics, authors Jim Mott and Don Kopriva noted Minnesota did not immediately join.) It should be noted, too, that the women had been competing for championships against the other conference schools prior to 1981 – in some cases they were referenced as "Big Ten titles" – but the results were not officially recognized.

(Although Tamara Flarup, the longtime women's sports information director at UW, recalled that they were at least unofficially recognized, and listed with an asterisk. "From my standpoint," Flarup said, "all those records that were established from those previous years [prior to 1981], I battled that they should be included in the Big Ten championship records, because they may have been unofficial championships, but how could we deny all the great athletes we had during that time? To my knowledge, they came in under an asterisk. Now they have all been bettered so it's not a big deal, but it was a big deal in 1981 because those were our records.")

The administrators of the conference's women's athletics programs, including Kit, were formally recognized as the Women's Program Group (WPG), and in May 1982, Phyllis Howlett was hired as the Big Ten's first assistant commissioner for women's programs.

Later, Kit would recall Howlett's early tenure with a touch of wry commentary: "Much of the time an unsung hero, Howlett added organizational skills to the conference. Utilizing diplomacy skills worthy of a Nobel Prize, often in an atmosphere which was not quite ready for a competent woman administrator, she was able to help the WPG and our programs to progress and develop. She and Mary Masters also organized the first Big Ten Championship Manuals for all sports, much of the groundwork having been done by the WPG."

Kit noted further that in 1982 a Conference Medal of Honor for Women – given to an athlete from each institution for combined excellence on the field and in the classroom – was instituted. Wisconsin's first winner: badminton champion Ann French, a four-year All-American from Elmhurst, Illinois. By 1983, conference rules and compliance procedures were put into effect for the women's programs; the first conference record book for women was published and a Big Ten female athlete of the year was initiated.

The conference's first woman athlete of the year was Judi Brown, a track athlete from Michigan State. But from 1985-90, in five of the six years, the Big Ten female athlete of the year was a Wisconsin Badger, all from track and field: Stephanie Herbst, Cathy Branta, and Suzy Favor (three times).

While ascendance to official standing within the Big Ten Conference was a positive for the women's programs, the fate of the AIAW and what the impact of a new administration in the White House in Washington might be were weighing on Kit when *Capital Times* sports editor Rob Zaleski caught up with her for a lengthy interview in November 1981.

Zaleski first took note of another positive: The men's football offices had been relocated inside Camp Randall Stadium, which freed their previous third floor space for women's athletics. The new digs, Zaleski wrote, "has given the women an identity of their own."

Kit's comments on the move had a touch of wry humor: "There was one room that was used for football films, and it was a real pit. But we fixed it up and turned it into a conference room, which is something we've always wanted. The guys had painted black over the windows, and there was a grungy old carpet on the floor. There was tape and film all over the place, and there was a moldy refrigerator. But we scraped the windows and put in new carpeting, and now it looks great."

Zaleski, who in 1981 was near the beginning of what would be a lengthy and distinguished career as a journalist in Madison, offered readers this perceptive take on Kit:

"Saunders, 41, is hardly a crusader in the Carry Nation mold. She is soft-spoken and cautious, friendly and demure, although it is obvious there are fires brewing within."

In the interview, Kit voiced concern about whether Title IX could survive the deregulation agenda of the administration of new President Ronald Reagan.

"If Title IX is eliminated," Kit said, "and the inflation rate continues to rise, and the economy continues to have problems, I can see a lot of sporting opportunities being dropped – for men and women. I don't see any immediate impact here at Wisconsin because we've made so much progress and I think there's a commitment.

"But down the line," Kit continued, "if things really get tight, they might be tempted to do away with non-income sports. This would hurt the women a lot, of course, but it also would hurt men's sports that don't make money."

Whenever it was brought up over the years that women's athletics did not generate income, Kit would politely point out that the same was true of most men's sports at UW, the exceptions being basketball, hockey and, especially, football.

If Kit didn't foresee any immediate impact from moves by the Reagan administration, the NCAA-AIAW controversy was of more immediate concern.

Zaleski set the stage in his article (which was titled "Women's sports rocky road"):

> "The NCAA, aware that women's sports are beginning to offer lucrative television possibilities, will hold its first officially sanctioned tournament (cross country) on Nov. 21 [1981]. Saunders says this is a first step in a power move to gain control of women's athletics and, subsequently, destroy the 10-year-old AIAW."

Zaleski then quoted Kit, who offered some of her most pointed criticism yet at the NCAA:

> "If you ask me what the NCAA's motives are, I can give you a biased answer. They want to have their own little monopoly. If they succeed in running their own women's championships and all the other things they've managed to take away from the AIAW, then the AIAW can't survive. And if that happens, the NCAA won't have any competition for membership.

> "Then a year or so down the line, they're perfectly free to do what they want with non-income sports. And I see them not caring at all about either men's or women's non-income sports. Eventually, I think they'll drop them."

Finally, Zaleski asked about the anti-trust lawsuit the AIAW had brought against the NCAA a month earlier.

"I think we have a good chance to win," Kit said, "but if we don't, I think it will be the end of the AIAW. For one thing, we don't have enough money for an appeal."

If – as it looked increasingly – the 1981-82 season might be the last for the AIAW, the UW women's basketball team made a late-season run that assured it would be memorable, at least in Madison.

Kit's high hopes when she hired Edwina Qualls as women's basketball coach in 1976 had never been fully realized. Kit continued to be supportive of Qualls, even after being blindsided by the coach's late 1977 Title IX complaint. Kit knew basketball was one women's sport – volleyball another – that had a realistic chance of producing income. She set a goal of drawing 1,000 fans a game to the Field House and took out ads promoting the games on the back of Madison city buses. But the goal wasn't reached, and two consecutive losing seasons ('79-'80 and '80-'81) didn't help.

Still, Kit being Kit, she didn't blame Qualls, at least not publicly. "Edwina probably puts more pressure on herself than I put on her," Kit told Zaleski.

The 1981-82 season brought a turnaround. The Badgers started slowly and had a 4-7 record after 11 games. But over the next 22 games, Qualls' team won 17. In the process they ended some notable winning streaks among their opponents. UW-La Crosse had won 23 in a row before losing to the Badgers. UW likewise ended a 13-game win streak of UW-Green Bay and 28 in a row for Miami of Ohio.

Their good play took the Badgers to the AIAW tournament in 1982, which included 16 teams in what was a depleted field owing to the NCAA holding its first women's basketball tournament. Smaller field or not, the Badgers were pleased to be in the tournament in what was their most successful season to date.

The Badgers competed in the Midwest Regional and in the round of 16 edged Colorado, 60-59. The highly ranked University of Texas was next, with the game to be played on the Longhorns' home court in Austin. Kit led an enthusiastic group from Madison to Texas for the game, with a spot in the AIAW Final Four going to the winner. The Longhorns – who were working on a 30-game winning streak of their own – proved too much for the Badgers, although it was competitive, the final score 72-61.

Three months later, at the end of June 1982, the AIAW disbanded operations.

"We are a dormant organization," Ann Uhlir, the organization's executive director, told the *New York Times*. "We will retain our members without further assessment of dues... pending the resolution of our litigation against the NCAA."

Kit gave an interview to *Capital Times* sports columnist Mike Lucas, who noted that Kit's term as AIAW vice president "expired at about the same time the organization did."

In the interview, Kit drew a beer analogy. "It's like Rolling Rock being taken over by Budweiser," she said. "What chance would they have? It's little versus big."

Kit's comments echoed the remarks of future NCAA president Judy Sweet, who, earlier in this narrative, called the takeover "a sub-merger."

Kit told Lucas: "What it means, essentially, is that the AIAW no longer exists. They're keeping an executive committee active just in case some miracle should happen and the AIAW should win its antitrust case with the NCAA. I don't think anyone really expects that to happen."

It didn't. On March 1, 1983, U. S. Judge Thomas P. Jackson ruled that the NCAA had not violated anti-trust laws and dismissed the AIAW suit. Kit had earlier stated that the AIAW did not have money for an appeal, but they did appeal, and a little over a year later, in June 1984, a federal appeals court upheld the district court ruling. It was truly over.

In her summer 1982 interview with Mike Lucas, Kit elaborated on her Budweiser–Rolling Rock analogy in analyzing what happened:

> "A number of women leaders in athletics swung over to the NCAA for the glamor of it. They run a first- class operation. It's nice to be taken care of in that way. The NCAA has real good bargaining power with the television networks and it will mean more visibility and publicity."

But Kit – correctly, in the event – predicted that the takeover would result in fewer women in top college administration positions.

> "It will be tough for women to establish leadership roles under the NCAA," she said. "In the govern-ing structure, the participation rate for women is pitiful – 20 percent. As a result, we have lost some opportunities to learn about the politics of sports government."

(Earlier in this narrative, it was noted that a fall 2019 *New York Times* story revealed women continue to lag behind in top athletics administrative posts: "Of the 65 colleges in the nation's five wealthiest and most powerful sports conferences," the *Times* noted, "only four have women leading the athletic department.")

"Some coaches," Kit continued in July 1982, "also are fearful that the field – and thus the participation for individual athletes – for national tournaments will be cut back under the NCAA. But at this point, it's fruitless to think about the pluses and minuses. The NCAA will be hearing our ideas and seeing more of us at the convention, that's for sure."

It was at the end of Kit's interview with Lucas that the columnist teased the likelihood of changes coming soon to the UW athletic department. Lucas didn't mention it by name, but UW had commissioned an evaluation of the athletic department's management by the accounting firm Arthur Anderson & Co. of Milwaukee.

"I really can't say much about it," Kit said. "No decisions have been made. We know we need to make some changes in the way we control budgeting and some things like that. We would be crazy if we wouldn't want to increase our efficiency and there are a lot of ways that can be done."

The news – when it broke about 10 weeks later – included a promotion and a new job title for Kit Saunders: associate athletic director for both men's and women's non-income sports.

Chapter 9
A NEW JOB TITLE,
A BASKETBALL CONTROVERSY
AND TROUBLE FOR TITLE IX

It was at a meeting of the UW athletic board on Sept. 17, 1982, that a plan to reorganize the administration of UW athletics was unanimously approved.

The restructuring included positioning three associate athletic directors beneath Elroy Hirsch, the current athletic director who would retain that title, while, as the next day's report in *The Capital Times* noted, relinquishing "most of his fiscal and administrative duties so he could concentrate on raising funds."

Around Madison and the state of Wisconsin, Hirsch was widely credited with rejuvenating a moribund men's athletic program in the 1970s. He was a football hero with an engaging personality, great at booster events. Hirsch was less concerned with – and less skilled at – day to day administration of the department. There were whispers about Hirsch's work ethic that grew louder in the early spring of 1982 when the search for a men's basketball coach to succeed Bill Cofield resulted in the naming of UW–Eau Claire head coach Ken Anderson. Within days, Anderson had second thoughts and withdrew from the post before he'd started. A new search was quickly initiated (the job went to Steve Yoder, coach of Ball State in the Mid-American Conference), but by then Hirsch was vacationing on a cruise. He participated by phone.

Still, under the new set-up, Hirsch would retain his title and final say on major decisions. The three associate directors directly under him included Otto Breitenbach, Hirsch's longtime second in command who would now be responsible for the department's income sports: men's football, basketball and hockey.

Kit Saunders was named associate athletic director for all non-income sports, men and women. Kit would have two assistant directors: longtime colleague Paula Bonner, promoted to assistant director for women's non-income sports (which is to say all women's sports), and Bob Lee, assistant director for men's non-income sports.

A third associate athletic director for administration would be hired, essentially to supervise the day-to-day running of the department.

Reaction outside the department centered on whether the new arrangement slighted Hirsch. *Milwaukee Journal* sports editor Jim Cohen's column on the new arrangement was headlined, "Is Elroy being shoved aside?" Cohen's answer: "Yes. Sort of."

Kit was not asked for comment in the immediate wake of the restructuring, but her salary – all three associate directors were to receive $50,000 annually – received a significant bump.

In a letter that year to her old college chum Kathy Riss, Kit noted, "I'm enjoying my new responsibilities as associate athletic director. I've had a crash course in baseball, wrestling, etc. It's been fun helping the men's non-income sports too. Also nice being in on more departmental decision-making than before."

In October 1982, a month or so after her new position was announced, Kit was able to recognize two Madison men who had helped her throughout her long and not always easy rise in the athletic department. It was at a meeting of WIS-Club, the booster arm of UW women's athletics, and Kit awarded a plaque to brothers Irwin and Bob Goodman, jewelers, philanthropists, rabid sports fans – and great friends to Kit Saunders.

"They always had her back," said Dale "Buzz" Nordeen, a Madison businessman and UW sports fan, who, before the decade was out, became Kit's husband. "Early on, Bob and Irv would take her to public athletic department events when department people didn't. She would go as their guest."

At the WIS-Club meeting on October 23, 1982, Kit stood and thanked the Goodmans.

"Most of us have only a few special friends," she said. "People we can always count on, no matter what. Bob and Irwin Goodman are two such people... They were right out front helping us before it was popular to do so... They have continued to speak quietly but positively in our behalf in the Madison community. Because of the respect which they have earned throughout the years, their steadfast support has lent status and respect to our program."

The plaque read:

> "In recognition of your generosity, support and boundless enthusiasm for the University of Wisconsin Women's Intercollegiate Athletics program. Thank you for all you have done and all that you continue to do for us. You are loved and appreciated."

The timing of Kit's new position heading all non-income sports coincided with the elimination of a varsity sport she'd help establish in the early '70s and which had enjoyed competitive success on the Madison campus – women's badminton.

When women's intercollegiate athletics moved under the purview of the NCAA in the early '80s, the organization decided not to hold a national championship in badminton and the number of schools fielding teams declined significantly.

For the decade prior, however, the Badger women had performed well, winning a WWIAC (the conference Kit also helped inaugurate) championship in 1977-78 under coach Sandra Norton and eventually – in 1983, their last year – a national championship.

One of the stars of that era – and a 1999 inductee into the University of Wisconsin Athletic Hall of Fame – was Ann French.

Growing up, French was part of a racquet-sport playing family in Elmhurst, Illinois.

"My parents met playing tennis," French said, from her home in the San Diego area, in an interview for this book. "My mom was a badminton player. They would bring us kids along to play. We figured out that if we just ran around screaming, things didn't go well. If we picked up racquets, they were much more encouraging." (French had a brother, Marty, who was a scholarship badminton player at Arizona State, and a sister, Linda, who followed Ann and played at UW.)

Illinois was just starting to have high school badminton when Ann was a junior – "I got to play two years," she said – but she was good enough to play adult tournaments starting at age 14. The Badgers' badminton coach, Sandra Norton, had eyed her during those matches and offered a scholarship.

"I wanted to be an engineering major," French recalled. "I thought, 'Go to a Big Ten university, on scholarship, and get to play badminton. What could be better?'"

French excelled in her sport, earning All-America honors from the AIAW every year from 1979-82.

"It was awesome," French said, of her time as an athlete on campus. "The Natatorium was fairly new. I think there were four gymnasiums upstairs and we had a nice gym with six courts and access to it five afternoons a week and on Sunday. There was plenty of training and plenty of play.

"It was a great group of women," French continued. "Between Kit Saunders and Paula Bonner, we all felt there was solid support for the female athletes and the women's program."

After French's sophomore season, Norton recruited Claire Allison, a young woman from the Toronto, Canada area. French and Allison became a very formidable doubles team. They won the AIAW national doubles championship two years in a row.

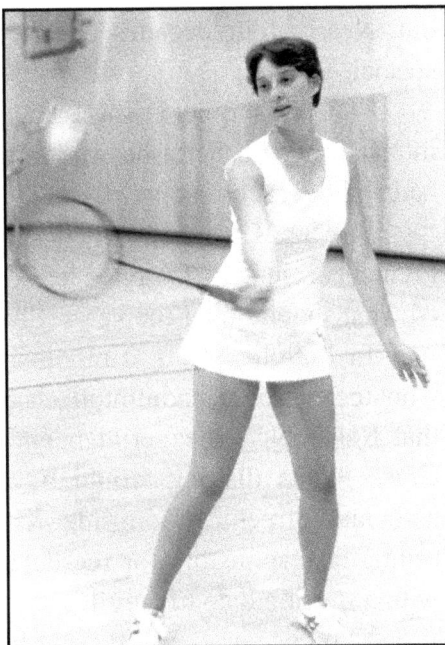

Ann French. (courtesy of UW athletics)

"The first year, people were surprised," French said. "They were like, 'Who are these girls?' The second year, they were prepared, and it was tougher."

That second national championship came in March 1982 at the AIAW tournament in Muncie, Indiana. The Badgers came in third as a team.

Everyone knew the 1983 badminton season would be its last as a varsity sport. French had used up her eligibility, but Kit came to her with an idea.

"Sandra Norton was retiring [as coach]," French said. "Kit knew the program was only going to exist for one more year. So they asked me to be the coach. I was a grad student trying to get my master's in civil engineering. They knew I was going to be on campus for another 18 months. They trusted me to coach."

They weren't wrong. The National Intercollegiate Badminton Championship was held in April 1983 and the Badgers captured the team crown. Claire Allison won the singles title. If the sport had to lose its varsity status, it was a great way to go out. Nearly four decades on, the memories for French are still special.

"Kit was quiet," she said, "but every time I had direct interaction with her, she was awesome. All the athletes felt we had a high level of support.

"I sent Kit a note when she retired from the University," French continued. "I wanted her to know how much we appreciated what she did over the years. She sent me a nice note back."

In March 1983 – a month before French and the Badgers won the national badminton championship – it was announced that Ralph Neale, superintendent of schools for the Middleton-Cross Plains district, would be the athletic department's third associate director (alongside Kit and Otto Breitenbach), and primarily responsible for the department's day-to-day operation, with a starting date of July 1.

News accounts stated that Elroy Hirsch, who would continue in the top job as athletic director, made the hire in consultation with UW Chancellor Irving Shain. The athletic board gave unanimous approval at a March 5 meeting.

Neale was a 1952 Montello High School graduate and earned a bachelor's degree from UW–Madison in 1957. He was a varsity wrestler and three-time letter-winner as a Badger and helped coached wrestling as a graduate student. Neale later started a wrestling program at Monroe High School and coached football there as well.

Neale knew athletics but his hire was widely perceived as an effort by the UW administration to professionalize the department and make it more accountable – by extension, a slighting of Hirsch. Neale, however, in an interview just a day or two after assuming his role that summer, rejected that scenario, telling the State Journal's Tom Butler he was "not a watchdog."

Neale continued, "I think the chancellor realizes that Elroy's contribution to the university is not running the business internally. His is out meeting people and [fundraising]."

Neale told Butler that he'd never considered the position until several friends urged him to send a resume.

"I sent it in and honestly forgot about it," Neale said. "A couple of months went by before I finally got a call to see if I'd be interested in taking an interview. I really thought I wasn't being considered. I was interviewed in January and then things moved rapidly."

That spring – prior to Neale assuming his new role – Kit made the difficult decision to fire Badgers baseball coach Tom Meyer. The move brought headlines, an indication that Kit's new position in charge of all non-income sports, including venerable men's programs like baseball, would bring increased scrutiny.

Meyer's dismissal as baseball coach in late May 1983 followed by four days the resignation of his top assistant, Steve Land. Kit told reporters that department protocol prevented her from commenting in detail on a personnel matter, but on May 26, two days after Meyer's firing, she spoke with *Capital Times* sportswriter Brad Fadulto. In the absence of an official explanation for the move, rumors had been swirling.

Kit said a combination of factors led to Meyer's removal, including the resignation of Land, which she said, "brought some of the general problems of the baseball program to our attention."

Meyer's win-loss record as coach was 229-276.

"It wasn't the record," Kit said.

> "But usually what you find with records is they're indicative of other problems in a program. If you look at Wisconsin and our record with retaining coaches, it takes more than a losing record for us not to renew a coaching contract. It has to be a lot of problems that are building up in a program… The resignations of the assistant coaches [two others besides Land, the top assistant, also resigned] brought a lot of things to our attention real quickly."

Kit conducted some player interviews in the wake of Land's resignation. So did reporters. One player told the *Capital Times* that Meyer was "a difficult man to play under... constantly on players... it got kind of hectic in the dugout."

State Journal sports columnist Tom Butler defended Meyer to the extent of saying baseball was always fighting uphill on the Madison campus, given the often-abysmal spring weather. Recruiting top players was never going to be easy.

No one was completely surprised when Kit announced in July that Steve Land, the assistant whose resignation prompted Meyer's firing, would return to the program as head coach.

That same season, under even more difficult circumstances, Kit filled a head coaching vacancy in the men's track and field program. In April 1983, coming back from a recruiting trip to Illinois, Dan McClimon died when his small plane crashed.

After a search, Kit tabbed McClimon's 30-year-old assistant, Ed Nuttycombe, for the job. Nuttycombe later said it was the last way he would ever have wanted to get a head coaching job, but he accepted. Both he and Kit made the right call. Nuttycombe went on to a storied career – including an astonishing 26 Big Ten conference championship teams – that landed him in the track and cross-country coaches Hall of Fame.

Meanwhile, the UW women's track and cross-country program continued to shine under head coach Peter Tegen. Their NCAA cross-country championship at Penn State in November 1984 – detailed in the first chapter of this narrative – was preceded by a Big Ten "triple crown" of 1983-84 titles that began with the cross-country team's conference winning performance at the Big Ten meet in Champaign, Illinois in September 1983. Cathy Branta won her second consecutive individual title to lead the Badgers.

Next up was the Big Ten indoor track season, and the Badgers earned the title narrowly over Indiana, with 104 points to the Hoosiers' 99.5. Branta won both the mile and two-mile competitions and was named the Athlete of the Championships.

Badger athletes Katie Ishmael (three mile), Dorothea Brown (long jump) and Sharon Dollins (triple jump) also were individual champions. At the Big Ten outdoor meet, it was again Wisconsin first, Indiana second. Branta won two events – the 1,500 and 3,000 meters (setting meet records) and Ishmael set a meet record in the 5,000 meters.

The stage was set for the Wisconsin women's program's first official NCAA championship later that year at the cross-country meet in Pennsylvania.

If 1984 was a year to celebrate unprecedented success for women's cross-country and track at UW, it was also a year when a major controversy in the women's basketball program was ignited, one that led to a painful decline in the program's fortunes and, within two years, a coaching change. Meanwhile, on the national level, a decision by the United States Supreme Court threatened to upend all the advances made possible by the 1972 passage of Title IX, causing considerable concern among the administrators – Kit, Paula Bonner, Tamara Flarup – who continued to build the women's program on the Madison campus.

Both events – an episode on the basketball court at the University of Minnesota and the troublesome Supreme Court decision – happened in February 1984.

The court decision had its genesis in a 1976 action by a Presbyterian school in Pennsylvania called Grove City College.

According to a summary of the case on the uscourts.gov website, in 1976 the federal government asked Grove City College to submit proof it was following Title IX regulations prohibiting discrimination by gender. The college refused, basing the refusal on the fact Title IX applied only to schools receiving federal funding, which the college claimed it did not. The government disagreed, pointing out that 140 of the college's 2,200 students received assistance through the federal Basic Educational Opportunity Grant program, widely known as Pell Grants.

An administrative law judge sided with the government, at which point the Pell Grants to Grove City students were discontinued. That resulted – in November 1978 – in a lawsuit by the college and some of its grant recipients asking a federal district court to overturn the decision.

The district court sided with Grove City College, but the government appealed, and the Third Circuit Court of Appeals reversed the district court, saying Grove City needed to follow Title IX guidelines if students were getting federal grants.

Appealed yet again, the case was accepted by the United State Supreme Court. Oral arguments were Nov. 29, 1983. The high court issued its decision on Feb. 28, 1984.

The uscourts.gov website describes the result:

> "A 6-3 majority of the Court held that when
> students received federally funded grants, Title IX
> requirements apply only to the specific program or
> activity that was benefited by the grants. In such
> instances, Title IX requirements do not apply
> across the entire institution."

Across the country, there was a collective shudder among women's intercollegiate athletics administrators.

"For those promoting sports for women," wrote Howard Chudacoff in *Changing the Playbook*, "the Grove City decision seemed to gut their efforts."

Later in 1984, as UW women's athletics celebrated its 10th anniversary of fielding varsity sports teams, new *Wisconsin State Journal* sports editor Bill Brophy – who was much more inclined to cover women's athletics than his predecessor – interviewed Kit and Paula Bonner about the state of play in Madison and beyond.

It was a largely positive piece – they had come a long way in a decade – but it was Bonner who brought up Grove City near the end of the column.

"I think it's ironic," Bonner said, "that our tenth anniversary ended up in the same year when the Grove City decision was made. What it means is that we have to be very conscious and very aware of what we're doing for women's programs and we can't assume everything is hunky-dory. It's incumbent on us to make sure women have an equal opportunity in athletics."

The dual interview with Kit and Bonner illustrates a potentially thorny dynamic that never became too much of an issue, largely because of the great mutual respect between the two women. Nevertheless, the 1983 reorganization of the department had placed Kit as associate director of non-income sports and Bonner assistant director for women's non-income sports (effectively all women's sports). Bonner reported to Kit, but it was Bonner who as of 1983 had more to do with the day-to-day operation of the women's program. She was thrilled with the assignment but disappointed not to get a women's director title.

"I didn't go to the Big Ten meetings," Bonner recalled. "Kit went to the meetings and was around the table talking about women's athletics. I wasn't. That was hard."

Yet Bonner valued Kit's friendship, institutional knowledge and deep commitment to women's athletics. In the end, the arrangement worked. Kit, for her part, was gracious in her assessment of Bonner's contribution.

In an unpublished essay written around the time of her 1990 retirement, Kit noted:

> "Bonner managed the women's program well,
> being a strong and effective advocate for improve-
> ment and change. She gave leadership to high
> schools, spearheading the 'Time Out Program' for
> coaches in conjunction with the State Department
> of Education and the Wisconsin interscholastic
> Athletic Association. She was also a force in the
> development of the first and one of the best
> student athlete support programs in the nation."

For women's athletics administrators across the country, the Grove City College case had a happy ending. It came through legislation, not the courts.

In his dissent of the 6-3 February 1984 majority decision, Justice William Brennan claimed it "completely disregards the broad remedial purposes of Title IX that consistently have controlled our prior interpretations of this civil rights statute."

Brennan continued:

> "According to the Court, the 'financial aid program' at Grove City College may not discriminate on the basis of sex because it is covered by Title IX, but the College is not prohibited from discriminating in its admissions, its athletic programs, or even its various academic departments....[the majority decision] severely weakens the antidiscrimination provisions included in Title IX."

Many lawmakers agreed. Chudacoff, in *Playing the Game*, noted:

> "A bipartisan group in Congress sponsored a bill that would reverse the Grove City decision and apply a collection of civil rights law, including Title IX, to all programs that benefited, directly or indirectly, from federal funds."

It was called the Civil Rights Restoration Act of 1987 and it easily passed both the House of Representatives and the Senate. President Ronald Reagan, however, vetoed the bill. Such was its popularity that both houses of Congress had the votes to override Reagan's veto. The override vote was on March 22, 1988. Title IX had its teeth again.

The U.S. Supreme Court decision in the Grove City case that temporarily altered the landscape of women's intercollegiate athletics was in February 1984. That month, an incident on the court of a University of Wisconsin women's basketball game turned the program upside down.

The Badger women, under coach Edwina Qualls, were having a good 1983-84 campaign (they would finish 13-5, good for second place in the Big Ten). They traveled to Minnesota for a game against the Gophers on Feb. 17 on a high note, having defeated first place Ohio State the previous weekend.

The game at Minnesota was highly physical. During the first half, Badgers co-captain Janet Huff suffered a black eye. By some accounts, the officials lost control of the game. Qualls was angry and felt all the calls were going in favor of the Gophers. Finally, with about five minutes left in the game, Qualls called a timeout. The team huddled around her. Qualls went on about the poor officiating. Then she told her players to go to the locker room – the Badgers were done.

Huff, who was a co-captain, said, "No. We are not leaving."

Heads turned toward the other senior co-captain, Mary Chrnelich. It was a fraught moment. Chrnelich nodded at Huff. "I'm with you," she said.

Chrnelich's name was familiar to Wisconsin basketball fans. Her brother, Joe Chrnelich, had a stellar career for the men's team in the late 1970s, twice a captain, and one of the top rebounders in the program's history.

Mary followed Joe to UW just as she had followed him to Milwaukee Pius High School, although unlike her brother, she didn't immediately gravitate to basketball at Pius. Prior to high school – she attended a Catholic school in West Allis through 8th grade – there had been no basketball for girls.

"The only sport we had was volleyball," Chrnelich, today Mary Chrnelich Nellen, recalled in an interview for this book.

"There was a boy in our grade school," Chrnelich continued, "whose dad was a lawyer. He wanted to fight to have me be on the boys' basketball team. I always played with the boys. I enjoyed doing athletic things. I loved to play. I didn't want to sit around and chat. But I didn't want [a lawsuit] to happen. I told my mom and dad, 'That would be terrible.' It didn't happen, even though [the lawyer] wanted it to."

Chrnelich had no organized basketball experience when she entered Pius. Summers, she'd been a competitive diver, with a coach who also coached at the public Nathan Hale High School. That's where Chrnelich hoped to go but her parents were adamant she attend Catholic high school.

"But, Mom, I'm a diver," Chrnelich said.

"You'll find something else," her mom said.

At Pius, the assistant girls' basketball coach approached her and said, "Are you Joe Chrnelich's sister?"

"Yes."

"Are you going upstairs tonight for basketball?"

"No," Chrnelich said, "I don't play basketball."

"Well," the coach said, "you can go up to practice or you can sit in detention."

Nearly four decades later, Chrnelich recalled, "I was a dumb little freshman. I went up there. And I never looked back. I fell in love with it immediately. I started on the freshman team. They pulled me up to varsity early in the season and we rolled from there."

Chrnelich played on the first girls' team at Pius to win a state championship. The program soon became a dynasty, winning multiple titles.

Chrnelich was also the first Pius female to get a full basketball scholarship to college, although that didn't go as planned.

Chrnelich had committed to play for Edwina Qualls at Wisconsin.

"At the last minute," Chrnelich recalled, "she pulled her offer. The girl she had originally recruited before me – I committed my junior year – somehow came back into the mix and [Qualls] wanted her. I ended up back in the recruiting pool."

UW men's basketball coach Bill Cofield, who knew Chrnelich through her brother, was a friend of the women's coach at Kansas. He alerted the Jayhawks that Chrnelich was suddenly available.

"They made me an offer on the spot," Chrnelich said. "I took it."

While she was unhappy with Qualls' pulling her offer – "it was terrible, that shouldn't happen" – Chrnelich's freshman year at Kansas was memorable. The Jayhawks' senior star was Lynette Woodard, destined to be one of the most decorated women players of all time.

"I got a starting spot," Chrnelich said. "I was a very good passer. If you could get Lynette the ball, you played."

Sophomore year, with Woodard gone, Kansas became less desirable, and Chrnelich learned a scholarship had opened at Wisconsin. She transferred and played her junior and senior years as a Badger.

"They were very welcoming," Chrnelich said. "Edwina and I got along just fine. It was like nothing ever happened."

That good relationship continued until the Minnesota game in February 1984, and Qualls' late-game order to the team to leave the court for the locker room.

"That came out of nowhere," Chrnelich said.

As noted, she and the other co-captain, Janet Huff, refused to leave. Three others, women who played sparingly – Ann Lederer, Cindy Slovak and Linda Stuessy – joined them. Five women: just enough to keep playing.

"We were vying to win the Big Ten," Chrnelich said. "We needed to win that game. We were only losing by 12. There was plenty of time left."

She conceded the game had been problematic. "The refs were not good. It was a rough game. It was not being [officiated] well. Janet Huff got clipped really bad. [Qualls] said, 'We're done.' We were like, 'Coach, there's still a lot of time left.' The game mattered."

In a *Capital Times* interview a few days later, one of the five who stayed, Cindy Slovak, recalled the moment:

"She told us all to go the locker room and not finish the game. I had walked all the way down to the locker room when I realized half the team was still upstairs. I went to get them and the seniors [Huff and Chrnelich] were standing there saying, 'We're not quitters.' Everything happened so fast. I didn't want to quit. I just didn't want to quit."

Chrnelich recalled: "The Minnesota coach came over to us and said, 'You're doing the right thing.'"

A comeback, however, was not in the cards. "We played the game out," Chrnelich said. "But we were obviously done. Emotions were way too high to expect we'd go back in the game and make it all happen."

Minnesota prevailed, 62-51.

Hard to believe, but the brief game stories in the *Wisconsin State Journal* and *The Capital Times* on Saturday, Feb. 18 recorded the Badgers' loss but made no mention of the drama that unfolded near the end. It was only a day later, in the Sunday *State Journal*, that the first whiff of the controversy surfaced, in a short story titled "Dispute strikes UW women." It named the five players who had ignored Qualls' directive and kept playing, and mentioned a team meeting scheduled for Monday, Feb. 20.

That afternoon, *The Cap Times* story revealed the first details of what had transpired, including the interview with Slovak.

Paula Bonner was quoted in the story, backing Qualls: "She felt the correct decision at the time was to pull the team for the safety of her players." She added that the department would back Qualls if the coach decided to discipline any of the five women who kept playing.

"The players have to follow the instructions of the coach during the game," Bonner said.

The stance was not as unwavering as it sounded. There were more meetings. Kit was involved, and eventually Elroy Hirsch. The *New York Times* ran a story on the controversy. By week's end – Feb. 24 – a *State Journal* headline read: "UW's Qualls reprimanded."

It was announced in a press release issued jointly by Hirsch and Kit.

> "We have determined Coach Qualls did not make a judgment that was in the best interest of the University of Wisconsin-Madison Athletic Department... Although the decision to pull the

team was perhaps in the 'heat of battle,' decisions such as this cannot be condoned."

"She took our captainship away," Chrnelich said. "She wanted to take our scholarships."

The reprimand reinstated the captaincies and ordered Qualls to allot the players court time as she had throughout the season. The latter didn't happen.

At Iowa on Feb. 24 – the night of the day the reprimand was announced – neither Huff nor Chrnelich played. Huff's absence was arguably justified – she was still recovering from the injury (which resulted in a slight concussion) at Minnesota. But Qualls said Chrnelich had an ear infection.

"Not true," Chrnelich said, in the interview for this narrative.

After the season, the athletic board's personnel committee was charged with making a recommendation to the board whether Qualls should be retained as coach. After what were reportedly heated discussions, the recommendation was made to renew Qualls' contract.

Chrnelich was saddened that the episode colored her last months as a Badger yet looks back on her overall experience at Wisconsin as "fantastic" and appreciates how the controversy was dealt with in the end.

"I felt proud that the school stood behind us," she said. "That was great validation for us. We were kids. We didn't know. We had everyone coming at us – reporters at our apartment doors."

Mary Chrnelich Nellen today runs Milwaukee-based 1 on 1 Teaching Hoops, a program that helps girls develop basketball skills. She briefly played professional basketball, coached at her alma mater, Milwaukee Pius, and watched her daughter, Nikki, develop into a talented player. Those months early in 1984 occasionally cross her mind.

"I look back and think, 'Would I do anything different?'" she said. "I don't think I would. I don't believe in walking off the court because the refs weren't good. It was one of those hard games that got very physical, but there was no reason to walk off."

Edwina Qualls stayed two more seasons as women's basketball coach at UW. The Badgers finished 11-17 and tied for seventh in the conference in 1985 and the bottom fell out completely in 1986. The Badgers finished 4-24 and last in the Big Ten.

That February – with another decision about renewing Qualls' contract coming in June (it would not be renewed) – a fair-minded assessment of her time at Wisconsin was offered by *State Journal* sports reporter Perry Hibner.

Conceding the program was then – in early 1986 – mired in an abyss, Hibner pointed out that "people forget more than 75 percent of Qualls' recruits have a degree. People forget Qualls' 1983-84 team finished second in the Big Ten and was the last conference team to beat Ohio State, a yearly powerhouse."

Hibner wrote: "People forget Qualls was largely responsible for getting funding for UW women's sports up to a level at which Badger teams can compete in the Big Ten."

While that last point might be overstated, it shouldn't be forgotten that it was Qualls who filed a Title IX complaint in 1977, making the case for more equity for women's sports and taking the heat for many in the program who felt the same way.

Still, as Hibner noted in his article, almost everything in the Qualls era was overshadowed by the incident at Minnesota, the pulling of her players from the court, the contentious aftermath.

Paula Bonner was quoted in Hibner's story: "It was the single most controversial thing to happen in Wisconsin women's collegiate sports. It's something I wished had never happened."

She wasn't alone.

Chapter 10

VOLLEYBALL ASCENDANT AND HOPES FOR A GOLF COURSE

T he celebration of the first 10 years of the varsity women's athletic program at UW-Madison in 1984 included an October banquet at the Field House which drew 575 people and saw Kit and rowing star Carie Graves inducted as charter members of the UW Women's Hall of Fame.

Tam Flarup, director of women's sports information, edited a silver-covered 32-page program that highlighted the accomplishments of the previous decade. Among them:

- The 11-sport program had 13 fulltime coaches and seven part-time assistants, with each coach and administrator having a newly remodeled office.

- Practice and competition facilities were remodeled and the women student-athletes benefit from full-time support staff personnel in athletic training, academic counseling, medical assistance and sports information.

- WIS-Club, the women's athletics booster group, counted 300 members and in 1983 raised over $50,000.

- In 1984, nearly 300 women athletes were in the program, with 104 receiving financial aid – nearly 1,000 had participated since 1974.

- Forty-one Badger women's teams had placed among the top 10 in national competitions since 1974 – with national championships in crew in 1975 and badminton in 1983 (and one in cross country about to happen in November 1984).

♦ Forty-eight Wisconsin women athletes had received All-American distinctions in several different sports.

One sport for which there had always been high hopes – both for success on the court and for its ability to attract a good crowd of spectators – was volleyball, yet across the first decade that success never materialized. Since 1975, the Badgers had finished higher than a tie for fifth in the Big Ten only once. In 1984, the third season under Coach Russ Carney, they were tied seventh with a conference record of 4-9. The following year, Carney's fourth as head coach, they slipped to a tie for ninth in the conference.

"The program was struggling," assistant director for women's sports Paula Bonner recalled in an interview for this book.

They decided to make a coaching change. "We went out to find somebody really good," Bonner said.

They did. Steve Lowe was a young man – just 30 in 1986 – on the way up, an assistant coach at the University of the Pacific, where he helped the Tigers to the 1985 NCAA volleyball championship.

Lowe, a native of Iowa City, met the Pacific head coach, Terry Liskevych, when each was doing post-graduate study in sports psychology at Pacific. Liskevych hired Lowe as an assistant coach in 1981.

"Steve is a special person," Liskevych would later recall. "He gets involved with his team on a personal level. He's a great human being who relates to people."

Paula Bonner, who led the search for a new Badgers volleyball coach, had Lowe on her radar early, though he was going to have to be truly special to get the job.

"I was very committed to letting women have coaching opportunities," Bonner said. "I still am. They are mostly going to happen coaching women's sports."

Meeting Lowe, it was clear his dedication to the women student-athletes was deep and sincere.

"Steve was one of the strongest feminists I could have hired for any coaching position," Bonner said. "He was so level-headed, so calm, he had tremendous credentials and background. I just thought – taking him as a whole person – he would be a tremendous fit for our program."

Bonner and Lowe shared a phone call and then he came to Madison for an interview. "A very special couple of days," Bonner recalled. "I remember so clearly driving him around and then taking him to the airport and talking some more while he waited for his plane."

Lowe got the job.

The results weren't immediate, although nearly so. Lowe's 1986 team finished tied for eighth in the conference. They tied fifth the next year. His 1988 team was the one that turned the corner.

"He made significant inroads recruiting in the Chicago area," Bonner said.

An hour outside of Chicago in Joliet, Lowe found Liz Tortorello, who would play for the Badgers, eventually earning a captaincy, from 1988-91.

Tortorello (today Liz Tortorello Nelson, and a volleyball commentator for the Big Ten Network), came from a family that was always talking sports. Her grandfather, Tony Tortorello, officiated Big Ten men's basketball for 22 years and was called "one of the Midwest's best known and most respected basketball referees" by the *Chicago Tribune*.

"I grew up talking about the Big Ten," Tortorello recalled, in an interview for this narrative.

Her high school sports experience did not start on a high note.

Liz Tortorello.
(courtesy of
UW athletics)

"The participation level wasn't the problem," she said. "It was pretty much everything else. The opportunities to play were there, but the opportunities to excel – good uniforms, marketing, anything girls now have in high school – we did not. It was a constant battle."

In Tortorello's junior year, she led her school, Joliet Catholic High School (now Joliet Catholic Academy), to the state tournament. They received volleyball uniforms to replace the softball shirts they'd been wearing and Tortorello got noticed by college recruiters offering scholarships.

One of them was Steve Lowe at Wisconsin.

"I knew I wanted to go Big Ten," Tortorello said, "probably because of my grandfather. My choice was between Northwestern and Wisconsin. It was Steve who tipped it to Wisconsin."

Lowe had come to watch her play in a tournament and then gone to dinner with the family at a Pizza Hut. "My little sister remembers it vividly," Tortorello said.

"He did a great job recruiting," she continued. "He was charming and personable. He made a huge difference, with his personality. He was a coach you definitely wanted to play for."

The decision was also helped by the fact one of Tortorello's Joliet Catholic teammates, Mary Penosky, got a scholarship with the Badgers a year earlier. Something was in the air in Madison.

"I cared about having a chance to win a Big Ten title and having a chance to win a national championship," Tortorello said. "Steve was someone you really got excited to play for. Not once did I ever think, 'Oh, they're in the bottom of the Big Ten.' He made us believe he was building something. That's what got me."

Lowe also fought for facilities. "We shared the Field House with the basketball team," Tortorello recalled, "and we rarely got to practice there. We practiced at the Nat[atorium]. Steve would battle for us. I caught him several times having heated arguments with the women's basketball coaches. He did everything he could for us."

Tortorello's freshman year, the volleyball team was still lucky to draw a couple hundred fans to the games. "But Steve had a vision," she said. "He paid members of the band $10 out of his own pocket to play at our games. He knew marketing. He started a booster club [the Wisconsin Avid Volleyball Enthusiasts – WAVE] and a summer camp and tournament."

Her first year – 1988 – Tortorello recalled the Badgers taking Illinois – which went to the Final Four – to five sets. "We were stubborn and feisty," she said.

In summer 1989, Lowe's Badger Volleyball Camp for Girls was held Aug. 7-11 and sold out all 120 spots. A mini-camp was held a week earlier for 60 girls who couldn't get in.

"Steve did a big fundraising booster club grass tournament every summer," Tortorello said. "A lot of us stayed on campus to do summer school and train. We were active with the booster club, which was a huge success."

Lowe's off-court promotional magic was matched by an uptick in the team's play in 1989. The Badgers did not make the NCAA Tournament field, but they were invited to the inaugural Women's Invitational Volleyball Championship, a tournament for the best teams not in the NCAA bracket modeled after the NIT tournament in men's basketball.

Tortorello recalled Lowe's talk before they made the trip – the tournament was held over several days at the University of Alabama–Birmingham. "We are going to this tournament," Lowe said, "and we are going to do extremely well because it is going to be a predictor of going to the NCAA tournament next year."

He was right. Lowe's Badgers won the tournament in Alabama. "It was playing multiple matches in a day," Tortorello said. "We were all sore and tired at the end – but we won." The Badgers beat Boise State 3-1 to win the title.

Brenda Williams, the coach at Alabama–Birmingham and one of the organizers of the tournament, said many years later: "Steve Lowe and that Wisconsin team were all tremendously classy. Winning our tournament provided them a springboard into the national program that the Badgers have become now."

Kit found the money for the team to make the trip to the tournament – unlike the NCAA, the Alabama event did not pay team's travel expenses. It proved to be the springboard Lowe predicted. The 1990 Badgers won their first Big Ten championship.

"It was a huge deal for Steve and our team," Tortorello said. "We got rings. It was very special. We got to host the first round of the NCAA tournament."

The Badgers played Illinois in that first-round match at the Field House, Nov. 30, 1990. It was a seminal night in the history of women's athletics at UW. Not only did the Badgers sweep Illinois in three straight sets to advance to the round of 16, the Field House crowd set an NCAA record for attendance. Never had so many – 10,935 – seen a collegiate women's volleyball game.

Tam Flarup, women's sports information director, was there. "I sat with Kit in the upper balcony," Flarup recalled. "We were looking at the people streaming in and we both had tears in our eyes. We always knew this would happen for women's sports at Wisconsin. We thought it would be basketball."

Two years later, the women's basketball team would fill the Field House when they hosted an NCAA tournament regional. But volleyball was first.

"That was crazy," Lowe said, in an interview after the Illinois match. "What a thrill that was. We were hoping we might set a [attendance] record and that was just fantastic."

The Badgers' dream season ended a week later, with a loss to Penn State in the Mideast Regional semi-final held at Lincoln, Neb.

While that was disappointing, there was great hope for the following season – indeed, the future of the program under Steve Lowe seemed limitless.

Then the unthinkable happened.

The following summer – 1991 – Lowe was treated for a blood clot in June and then in July was hospitalized in Madison for what a newspaper headline speculated might be pneumonia. The story said he felt tired, his lungs were congested. By early August, a *State Journal* headline read: "UW's Lowe Critical." Though he never smoked, cancer had been discovered in the lining of a lung.

"It went so fast," said Tortorello, who was in Madison with her teammates getting ready for her senior season. "Our coaches set up a camera at the end of the court at practice – probably a VHS – and they would give Steve tapes so he could watch them in his hospital room."

The team made a visit.

"We were all nervous," Tortorello said. "We hoped we could cheer him up. But it was awful. He had a ventilator. We just panicked. He was so fragile. Our coach?"

Steve Lowe died Aug. 22, 1991, age 35.

Nearly three decades after his shocking death, Lowe's legacy at the University of Wisconsin is secure, both in the success of the women's volleyball program through the years and in the way the campus has not allowed his memory to be forgotten.

Each year, the Big Ten home opening match is recognized as "Steve Lowe Night" at the UW Field House. In 2016, the 25th anniversary "Steve Lowe Night" was held in front of a sellout crowd. The Badgers, facing Ohio State, were rated third in the nation and had sold 3,000 season tickets.

"UW is living the dream Lowe surely had for the program he inherited in 1986," wrote Madison sportswriter Andy Baggot in advance of the 2016 event.

Three years later, in December 2019, the Badgers reached their highest plateau yet and played a match for the national championship, losing in the final to powerhouse Stanford. In December 2021, Badger volleyball reached the summit, winning the NCAA championship, beating Nebraska.

While Paula Bonner was hiring Steve Lowe, Kit was busy in her role, still relatively new, heading all non-income sports. She did a lot of public speaking in the mid-1980s, including many Founders Day events, the spring gatherings across that country that served to both raise funds and keep UW athletics in the minds of its far-flung alumni. Kit would give as many as three Founders Day speeches in a season: in 1985, she spoke in New York City, the Quad Cities, and Cedar Rapids.

The draft of Kit's 1986 Founders Day remarks does not include the cities where she spoke, but it nonetheless provides a lens into why she was such an effective speaker and advocate for the value of UW athletics and sports in general.

Her speech also references the recent search and hiring of a new women's volleyball coach – Steve Lowe.

"As I talked with some of you before dinner, I could tell that you are here because you are proud of the University of Wisconsin," Kit's speech began. "I am here tonight because I am also proud of the University of Wisconsin and because I believe in sports and athletics."

Kit told the audience that she'd recently met new UW System President Kenneth Shaw – he started Feb. 1, 1986 – at the annual NCAA convention in New Orleans in January. Shaw was receiving the NCAA's Silver Award – Jack Nicklaus was another recipient – given to student athletes who have distinguished themselves 25 years after competing. Shaw was a standout basketball player at Illinois State.

"He's a man who believes he has benefited from his sport experiences," Kit said of Shaw.

Kit told her audience she'd been reading an early novel by James Michener, *The Fires of Spring*.

"I'm a great Michener fan," Kit said, noting that the novel "is the story of a poor-house boy growing into an intelligent, sensitive man. In this young man's life, playing basketball in high school is one of the first experiences that keeps him on a path which goes in the right direction."

Kit quoted from the book: "Many words are wasted about high school athletics: body building, character formation, sportsmanship. Rarely do sports achieve these flowery ends, but what they do achieve is something even finer. They help boys find a place in society" – here Kit added, "and girls now too" – "especially [those] who might otherwise live on the fringes of the world."

"To paraphrase," Kit said, "some of them like the taste of the glory and the experience of sport so much that they determine that they want to make something of their lives. Michener was talking about high school sports, but don't make the mistake of thinking that young people are all through developing when they come to college."

Which is why, Kit said, the coach in college has such an important role to play.

"With that in mind," Kit said, "you can see why a big part of our job is to be sure that the coaches we hire are the best people we can find and why we are concerned about how each student is treated and what kind of experience he or she has."

Kit then talked about the hiring of Steve Lowe.

"We have just concluded a search for a new head coach for our women's volleyball team," she said. "As always, the experience of interviewing the fine individuals whom we invited to Madison was extremely interesting. I find it to be a kind of 'seminar' not only in where a particular sport is today on the national level, but what the world out there thinks of Wisconsin and the Big Ten Conference, and what the philosophies are of those we deem to be outstanding."

Kit said the recent volleyball coach search provided gratifying feedback of how UW and the conference were regarded: the applicant pool was stellar, the job clearly regarded as a plum.

"I am happy," Kit said, "to say that the gentleman who was our number one choice [Lowe] has enthusiastically accepted our offer. We are well on our way to developing our volleyball program to best serve our student athletes and to represent Wisconsin in a superior way."

One athlete who was representing UW women's athletics well in the late winter and spring of 1986 was a freshman named Beth Benevente, later Beth Benevente Miller. Her sport was gymnastics and on March 7 in a dual meet against Iowa, she set a UW freshman record by scoring 36.60 (out of a possible 40) in the all-around, the combined scores of four events: vault; uneven bars; balance beam, and floor exercise.

Benevente was from Glendale Heights, Ill., and in an interview for this book said she got her start in the sport when her parents enrolled her in a tumbling class when she was 6 years old.

Benevente attended Glenbard North High School and was a two-time state champion in the vault and all-around champion her senior year.

She was recruited by UW and came to Madison for a campus visit. She was also considering Utah State.

"I looked at Utah State and Wisconsin," Benevente said. "I think the city of Madison, as a whole, was just so beautiful – Utah had the mountains, but Madison was beautiful, too, and closer to home for me."

The Big Ten women's gymnastics championships were held in late March 1986 at the University of Minnesota. The competition was held in a large basketball arena with a raised floor and while practicing for the vault Benevente soared to the edge of the floor and rolled off into the spectator seats below.

She wasn't hurt. "But the next day they moved the whole thing back a little."

It was in the uneven bars – not traditionally her strength – that Benevente excelled during the competition, tying with Mary Olsen of Ohio State for the Big Ten title.

"It was a huge surprise for me," she said. "We shared the podium. There wasn't a lot of room up there."

By the following year, Benevente had set UW records in the vault, floor exercise and all-around; she'd put up the second-best score in balance beam and third best all-time in uneven bars.

It was her senior year, March 1989, when Benevente achieved a personal goal, scoring a 38 (out of 40) in the all-around during a triangular meet with Iowa and Michigan.

The meet was held in the Armory on Langdon Street, a facility referred to as the "Red Gym" by nearly everyone. Around that time, Kit wrote that she felt the Red Gym was "the best gymnastics facility in the Big Ten. It provides over 15,000 square feet of training space, including up to date equipment, a large foam training pit, 10 balance beams, 4 sets of uneven parallel bars, and spectator seating for about 1,000."

Benevente liked her coach, Terry Bryson – "she was a good coach with a strong Tennessee accent" – and stayed on as a volunteer graduate assistant coach once her competitive eligibility was finished. Her only negative memory of those Madison years is how the curtain came down: women's gymnastics was one of five sports eliminated by UW in a budget repair move in 1991, a year after Kit's retirement.

Benevente was helping coach and was with the Badger team in a hotel room in Champaign-Urbana, where the University of Illinois was hosting the 1991 Big Ten championship, when Bryson delivered the news. Rumors had been flying so it couldn't have been a shock, but the cold finality hit hard.

"It was tough for everybody," Benevente said. "Terry felt like she needed to tell everybody, so they didn't hear it from somebody else." The team, deflated, finished sixth, having gone in as one of the favorites.

In the same month Beth Benevente set a UW gymnastics scoring record for freshmen – March 1986 – Kit was named by UW Chancellor Irving Shain to a committee that would attempt to make a long-gestating plan for a University of Wisconsin golf course a reality.

Kit's appointment was notable in that she was the only woman on the 11-person committee that included Madison's two-time United States Open champion, Andy North. She was also the only representative of the UW athletic department on the committee, which may seem odd at first, until one considers that the funding for the course was coming from the University of Wisconsin Foundation, not the university proper. The plan was for UW athletics to operate the course once it was open, at least initially.

As the only committee member from athletics, Kit's role was large: she chaired the policy committee that would formulate general operating procedures, subject to approval of the chancellor's office and UW athletic board.

It also seems worth noting that golf was one of the few sports Kit played only sparingly – although by 1986 that was about to change, and not only due to her involvement with the UW course.

In November 1988, Kit addressed the Dane County Builders Association, providing both an interesting account of the checkered history of trying to open a UW golf course – it dated to the

1940s – as well as a progress report that included a prospective debut for the course in spring 1991.

In her talk to the builders, Kit noted that there was a mention in the minutes of a 1945 UW Board of Regents meeting that the Nakoma Golf Club course on Madison's west side had been offered to the UW for $110,000, a price deemed excessive by the university administration. A decade later, in 1955, there was discussion about a course to be situated on 150 acres between Picnic Point and Eagle Heights.

The course would be named for Guy Sundt, who had just died. Sundt was a star athlete and coach at UW, ending his career as athletic director. He so identified with UW athletics that after he was cremated, his ashes were dropped from a plane into Camp Randall Stadium. In her builders talk, Kit noted that the Sundt course was approved by UW athletics and its board, but vetoed by the university administration, which felt that prime campus land could be put to better use.

Yet another decade later, in 1965, the University of Wisconsin Foundation purchased, for $900,000, 326 acres in the town of Westport, just north of Madison, with a golf course in mind. The money came from the estate of Harry Culver, a real estate mogul and founder of Culver City, adjacent to Hollywood in southern California. Culver's father, Jacob Culver, grew up in Wisconsin and attended UW. But instead of using the Westport land for a golf course, the foundation ended up selling the property at a considerable profit.

In 1971, the foundation purchased the land – 585 acres north of Verona – that would finally become the UW golf course, though it would take another two decades to reach fruition. The saga of those 20 years, with starts and stops and all manner of intrigue, could likely fill a book itself. It was only when Chancellor Shain appointed the committee in 1986, Kit told the builders, that reason for real hope emerged.

"The committee began to meet in earnest and things began to happen," Kit said.

With a budget of $4.5 million and a well-regarded course architect, Robert Trent Jones, Jr., on board, ground for the new course was broken in fall 1987. It wouldn't go altogether smoothly – by summer 1988, construction was delayed when some budget estimates of the Jones design proved insufficient for the actual construction – but the problems were addressed promptly and when Kit, in her builders speech, suggested a spring 1991 opening, she said it with reasonable confidence.

"I think you can see," Kit said in closing, "that it will be an exciting facility for the university, for the Madison area and for the state of Wisconsin. It should be a magnificent course."

She was right. University Ridge Golf Course opened June 1, 1991, to excellent reviews. Its standing was confirmed just seven years on, in 1998, when University Ridge hosted the NCAA Division I Women's Golf Championship, the biggest event in women's college golf.

In May 1986, two months after Kit was named to the chancellor's committee on a university golf course, she was one of five Madison women named a "Woman of Distinction" by the YWCA. The annual awards celebrate women who have made a positive difference in Madison. The awards were presented at a June luncheon at the Concourse Hotel and one of Kit's co-recipients was Katharine Lyall, executive vice president of the University of Wisconsin System (Lyall would serve as UW System president from 1992-2004.)

It was one of the first – preceded by Kit's 1984 induction into the UW Women's Athletics Hall of Fame – in what would be a series of official recognitions of Kit's pioneering role in advancing women in sport. Among the others that followed were induction into the Madison Sports Hall of Fame, and, in 1997, a Lifetime Achievement Award from the Women's Sports Advocates of Wisconsin.

In June 1986, two weeks after Kit received her YWCA award at the Concourse, she sat down with Ralph Neale, deputy director of UW athletics, for her performance review. The copy

Kit kept for her records shows she received an excellent evaluation, starting with her role supervising Paula Bonner and Duane Kleven, assistant directors of women's and men's varsity sports, respectively. (Kit's title of associate director placed her in charge of men's and women's non-income sports.)

Neale wrote:

> "The stress you have placed on coordination and communication between women's and men's programs for Division unity and effectiveness of operation has resulted in both Paula and Duane checking between themselves on day-to-day operational matters."

Neale went on to praise Kit's administrative role:

> "Your strong assets... have greatly assisted the Division in our attempt to develop a coordinated, effective and efficient management approach to all Division responsibilities." And her public relations efforts: "You have demonstrated a positive public image for the Division and yourself. Your participation with community and alumni activities is meaningful and appreciated."

The evaluation is worth quoting not because it holds any surprises – Kit had been a high achiever since high school – but because before the year was out, her role within UW athletics was substantially altered, a change Kit did not appreciate or think appropriate.

Chapter 11

BUZZ

That fall, one of the greatest athletes ever to compete for the University of Wisconsin arrived on the Madison campus. Suzy Favor was a freshman in 1986 but she was already an accomplished runner, having been highly recruited out of high school in Stevens Point.

"I was lucky," Suzy Favor Hamilton – she married Mark Hamilton in May 1991 – said in an interview for this book. "In our small town, some of the parents started a running club. I think I was in middle school when that started."

She remembered competing in a Junior Olympics, and another junior national championship in Nebraska. "We were all over the Midwest," Favor Hamilton said. "At one of the races we had we ended up staying in a church – we didn't have a lot of money. We slept on the church floor in sleeping bags. One of those memorable moments – quite fun."

Favor Hamilton said she hoped to go to UCLA but her great high school success put pressure on her to stay closer to home.

"Everybody wanted me to go to Wisconsin," she said. "Inside, I really wanted to spread my wings, try something new and sort of be on my own. But at the same time, I don't think I had the courage. I was the hometown girl. Everybody wanted me to stay."

In Madison, Favor Hamilton bonded with another standout freshman runner, Mary Hartzheim. They roomed together.

"She and I dominated coming in," Favor Hamilton said. "We beat all the top runners at Wisconsin. We actually had quite a hard time from the other women on the team, because we came in and were dominating. There was a lot of jealousy and cattiness, which Mary and I didn't have time for. We just went out and kicked their butts. We were like, 'I'm not going to slow down for you people.'"

Favor Hamilton's track and cross-country record at UW was so staggeringly successful a check of the record nearly defies belief. A partial list of accomplishments: Nine individual NCAA track titles; 23 Big Ten track titles; 14 times an All-American; three straight Big Ten Female Athlete of the Year Awards.

"Her name has become a household word in Wisconsin and in track nationally," Kit wrote, shortly after Favor Hamilton's college career concluded. "She has brought great honor to the University and to the state of Wisconsin and has served as a role model for countless young women."

Of course, the world now knows that two decades later, Favor Hamilton earned not honor but lurid tabloid headlines when it was revealed she had worked as a sex escort in Las Vegas. Her name was removed from the Big Ten Female Athlete of the Year Award (it had been renamed for her in 1991). She was diagnosed as bipolar, wrote a memoir – the subtitle was *A Life Spent Running from Madness* – and when interviewed for this narrative in 2020, pronounced herself happy with her current life in California. "It has been the best thing in the world to be out here."

Her UW memories? A mixed bag, Favor Hamilton said.

"When I was in college," she said, "I loved it at Wisconsin. I met my husband my freshman year in college. We've been married almost 30 years. So the best thing in my life came from Wisconsin."

She also mentioned Mary Hartzheim, her former roommate and best friend, who died, in 2005 at 37, of cancer.

"I was blessed," Favor Hamilton said, "with the most important thing in life – incredible people. So I felt very fortunate [at Wisconsin]. But it's interesting, because there were negatives that I wish could have been resolved."

Favor Hamilton continued: "I have some issues with the athletic department. Things that really hurt me. That's why I often stay back from people wanting to talk to me about my athletic career at Wisconsin."

Favor Hamilton said she learned that an assistant coach on the men's track team had taken a film of her running that showed only her breasts. Another coach showed her a letter from a program supporter suggesting she wear two sports bras when competing.

"The focus on my body caused me a lot of emotional problems," she said. "I didn't realize how traumatic that was at the time. I've always been so good at burying things, letting them pile up inside, believing that if I didn't think about it, it would just vanish."

Other issues included academics, where, she said, her athletic greatness got her passing grades she didn't deserve. Favor Hamilton was diagnosed with ADHD (attention deficit hyperactivity disorder) at age 42. "Ever since taking medication, I can learn, I can read. It's sad it didn't get done earlier."

Asked if she sought help while at UW, Favor Hamilton said: "I was the perfect athlete. I couldn't stir anything up because then I wouldn't be the perfect image everyone wanted me to be."

During Favor Hamilton's time at UW-Madison, the athletic department itself underwent seismic changes, including some personnel moves – a new athletic director and football coach among them – that, viewed in retrospect, proved unfortunate at best. New head football coach Don Morton (hired in November 1986) and athletic director Ade Sponberg (hired in May 1987) presided over a several-year period in which the football team's on-field performance was historically poor, and that in turn produced empty seats at Camp Randall Stadium and a budget crisis for UW athletics.

That was still to come when another athletic department personnel move, announced in October 1986, drew less attention but had a disheartening effect on Kit.

A *Capital Times* story from Oct. 3, 1986, began with the following:

> "A restructuring of job duties within the University of Wisconsin athletic department was expected to be approved today at a meeting of the school's athletic board."

The story continued:

> "The changes involve the exchange of some responsibilities between deputy athletic director Ralph Neale and Associate Athletic Director Kit Saunders [and] the addition of fundraising coordination to Saunders' duties."

Kit's role would now involve personnel (hiring and non-renewals); public relations; and, as noted, fundraising. Neale, relinquishing his personnel duties, took over the direct reports of Paula Bonner (heading women's varsity sports) and Duane Kleven (heading men's varsity sports).

The *Capital Times* story noted, "Saunders said she isn't elated about the changes."

Then it quoted Kit: "Well, of course," she said, "varsity sports has been a big part of my life for a long time, so I'm going to miss having director relationships with those programs. But the other thing is that those programs will benefit from the organizing of the fundraising."

Privately, Kit went further. After her 1990 retirement, Kit worked on a sequel to the chapter on UW women's athletics that she wrote for Volume 3 ("Women Emerge in the Seventies") of a series titled, *University Women: A Series of Essays*. Kit's original essay on UW women's athletics left off at 1977; her sequel (apparently never published but included with her papers), covered the years 1977-1990.

In the unpublished essay, Kit wrote that she viewed the 1986 restructuring as Neale "consolidating his power." Salaries were in part determined by the number of people reporting either directly or indirectly to a supervisor, and, as Kit noted, "a great number of individuals" were on the coaching staffs of teams supervised by Bonner and Kleven (and, under the new structuring, by Neale rather than Kit). Perhaps more important, Kit noted, "Neale gave tacit approval for some measures which this writer sees as having long-term, damaging effects on women's programs."

Kit added: "Neale also resisted proposals and plans from Bonner to close the expenditure gap between men's and women's non-revenue sport budgets."

Much more happily, in the late spring of 1987, Kit was invited to a tennis date that changed her life.

"Tom and Marietta Fox were playing tennis with Kit and wanted a fourth," Dale "Buzz" Nordeen recalled, more than three decades later, in an interview for this book. "I joined them, and that's how I met Kit."

Kit was living on Madison's southwest side in a one-story home on Prairie Road, and Buzz recalled that first meeting was at tennis courts near Kit's home. It was June 1987.

By July, they were writing each other friendly, cheerful letters, slightly tentative, as if they were wary of overreaching too soon. Buzz's wife of 36 years had died the previous July. As for Kit, Buzz said, "At the time she was dating a couple of other gentlemen."

Yet, early on, each sensed something in the other, a kindred spirit, soon much more. By early August, the letters were more personal.

"One thing led to another," Buzz said. "We started communicating back and forth and spending time together."

Buzz Nordeen was 59 that summer, a successful banking executive, and – it wouldn't have been lost on Kit – an enthusiastic supporter of University of Wisconsin athletics.

Dale "Buzz" Nordeen.
(courtesy of the
Nordeen family)

"I guess," Buzz said, with a chuckle, "I would have been considered one of the good old boys that Kit had to deal with."

He was much more than that.

Buzz was a Madison native, and grew up in the Nakoma neighborhood, in a house his father, Frank Nordeen, who worked for General Electric, built in 1932. Buzz got his enduring nickname, according to longtime family friend Ruthie Bartlett, because as a boy he wouldn't stay still, buzzing one place to another, always on the go. His mother, Pearl Day Nordeen, told Ruthie later it was impossible to keep up with him.

Buzz attended West High School, playing quarterback for the football team, a pursuit to which he was more devoted than his studies. His grades were marginal enough that prior to graduation he enlisted in the Navy. It was 1945, World War II was winding down. Stationed in Hawaii – "working in a chow hall," he grumbled later – Buzz had a personal reckoning.

His daughter, Katherine Nordeen Snyder, heard the story from her dad. "He said to himself," Kathy recalled, "'I can either work in a mess hall the rest of my life or knuckle down and try to make myself better.' He knocked the top off college."

That was at the University of Wisconsin–Madison, on the GI Bill. Buzz graduated with honors in accounting – while working nights in the mailroom at Oscar Mayer – and then entered GE's business training program. On Aug. 26, 1950, at the Grace Episcopal church in Madison, Buzz married Nora Ellen Haley, who, like Buzz, went to West High and had graduated from UW the previous spring. After a honeymoon in northern Wisconsin and Canada, the couple in September 1950 established a home in Schenectady, New York, where Buzz worked as an accountant. Before too long, the couple returned to Wisconsin.

"My father-in-law was president of First Federal Savings and Loan [in Madison]," Buzz said. "He wanted us to come back to the Midwest. And I promised him I'd take the CPA exam."

Buzz applied at several Madison accounting firms but ended up with Ernst in Milwaukee, where he passed the CPA exam. In short order, Buzz and Nora returned to Madison, where Buzz accepted an auditor's position at First Federal and worked in real estate with his father-in-law's firm, John W. Haley and Sons. Madison's west side was beginning a decades-long real estate boom. Buzz was on point for his firm's development of 600 acres of residential home sites in the Hill Farms, west of Midvale Boulevard.

Buzz had been working his way up the executive ladder at First Federal when his father-in-law died in 1962. John Haley's death, at 63, was front-page news in the both the *Wisconsin State Journal* and *The Capital Times*. Buzz assumed the presidency of First Federal, a post he would hold for the next 27 years. He combined his successful business career with civic and charitable engagement in Madison, serving as president of the Greater Madison Chamber of Commerce and holding leadership positions in Downtown Madison, Inc. and the Greater Madison Foundation for the Arts, among many others.

Buzz and Nora raised three children, Katherine, Christopher and Andrew. Nora was a tireless volunteer in the Madison area, giving her time to numerous causes that included Attic Angels, Methodist Hospital, Mobile Meals and the Red Cross. She played tennis and was a skilled craftswoman.

But in the second half of the 1970s, not yet 50, Nora began having memory issues.

"Some of her friends were noticing," Nora's daughter, Kathy Snyder, said. "She'd make an appointment for tennis and not show up."

It was early-onset Alzheimer's disease, a terrible diagnosis, for Nora, for Buzz, for all the family.

"I remember being at home with her," Kathy said. "She was a sewer and weaver and she couldn't remember how to backstitch while she was sewing."

Kathy continued: "There was a horrendous period when she knew she was forgetting. It frustrated and angered her. It was a torment. A little further on with Alzheimer's, she didn't remember that she didn't remember. There's maybe some peace with that."

In October 1985, Buzz and Nora took a trip to Hawaii with two of their closest friends, Dick and Ruthie Bartlett. Dick and Ruthie were celebrating their 40th wedding anniversary. The couples had traveled previously, including ski trips to Colorado, where the Bartletts had a place in Steamboat Springs. The Hawaii trip went well but there was an elegiac feel to it. Besides Nora's Alzheimer's, Dick was battling cancer.

"Nora rode on the golf cart while Dick and Buzz and I played," Ruthie Bartlett recalled. "She enjoyed the flowers and the trip."

Dick Bartlett died, age 59, not a year later, July 6, 1986.

When Nora died, age 58, just two weeks later, the official cause was leukemia. It was a wrenching period for Buzz. He was aided by the support of his adult children and by his decision to quit alcohol. In recovery, a gentler side of Buzz emerged, a willingness to share feelings that often went unexpressed by men of his generation. It was around this time he was introduced to Kit Saunders.

Buzz had remained close with Ruthie Bartlett. "He said, 'You're the sister I never had,'" Ruthie said.

One day Buzz phoned with a question. "Do you know anything about this Kit Saunders?'

Buzz explained he and Kit were going to be tennis partners.

"I know her real well," Ruthie said. She'd met Kit through the Bartletts' support of UW athletics. Ruthie was a longtime member of WIS-Club. "She's a nice lady," Ruthie said of Kit, "and doing a good job at the university."

The meeting of Buzz and Kit on the tennis court quickly led to a friendship and then – again quickly – something more.

On July 13, 1987, Buzz sent Kit a card that pictured a small boy on the cover opening a mailbox with the line, "Thinking of You."

"Dear Kit," Buzz wrote. "I forgot to thank you for the berries. They were great and are now gone. I truly enjoyed being with you…"

Buzz then noted that he hadn't "been in unfamiliar situations" in quite some time. He added, "I hope I don't get off base and make you feel uncomfortable with my crash bang way of doing things. It seems we both like a lot of the same things and activities."

Buzz then conveyed his travel schedule over the next several weeks, noting he had golf events and out-of-town weddings: "As I look this over it's nuts to be this committed."

In closing, Buzz wrote, "Let's stay in touch and call each other when you have a quiet time…."Thanks again for fun times. "Buzz."

Kit answered immediately, July 15.

> "Dear Buzz, Your note was very thoughtful and much appreciated. Please don't worry about your 'crash bang' way of doing things. I appreciated

your choice of words about having some quiet and
also some quality time to fill in with good company, fun active things to do and good conversation.
We've had a good start on that and will take
advantage of what opportunities we can make in
the future. It's a good feeling and lots to look
forward to....

Sincerely, Kit."

Buzz was right back, again, with a note he ended, "Love,
Buzz."

Kit's answer on July 21 mentioned that "meeting your kids
sounds like fun" and noted that she was trying to end "the
relationship I told you about" in a way that would "preserve a
good friendship."

She ended with, "Love, Kit. (Thanks for signing off that
way!)"

Things were moving fast. Later that summer, Andy Nordeen
got married and Buzz brought Kit to the wedding.

"That was hard for me," Kathy said. "I wasn't really ready
for that. But he [Buzz] taught us to be accepting, and we were."

Into fall, Buzz and Kit grew closer. And before too long, the
kids realized their dad had found someone special.

"She was very generous," Kathy said of Kit. "She didn't
have to be so accepting of us. But she stepped right in, we were
accepted, we talked, we did things together."

That Christmas, Kathy sent Kit a note from the home Kathy
shared with her husband Bill in New Jersey.

"Dear Kit," Kathy wrote.

"Thanks for the card and the note inside. I appreciate your honest sharing and the way in which
you've encouraged Dad to communicate his
feelings. He seems content and his contentment
and happiness show to other people... In your note
you thanked us for being glad for Dad – we are
also very happy for you. There is nothing better

than finding someone with whom you can share
your life – all of it."

The following month – Jan. 12, 1988 – Buzz wrote a letter
to Kathy, Chris and Andy which he began by discussing a skiing
trip he and Kit had just made to Colorado. Then:

"The real reason for [this] note is to update you on wedding
plans," Buzz wrote.

Buzz recalled that he'd asked Kit to marry him in December
1987. "I think we were at an athletic event," Buzz said. "I just
said, 'You know, we've been together long enough to know and
understand each other. How would you like to become my wife?'
She accepted."

In his letter to the kids, Buzz said he and Kit would be
married in April. They'd looked at a charming 19th century little
white church at the corner of Old Sauk and Pleasant View Roads
in Middleton. "But they have no heat and won't let people use it
until May or June," Buzz noted. He and Kit had decided on the
Frank Lloyd Wright-designed Unitarian Meeting House in
Madison. "We want all the family there and hope it fits your
plans," Buzz wrote.

Dale "Buzz" Nordeen and Katherine "Kit" Saunders were
married April 9, 1988. Kathy was the bridesmaid and Chris and
Andy were groomsmen. A reception was held at the Pool Terrace
of the Concourse Hotel, with music by the American Jazz
Express.

"We love each other, have fun together and want to share
our lives," Kit told the *Wisconsin State Journal*. "We enjoy
tennis, skiing, golf, biking and other outdoor pursuits. We plan to
share our lives in Madison and continue to enjoy each other's
company."

Professionally for Kit, the months that followed the October
1986 athletic department restructuring were marked by still more
change. The October 1986 move had placed her in charge of
personnel, public relations and fundraising, a change, it should be
remembered, that Kit did not greet with enthusiasm. The other
changes, while not affecting Kit directly, involved high-profile

positions of great importance to the athletic department. Their success – or, as it turned out, lack of success – would impact the entire department and lead to turmoil.

"While the UW athletic program has been characterized by great stability with respect to coaching and most support staff," Kit wrote, in her summary report of the years 1977-1990 and referring to the second half of the 1980s, "the same has not been true for the top administrative positions."

While Kit referenced the overall stability of the coaching and support staffs, there was one key coaching change – a new hire in November 1986, one month after the department reorganization lamented by Kit – that in one sense begat much of the upheaval that roiled UW athletics through the rest of the 1980s.

The football program was and likely always will be the engine that drives major college athletic departments, generating by far the most revenue.

Wisconsin hadn't been to a Rose Bowl since 1963, but throughout the first half of the 1980s, the football Badgers had been respectable and sometimes better than that, under head coach Dave McClain. His teams won seven games in each season between 1981-84, and though they dipped to a record of 5-6 in 1985, average attendance at Camp Randall stayed above 70,000, where it had been for a dozen years. Fans might appreciate the marching band and the Saturday afternoon spectacle as much as the play on the field, but for an athletic department never flush with funds, that football attendance was hugely important.

In spring 1986, just a few days after the annual Badgers' intrasquad football game, McClain rode a stationary bicycle at Camp Randall Stadium and then got in the sauna, where he chatted with a friend and mentioned that he felt like he might have the flu. Within minutes, McClain suffered a heart attack and was taken to St. Mary's Hospital, where his death was pronounced. He was 48.

Athletic director Elroy Hirsch promoted McClain's defensive coordinator, Jim Hilles, to interim head coach, and Hilles was one of two finalists for the permanent position in November 1986. His returning players supported Hilles, but the 1986 season under Hilles – the Badgers finished 3-9 – wasn't good enough. Hirsch hired University of Tulsa head coach Don Morton, who prior to his two seasons at Tulsa had shined as coach of North Dakota State, admittedly a smaller stage – Division II – than Madison and the Big Ten.

Morton was best-known for a run-oriented offense he called the "veer," and once he arrived in Madison he put VEER on his car license plate. It wasn't long into Morton's tenure as head coach that one wag suggested the plate should read "third and ten."

But Morton was young, personable, and energetic, and his team hadn't yet played a game in spring 1987 when it was announced Elroy Hirsch would be retiring as athletic director. In May, word arrived that Ade Sponberg, athletic director at North Dakota State – where he had teamed with Don Morton – would be the new director of athletics at UW. It was a vast move up in class for Sponberg – the budget for Badgers athletics was 10 times the budget in Fargo.

The following month – June 1987 – it was announced that Donna Shalala would be assuming the position of chancellor at UW–Madison, replacing Irving Shain, who had resigned. In hindsight, it was an excellent hire for the university and especially UW athletics – Shalala knew the value of a successful sports program. In that sense she was the anti-Shain. Her predecessor had been ambivalent at best about athletics.

At a press conference in Madison in June where Shalala's hiring was announced, Kit handed her a tennis racquet with a red UW cover. They would stay friendly throughout Shalala's time in Madison. At one point, not long after Kit's 1990 retirement, Buzz and Kit attended a charity silent auction where one of the items up for bid was a tennis match against Shalala and her mother, Edna. Buzz and Kit bid on the tennis date and won it.

"Some time later," Buzz recalled, "Donna called to say her mom was in town. We went out to Powless [the tennis center named for former basketball coach and tennis star John Powless] and played."

Buzz said he and Kit hadn't realized who they were up against. Edna Shalala had been one of the top-ranked female tennis players in the country. Outside on the clay courts at Powless, Edna – in her late 70s – dazzled everyone with a slicing backhand that seemed to jump backward as it landed. The Shalalas won going away, there was considerable banter back and forth, and a grand time was had by all.

"Donna would yell, 'Mom, get those damn Republicans!'" Buzz recalled.

While Shalala's hiring in spring 1987 was widely applauded, the fact a new chancellor was hired in the immediate aftermath of the hiring of a new football coach and athletic director was deemed "a backwards hiring procedure" by the sportswriter and author Rick Telander in his later book on UW athletics, titled *From Red Ink to Roses*.

In the meantime, Shalala from the outset prioritized athletics.

She didn't begin as chancellor until the first week of 1988. On her first day, she showed up at Bascom Hall just a few minutes after 6 a.m. A security guard said, "You must have a tough boss." Shalala laughed. "Truth is," she said later, "I couldn't sleep."

What was significant for those involved with or following UW athletics was what Shalala did her first night on the job. She went to a hockey game at the Dane County Coliseum between the Badgers and Lowell. It was first hockey game Shalala had ever attended.

"I understand this is one of the best Wisconsin athletic teams," she said. "Mostly I've been going to losing games."

Just a week later, Shalala acted as guest coach at an alumni basketball game preceding the Wisconsin-Illinois men's game at the Field House. Each weekend throughout January, Shalala had brunch at the Wisconsin Center with high school seniors who were being recruited to play football for the Badgers in the fall. It is impossible to overstate how much different this made her from her predecessor as chancellor.

It's also impossible to overstate the dire financial situation the athletic department was quickly finding itself in, not least because of the collapsing football fortunes. Don Morton's first team had a 3-8 record in fall 1987, and the last home game, Nov. 21 against Michigan State, drew barely 45,000 fans to Camp Randall.

"A stunned Shalala," Telander wrote, "was greeted with the news that football revenue for the 1987 season was $700,000 short of budget and the athletic department's resources were gone."

A *Wisconsin State Journal* article, Nov. 10, 1988, noted: "Yet in the midst of a budget crisis, another issue is quietly coming to a head: A concern for equity between male and female athletes."

A month earlier, in October 1988, UW athletic board chairman Barney Webb assigned a task force on sex equity, with a charter to evaluate the status of women's athletics at UW–Madison and the school's compliance with Title IX.

Title IX was back in play in 1988 after four years in the wilderness brought about by the 1984 Grove City decision by the U.S. Supreme Court that ruled Title IX gender equity requirements applied only to particular units in a university that received federal funding, not universities as a whole. In 1987, Congress passed the Civil Rights Restoration Act, restoring the entire university mandate regarding Title IX – but President Ronald Reagan vetoed the legislation. In March 1988, Congress overrode the Reagan veto: Title IX was back.

Its revival reinvigorated women's athletic programs around the country and some schools found themselves on the receiving end of Title IX complaints and lawsuits. One famous case that

was instigated in the 1970s but took nearly a decade to completely wind its way through the court system was Blair vs. Washington State University. The lower courts had sided with the women
at the school who were asking for more equitable financial
resources – but those rulings had exempted men's football,
accepting the argument that only men play football and the
program subsidizes many non-income sports.

In 1987, however, the Washington Supreme Court ruled that
football should not enjoy singular status. Justice John Dolliver
noted that the law "contains no exception for football. The
exclusion of football would prevent sex equity from ever being
achieved since men would always be guaranteed many more
participation opportunities than women."

Women on the UW–Madison campus were paying attention.
Recalling that moment, Paula Bonner said, "I'd reached a point
where comparing women's sports only to the non-income [men's]
sports had to end."

As noted, it was in October 1988 that the UW established a
sex equity task force. Bonner told the *Wisconsin State Journal*:
"Women make up half of this university, but only 33 percent of
athletes on campus are women."

Bonner noted further that male Badger athletes received 195
athletic scholarships while women athletes got 77; and that
spending on travel, recruiting and supplies was likewise lopsided
in favor of the men's programs.

In the *State Journal* article, UW deputy athletic director
Ralph Neale pushed back, citing the department's budget woes
triggered by the decline of UW's football fortunes.

"If we have to shift money around to existing programs, it
would be like robbing Peter to pay Paul," Neale said. "The
problem now is that we don't have any financial ability to put any
quick fixes on our budget problem or equity. There is no immediate solution."

Bonner, however, had seen enough delays. "I think now is as
good a time as any," she said. The sex equity task force appeared

to agree. Established in October 1988, it would issue its recommendations in a 26-page report released in May 1989.

Meanwhile, the department's administrative changes alluded to by Kit in her 1977-1990 written summary were beginning.

Shortly after Ade Sponberg was hired in May 1987 to replace Elroy Hirsch as athletic director, Otto Breitenbach, Hirsch's top assistant and someone much appreciated by Kit during his nearly 15 years with the department, announced his resignation. It came in December 1987 and was not a complete surprise – Breitenbach thought he deserved to replace Hirsch in the top job and had earlier been a finalist for the University of Denver athletic director position. He left to become executive director of the Badger State Games, a popular statewide amateur competition. (Kit sat on the executive committee of the Games' sponsor, the Wisconsin Amateur Sports Corp., and competed, too, winning the 1987 Division B doubles tennis title with Ann Jackson.)

To some observers, Breitenbach's departure soon began to resemble a successful escape. The Badger's dismal 1987 football campaign – remember that final game attendance barely topped 45,000 – begat the budget crisis referenced by Neale in response to the October 1988 establishment of the sex equity task force.

That same month – October 1988 – state auditor Dale Cattanach made headlines when he announced an audit of the UW athletic department. The Legislative Audit Bureau wanted to see the details of the department's $1.3 million 1987-88 shortfall and the projected budget deficit of $821,000 for the fiscal year ending June 1989.

The audit brought shockingly bad news. A *State Journal* headline in February 1989 read: "Athletics deficit is $4 million." In *From Red Ink to Roses*, author Rick Telander wrote that the audit "described the department as a mess beyond belief."

Someone who had worked for the Legislative Audit Bureau early in his career would soon play an important role in helping UW athletics turn that around.

Alan Fish in early 1989 was head of the Division of Policy and Budget for the Wisconsin Department of Health and Social Services. When he read the athletic department audit, he sent Chancellor Donna Shalala a letter outlining a plan to right the ship, a proposal that included increasing ticket sales, advertising and promotion; expanding fundraising; and tapping the state coffers – and current UW students – for additional assistance.

"This crisis can be an opportunity," Fish wrote. "The fact that it has been a high-profile story in the media can be used to involve more people and organizations in the solution."

Shalala hired Fish as the department's director of finance in March 1989.

In an interview for this narrative, Fish recalled his conversation with Shalala about taking the job.

Shalala said, "What kind of experience do you have with intercollegiate athletics?"

Fish replied, "Well, I played golf for Luther College, Division III."

"She laughed, thank goodness, instead of throwing me out of the room," Fish recalled. "She was desperate. She wanted someone to be embedded in there. Because I had done budgets, politics, marketing, and communication, she wanted someone with that skill down there reporting to her."

Just two months later, in May 1989, the 10-member task force on sex equity in the department released its report.

It should be noted that amid the budget woes and the release of the task force report, women's athletics at UW enjoyed some on-the-field success. In March, two months before the report's release, Suzy Favor won the NCAA indoor mile run competition at the Hoosier Dome in Indianapolis. Favor's time of 4:30.63 was the second-fastest time ever recorded by a female collegian.

The previous fall, the UW women's soccer team qualified for the NCAA Final Four, and headed for Chapel Hill, N.C. for a semifinal match with perennial powerhouse the University of North Carolina. The Badgers' coach, Greg Ryan, had drawn praise since assuming the job in 1986, with the North Carolina coach, Anson Dorrance (winner of multiple national titles), telling *The Capital Times*, "Ryan's doing a great job up there."

North Carolina beat the Badgers, 3-0 (and went on to win the championship), but Badgers' goaltender Heather Taggart didn't allow a goal until 74 minutes into the semifinal match and was named to the all-tournament team.

In June 1989, the Wisconsin women's crew hosted the Women's National Rowing Association Championship on Lake Wingra, near Vilas Park. Since the NCAA didn't offer a women's championship, the association's regatta was the biggest prize in collegiate women's crew. It was prestigious for the Badgers to host, but as coach Sue Ela told the *Wisconsin State Journal*, a little of the shine was taken off because top-ranked Radcliffe had eschewed Madison for a regatta in England and some other top schools were missing as well. "If Radcliffe doesn't care about winning a national title," Ela said, "I guess that's their choice."

Perhaps more telling, Ela noted that among the other teams not in attendance, the primary reason was a lack of money for travel, a circumstance that never seemed to stop collegiate men's teams.

And that, of course, was the exact circumstance the UW's task force on sex equity was hoping to correct when it released its report on May 8, 1989.

With everything else going on at UW athletics, perhaps it's not surprising the release of the report didn't generate major headlines. Although all the recommendations of the report were accepted unanimously in a vote of the UW athletic board on May 12, the first news story related to the report came May 21, on page 5 of the *Wisconsin State Journal* sports section. Along with the main story, titled "In search of equity," there were two sidebar stories, one giving Kit's reaction to the report, the other an assessment by Alan Fish.

The *State Journal* listed three major recommendations from the report:

1) "Add 14 to 18 women's athletic scholarships 'to achieve an appropriate ratio of men and women on scholarship.'"

2) "Provide better financial support for women's athletic programs. The total cost of upgrading six sports, as outlined in the report, would be $290,000, in addition to the scholarships."

3) "Establish a committee that will continue to review how well the UW is moving toward its goal of sports equity between men and women."

The newspaper quoted Paula Bonner: "The report is an important blueprint for the future of the women's sports program," she said. "It's a thoughtful and progressive documentation of where we should be taking the women's program."

Fish, the interim finance officer for the athletic department, said he thought that even with the current budget crisis, a goal of significant improvements for women's sports was "overall, quite realistic." He noted the improvements might pay dividends, should women's basketball, volleyball and soccer begin drawing a larger, paying fan base, a hope he felt was realistic.

"(There's) real potential for increasing spectators," Fish said, "and so increasing revenue. These can be investments. The trick is, fold the goal of Title IX into our overall five-year financial plan." (In April, the UW Board of Regents had approved a five-year plan that included a three-year, $10-per-semester student fee and administrative cuts beginning in 1990-91 and totaling $250,000 annually. It also listed increasing football attendance as a top priority.)

Interviewed for this book, Fish noted that he had family encouragement to take the equity report seriously. "When I started working in the athletic department," he said, "my wife and two daughters were all talking to me and saying, 'What are you going to do about women's sports?'"

Interestingly, Kit's reaction to the sex equity report was somewhat more muted – or perhaps more realistic. She spoke about it at length with State Journal sportswriter John Aehl:

> "The report does point out that we've got a good, comprehensive program, and that we've done a pretty good job of keeping pace with other Big Ten schools. Although some of the other schools that have decided to invest in some of their key sports, like basketball, have zoomed ahead of us, like Iowa.

> "The committee was cognizant of the fact that we've got serious budget problems. The biggest challenge facing us right now is taking care of the budget deficit in the Athletic Department."

Alan Fish said that when he first came into the athletic department, he sat down all the stakeholders to get their take on how things stood. Among those conversations, Fish said, his talk with Kit stood out. It was focused, unsurprisingly, on gender equity and the May 1989 report.

"Kit was the person," Fish recalled, "who had the vision to say, 'Look, we've come this far. Now we're at another inflection point with this [Title IX reinstatement] court decision. And we have to take advantage of it.'"

Fish continued:

> "Kit was the velvet hammer. She knew her stuff. She was always leaning in. She was never offensive. She was always professional. But she never let up. She was both patient and relentless, which was exactly the right political take on trying to make progress back then on gender equity."

In her public statements, Kit usually found some reason for optimism, and concluded her *State Journal* interview on the equity report by saying that even amid the budget crisis, women's sports were far more highly regarded and faring much better than when she first became director of women's athletics in Madison in 1974. Kit said,

> "The first time we started talking about Title IX, when we were just starting the program, there weren't a lot of people who had a lot of empathy for what we were trying to do. But now that the program has been in existence for 15 years, there is an awful lot more support for helping the women's program along. There's a real positive attitude on the part of the Athletic Board. It's really nice to see, 15 years later, even in the face of budget problems."

Just a month later, in June 1989, Paula Bonner announced her departure from the athletic department, to take the position of assistant executive director of the Wisconsin Alumni Association (WAA). That organization was undergoing change: its longtime director, Arlie Mucks, was retiring after 28 years and would be replaced by Gayle Langer.

The relationship between Bonner and Kit had not been without friction, especially once Kit moved into a role that placed her in charge of all non-income sports, men's and women's both. But the friendship and respect that grew out of their years working together carried the day; they got past their differences.

"I was feeling a little antsy," Bonner said of her decision to leave, in an interview for this narrative. "I had done a lot on campus, knew a lot of faculty, and I was starting to feel a little penned in being focused specifically on athletics. We'd made a lot of strides. But I was interested in working on a bigger, broader scope with higher education and the university."

Bonner's background in athletics would only help as she transitioned to engaging with UW alumni – following the Badgers is a primary way graduates stay connected to campus. Langer thought Bonner was a natural for the WAA.

Donna Shalala, the new chancellor, thought so, too. She reached out to Bonner. "Come have a hot dog with me," Shalala said. They met one noon at a campus food cart. "You'll meet so many people," Shalala said, adding that Bonner could always return to athletics if she chose to. In the end, Bonner stayed with WAA, moving up to the executive director post where she remained until her 2017 retirement.

For Kit, there were ramifications from Bonner's departure. The athletic department asked her to assume Bonner's assistant director for women's sports duties, while keeping her personnel and public relations responsibilities. That would provide a much-needed reduction in administrative costs for the department.

"Another factor, though," said finance director Alan Fish, "and of equal importance, is Kit's enthusiasm and experience."

Veteran *Capital Times* sports columnist Mike Lucas made that case in a July 1989 story titled, "She's UW's top team player."

Lucas's playful lead captured how often Kit had been required to change hats.

"If she had her own workout video," Lucas wrote:

> "Kit Saunders-Nordeen would be shown running the steps at Camp Randall Stadium. The exercise, in team play, has involved a series of moves within the administrative structure of the University of Wisconsin athletic department, dating back to when Saunders-Nordeen was just a Saunders.

> "She has added a hyphen, a husband, and a number of different responsibilities since starting on the ground floor with the women's program in 1974. She was the director then and she's the director again, completing the circuit by replacing one of her first graduate assistants, Paula Bonner, who replaced Saunders-Nordeen in 1983."

Kit did not dispute Lucas' assessment.

"I've been upstairs-downstairs more often than the owner of a local deli," she said, referencing Madison's popular Upstairs Downstairs restaurant.

Later in the Lucas interview, Kit made a passionate case for an athletic department that integrated men's and women's programs, the better for each to succeed.

"I feel everybody ought to care about everybody else," Kit said. She said she'd heard a booster club refer to women's sports as the "women's department."

> "There isn't a women's department. There is an athletic department. Before I leave here, I want to get that principle across."

(Kit's vision didn't happen immediately, but almost. By 1992, each of the department's associate athletic directors were assigned responsibility for an equal number of men's and women's sports. "The intent of this reorganization," a board equity committee's report noted later, "was to share commitment, understanding, and responsibility for men's and women's sports within the administration and to minimize internal struggles for attention and resources on a gender basis.")

If anyone knew its importance, Kit did. "By working across the board, I've gotten a feel for the whole picture. And it's harder to be critical when you're part of the whole. Hopefully, everybody will get that feeling someday."

Kit continued: "It has been really tough in the last year or so with all the budget problems. The coaches are the most demoralized. They wonder if their budget is going to be cut in half, and if they're going to spend the summer fund-raising. I want to let them know they still have somebody who cares about them.

"One thing I am," Kit concluded, "is a team player."

There was a nice moment in November 1989 when Kit introduced women's track and cross-country coach Peter Tegen prior to Tegen's induction into the UW Women's Athletics Hall of Fame. It came during the women's program's annual recognition banquet at Lowell Hall. Kit, of course, had been a charter inductee (alongside Carie Graves) when the hall was established in 1984. In her remarks Kit noted that Tegen had coached two national championship teams, 22 national championship individuals or relays and 122 Big Ten champions – an amazing record. Tegen then introduced the night's other inductee – the UW women's first track All-American, Cindy Bremser.

While Kit spent the months of late 1989 and early 1990 once again hands-on with UW women's athletics, the department leadership – apart from Kit – underwent a sea change. In August, Ralph Neale, who was brought in as Elroy Hirsch's deputy – to read the budgetary fine print that was never Elroy's strong suit, only to get hit with a full-on budget crisis – left the department to become superintendent of schools in Westfield.

Chancellor Donna Shalala, meanwhile, had seen enough of UW athletics under Ade Sponberg. "A fine human being," Kit wrote later of Sponberg, but over his head with the athletic director job at a Big Ten campus. Shalala and Sponberg announced his pending departure at a joint news conference in mid-November. Two weeks later, Shalala accepted the recommendation of the UW athletic board – in a 10-0 vote – that head football coach Don Morton also be terminated. Morton, bitter, declined an opportunity to work elsewhere in the department. He was unpopular in Madison and returned that sentiment, soon leaving the city. His won-loss record with the Badgers was 6-27.

The following month, on Dec. 15, 1989, Shalala pulled the ultimate rabbit out of her hat and immediately had the entire state of Wisconsin looking beyond the past few painful years of UW athletics. She announced a stunning new hire: Pat Richter, a homegrown Madison boy and three-sport hero as a Badger during the early 1960s, would be the new UW athletic director. Richter was everyone's first choice for the job, but few thought he would accept it. Richter had to take a pay cut from his job as a top executive at Oscar Mayer in Madison to return to Camp Randall. Shalala, proving herself a force of nature, convinced him to do it.

On the day Richter addressed the media in Madison about his new position, he met first with the department personnel. In that private meeting, Richter pledged to unite the department. Kit was one of many who left the meeting impressed.

"It doesn't feel so much like an upheaval as it does finding solutions," Kit noted. "Everything he said was what our people needed to hear, and they knew he really believed it. He recognized the excellence that's here."

A month later, on Jan. 17, 1990, Kit helped host a news conference where the women's athletics booster club (WIS-Club) unveiled a new logo and theme for the decade of the '90s. The theme: "The Women with the Winning Ways."

WIS-Club president Barbara Wegner said, "We feel the excitement of change. Times are changing right here for the University of Wisconsin Athletic Department, and enthusiasm is soaring throughout the state."

Wegner's assessment of the enthusiasm for the department's future was not misplaced: Richter had acted decisively (and quickly) as athletic director, announcing a new head football coach in early January: Barry Alvarez, an assistant at Notre Dame. With Alvarez's arrival in Madison, the all-important football program was soon in ascendance.

Wegner continued, "We have created a unique new concept for WIS-Club and our women athletes that will take them into the '90s with a feeling of energy, strength, pride and tradition."

Kit offered WIS-Club the department's thanks:

> "Every single women's sport has been helped at
> some point time by WIS-Club's financial and
> moral support. The new theme, poster and logo
> combine to give WIS-Club an immediate identifi-
> cation with Badger women's sports. The total
> package also gives us an appealing, upbeat vehicle
> to help promote all of our sports. It's a great step
> into the '90s and complements the positive outlook
> for Wisconsin Athletics."

Booster clubs are one thing, skeptical newspaper reporters are another. In the wake of the WIS-Club announcement, the *Wisconsin State Journal* ran – on the first sports page of its large Sunday paper, Feb. 18, 1990 – an examination of the 17 years of varsity women's athletics. Because no one was more associated with the program over those years, the lengthy article in a way served as a report card on Kit's performance.

"A few weeks ago," reporter John Aehl began his piece, "the University of Wisconsin, with fanfare, exhibited proudly a new look for its women's sports program, leaning heavily on the slogan, 'The Women with the Winning Ways.'

"Fine words," Aehl continued, "but a legitimate question in this 17th year of organized intercollegiate sports at the UW is: Just how winning have been the ways?

"The answer is that the program has done pretty well."

Aehl then revealed statistics that made his "pretty well" assessment of the program seem understated:

> "According to a rating system used by *USA Today*, the UW women's program ranked 17th in the nation in overall quality in 1988-89. In the Big Ten Conference, only Iowa (16th) was ranked higher… Wisconsin's women's teams compete with other Division 1 colleges in 11 sports; four UW teams were ranked in the top 25 nationally in 1988-89 – soccer, tennis, cross-country and track and field."

Historically, the numbers were even better. According to the *State Journal* article, the Badgers' 33 conference championships (plus one tie) led the Big Ten for the period 1974-1989. Seventy-three women UW athletes attained All-American status; 42, including relays, were national champions.

Interviewed for the story, Kit said,

> "We have consistently improved our scholarship situation and we are improving in sports that have less of a winning tradition. We have greatly

improved our facilities, and we have an excellent
group of coaches. And the records of our teams
have generally been good."

If it sounded like a summing up, well, that may or may not have
been intentional on Kit's part. Within weeks, however, she was
ready with a major announcement of her own.

Chapter 12

STEPPING AWAY

B
uzz said, "I was having so much fun in retirement she decided to join me."

On March 7, 1990, the University of Wisconsin News Service sent out a press release announcing Kit's retirement from UW athletics, effective June 30.

Buzz's comment – made nearly three decades later in an interview for this narrative – wasn't strictly accurate. Buzz wouldn't officially retire until fall 1990, but his workload was significantly reduced in the wake of a June 1989 merger of First Federal Savings Bank of Madison with First Federal Savings of La Crosse. Buzz was named vice-chairman of the new entity, but his day to day duties were not as pressing.

Both privately and in interviews at the time, Kit expressed at least three reasons for choosing to retire at age 49. First among them was what Buzz was alluding to: She wanted to spend more time with her new husband. Indulging their shared passion for skiing, boating, travel and more – as well as spending more time at a beloved farm property southeast of Madison – was not feasible while Kit was associate athletic director.

"While she was still there, we went to many, many sporting events," Buzz said. "Gymnastics, baseball, wrestling, fencing – she was expected to show up at most of them."

Buzz recalled accompanying Kit to a football game at Camp Randall, where they had seats in the press box. There is a long history of not cheering in that facility, a circumstance Buzz tried but could not abide.

Kit and Buzz at a Badger sporting event. (courtesy of the Nordeen family)

"My vocalization was not acceptable," he said, chuckling. "We ended up sitting outside."

Kit was tired, too, of the high-profile, increasingly high-scrutiny life of a top Big Ten athletic administrator, one who in her case had needed to fight nearly constantly for equitable treatment. Her hugely successful track coach, Peter Tegen, later said he felt she was probably exhausted from the battle.

Finally, she would be leaving the department as it embarked on a new era under the leadership of Pat Richter. Buzz said Kit told him, "Pat should have the opportunity to select his own people."

In the UW press release, Kit touched on all those themes.

"This job requires and deserves a 150 percent commitment of time and energy," Kit said. "I'm at a point in my life where I need more flexibility.

"I have great confidence in the leadership being provided by Pat Richter as our new athletic director," Kit continued. "It's an exciting time for intercollegiate sports at Wisconsin."

She concluded, "I'm proud to have played a part in developing a program from absolute scratch. It hasn't always been smooth, but we've made great progress, and had a lot of help along the way. Today, there is a real acceptance of girls and women as athletes."

Kit told the *Milwaukee Sentinel*:

> "This has been a big part of my life for a long, long time and I'm sure I'm going to miss it. I'm sure I won't be bored, and I'll continue to be a big supporter of our sports programs... I feel very good about what's happening in the athletic department and the direction it is going. The department has turned the corner with Pat Richter."

Richter was one of dozens – scores – of people who sent Kit appreciative notes, either in March, when her pending retirement was announced, or a few months later, when it took effect.

"I just wanted to drop a note to tell you how much I appreciated your assistance over the past seven months," Richter wrote.

> "Coming at a time when you, yourself, were wrestling with important personal decisions makes your contributions even more significant.
>
> "You obviously have been a key player in moving the U.W. Women's Program to national prominence... Somehow, 'retirement' doesn't seem like the right word and I'm sure you and Buzz will be as active as ever."

University of Wisconsin System President Kenneth "Buzz" Shaw wrote too:

> "You're far too young to retire! I am always surprised when someone leaves the university in her prime. And yet, it seems that you have done everything else right, so you must have the right idea about this too. Thank you for choosing to

dedicate your career to higher education and
particularly to women's athletics."

And Judy Sweet, director of athletics at the University of California, San Diego, and just a year away from being the first woman
president of the NCAA:

> "In all sincerity, I have been privileged to enjoy a
> variety of positive professional opportunities and I
> truly believe that my experiences at Wisconsin
> under your leadership were the most influential in
> my career. I feel fortunate that our paths crossed
> and that I was able to learn so much from you. I'm
> delighted that you are looking forward to retire-
> ment, but I'm disappointed for the young people
> who will miss out on your guidance. Again, for
> those of us who were lucky enough to have you as
> a mentor, a most sincere thank you."

One letter that stands out came from Duane Hopp, whose quarter
century as a UW-Madison photographer meant he spent abundant
time with the famous and infamous. He photographed both Frank
Lloyd Wright and Louis Armstrong at the Memorial Union
(Armstrong in his underwear). Hopp knew class when he saw it
and was not easily impressed; Kit impressed him. Hopp wrote,

> "The winds of change have been blowing in the
> Athletic Department. Before you clean out your
> well-used desk, I just would like to say that I
> found working with you during my days with a
> camera most enjoyable. You had such a major role
> in building the women's sports program into the
> excellent program it now is, and I was fortunate in
> being able to watch it grow under your leader-
> ship."

Hopp continued:

> "The women's program started out with a lot of
> heavy problems in funding and facilities. I will

have to confess that I enjoyed photographing the
athletes in your program more than the men, in
some respects. A photographer didn't have to
contend with head problem athletes! When it was
time to work up the team and individual head
shots, the gals were there on time, and anxious to
assist you so that the final result in print was up to
their expectations. In all those years, I didn't run
into any prima donnas, and when they competed,
that fierce determination showed on their faces!
Working with the coaches and administrative staff
you developed was a super experience, and there
are many memories that will linger from those
years photographing women athletes at UW!

"My positive experiences," Hopp concluded, "are
a direct reflection of the leadership you gave to the
athletic department. The personal and professional
relationship we had was a highlight over the years,
and I wish you well as you take a break from the
pressure of building a sports program and enjoy a
little leisure. You have earned it!"

One letter that surely stirred memories for Kit came from Murray
Fowler, the linguistics professor who was appointed to chair a
committee on women's athletics at UW in 1973, in the wake of
the original Title IX legislation. There had been an earlier
committee, chaired by Elroy Hirsch, that met once in eight
months. Fowler's appointment by Chancellor Ed Young was a
rebuke to Hirsch's leadership on the equity issue.

"A wonderful person," Kit, who served on the committee,
called Fowler. Effective, too. They met 18 times in the space of
one year.

"I see that you have decided to retire," Fowler wrote.

"You have done a superb job under not always the
most comfortable of circumstances; so I am not
quite certain that I want to say that I unqualifiedly,
wholly approve of your decision. But I suspect that

if you are thinking of leaving, then this was the moment to grab.

Fowler continued,

> "I enjoyed getting to know you and working with you (so long ago now) on that committee. It is long since I have seen you. I wish you well."

The two women Kit worked most closely with over the last decade and a half of her career wrote too. Paula Bonner thanked Kit

> "… for all the support you've given me through the years. I know our relationship has had its moments, its times of 'push and pull,' agree and disagree, shared views and opposite views. However, I know we always tried to do what we thought was right… I want to wish you the very best in your retirement and I know you're looking forward to having more time for yourself and to spend with Buzz. You've worked long and hard to get to this point and deserve to have lots of fun and satisfying times."

Long-time women's sports information director Tamara Flarup wrote,

> "Today is your last 'official' day in a career of 'firsts' and 'bests.' You have been responsible for establishing the nationally ranked women's program at Wisconsin. Your foresight, your battles, your insight provided the direction for others to follow, and we are most appreciative.

> "I am also pleased to be part of your history. You gave me a chance 13 years ago. I have been very proud to work with you these years. Thank you for your continued guidance and support."

In June, as Kit officially exited the athletic department stage, there was a long article in the *State Journal* headlined, "Final report is thumbs up: Saunders-Nordeen leaves UW women's program in good shape."

Fred Haberman, chairman of the athletic board in the early 1970s, was quoted: "Kit did a superb job... She was assertive without being uncompromising. She had a very good vision of where the program was going to go."

In the article, Kit articulated a vision of where she wanted to go in the early days of retirement.

> "On July 1, I'm going to be out putting my sailboat in Lake Mendota," she said. "I'm going to keep that boat close to the water this year, rather than in the barn on the farm. I'll have more flexibility to do more things. My friends have bike trips planned, and tennis outings. And I'll be able to just mess around."

In this "exit" interview, Kit recalled the struggles of her early days in the department, but also sounded gratified to have worked on one much more recent project.

> "Probably the one project I have enjoyed the most is the new golf course... During times we were changing leadership in the department I was the only one hanging in there on the golf course. I was climbing around on that land before it had any golf course features. It is very satisfying to see what has come out of it."

In a similar *Capital Times* story, Kit referenced the departure of basketball coach Edwina Qualls as one of the hardest times of her career.

"That was administratively the toughest thing I had to go through," she said. "We all knew what needed to be done... And it was very messy. It was difficult for me. Hey, I hired her."

No question, though, that overall Kit left with good memories.

"One thing that was really nice for my last year," she said, "was to go and get back and work with the women's program. Which is what got me into the whole thing in the first place."

The *Cap Times* reporter asked if she had any regrets. Kit said,

> "I don't really have any regrets. I'm glad I got into intercollegiate athletics when I did. It was where the action was. To see a program grow… I don't know that there are a lot of people that are in a profession for 30 years and really see a lot of progress. I'll miss working with the coaches and seeing the results. It has been fun."

In July, Kit and Buzz established the Kit Saunders-Nordeen Endowment Fund to benefit the UW's women's athletics program. The announcement included an opportunity for others to donate to the fund and more than 60 of Kit's colleagues, friends, and family stepped up with donations. In December 1991, Kit and Buzz enhanced the fund with a $10,000 additional gift. (In 2007, the endowment exceeded $100,000.)

UW Chancellor Donna Shalala – the endowment fund was her idea – hosted a reception for Kit at Olin House on July 26, 1990 to announce the endowment.

At the time it was established, Kit was quoted in the Badger Women's Sports Connection newsletter: "The establishment of this fund is an honor, but it will be even more gratifying to see it grow as individuals who love and respect this fine athletic program contribute to the endowment."

That same September 1990 issue of the newsletter announced the August appointment of Cheryl Marra as the new associate athletic director for women's athletics at UW. She'd previously directed women's athletics at Denison University in Ohio.

The following summer, 1991, Kit began doing interviews for a history of the farm Buzz and his first wife, Nora, purchased in November 1970. It was near Stoughton in southeastern Dane County. The eventual narrative Kit produced honors the Nordeen family's early years on the farm – through interviews with Buzz's kids, Andy, Chris and Kathy – and segues to the great joy and serenity it brought Buzz and Kit during their marriage. Kit's love of nature is palpable in her prose.

> "One of the most enjoyable activities on our farm is walking the trails or along the edges of our woods," she wrote. And at another point: "One of the most wonderful things about our farm is the abundance of wildlife that we can observe firsthand or through the 'stories' left by their tracks."

"Their little farm near Stoughton was important to both Buzz and Kit," noted their neighbors and good friends, John and Norma Magnuson, in a later appreciation. "Kit loved her hikes along the trails through the woods with the dogs [and] the cross-country skiing. Buzz loved to care for the trails, interacting with local farmers, and making folk art such as stone- studded birdbaths and quaint wooden mailboxes. The farm was Kit and Buzz's wonderful woods, small stream, farm fields, and little old farmhouse and barn. They share it with each other and with family and friends."

The Magnusons elaborated on Kit's great fondness for dogs:

> "Kit loved dogs, big ones like Trudy, their loveable German shepherd; little ones like Oscar, our wiener dog, and many in between sizes such as Cami, Kit's black cocker spaniel. An aside about Cami's name. Kit had strong thoughts about Camilla Parker Bowles' mistreatment by the British Crown. Kit, in all things, objected to mistreatment by the powerful. Kit cared and loved Cami, the dog, with love and attention."

In 1992, Kit was inducted into the Madison Sports Hall of Fame in a dinner ceremony at the Holiday Inn–Southeast. Besides Kit, the class of inductees included former UW hockey coach John Riley; former UW football coach John Jardine (who was inducted

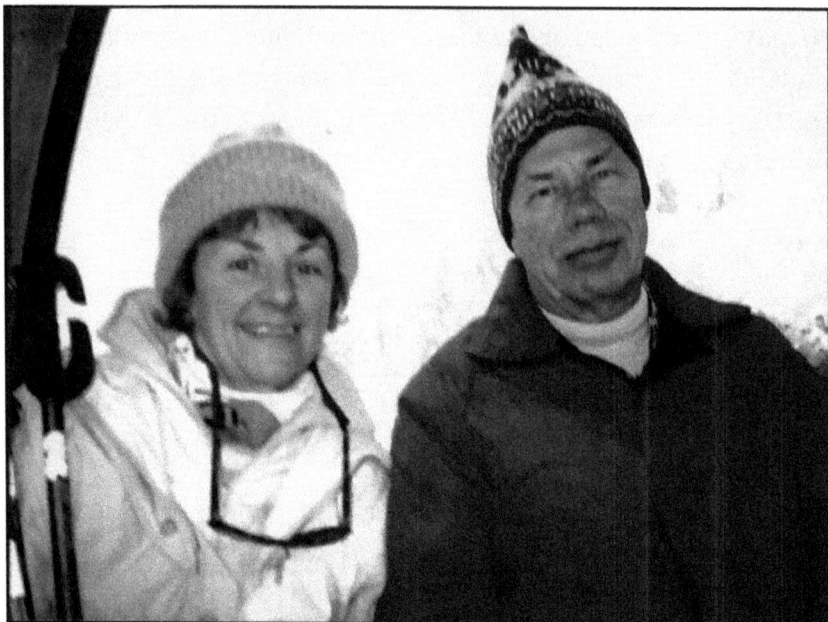

Kit and Buzz on a ski trip. (courtesy of the Nordeen family)

posthumously); and retired Madison West boys basketball coach Jim Stevens.

In September 1994, the 20th anniversary of women's athletics gaining varsity status at UW-Madison was observed with a three-day celebration that included Kit hosting a panel discussion titled "They Came to Stay...and to Play." Among the panelists was Gilda Hudson-Winfield, a Chicago attorney and UW athletic board member who was a member of the inaugural women's track team and one of the first women to earn an athletic scholarship. Also on the panel, two pioneers interviewed for this narrative: Kathy Tritschler, chair of the Department of Sports Studies at Guilford College in North Carolina; and Nancy Page, associate athletic director at UW-Stevens Point. Judy Sweet, the first woman president of the NCAA, gave the keynote address in Memorial Union's Great Hall.

Kit was interviewed as part of the 20th anniversary and asked about the obstacles the women's program had to overcome.

"In the beginning," she responded, "the major obstacle for incorporating women's athletics was a question of educating people and their attitudes... to really believe that we were serious and that we were here to stay. And then later on, I think, the most serious obstacle was competing for scarce resources and being seen as competing against the men's sports for those resources."

Asked about the future, Kit said, "What I see in the future for women athletes kind of parallels what I see for women and their accomplishments in any other field. I see fewer and fewer differences and expectations for girls and boys [in] developing their talents, no matter what they may be."

Long-time women's sports information director Tam Flarup pulled together a list of the program's accomplishments across the first 20 years – an extraordinary record of achievement that included the following:

- Five national championship teams in three sports.
- Eighty-nine athletes earned 227 All-American honors in nine different sports.
- Thirty-two teams won Big Ten titles in four sports.
- Individual athletes won 191 Big Ten championships in five sports.
- Three hundred forty athletes were named to the Academic All- Big Ten teams in their respective sports, more than any other Big Ten school.

For Kit, the years of slights, bruised feelings, and fighting for an equal chance to compete gave way to an extended award season honoring those years.

In October 1996, Kit got a letter informing her that she would be the recipient of the 1997 Women's Sports Advocates of Wisconsin's (WSAW) Lifetime Achievement Award. Tam Flarup nominated her. The WSAW was established in 1980 to recognize, promote and support girls and women in sports in Wisconsin.

At the WSAW annual award banquet the following February, Kit received an award sculpture and a 14-karat gold diamond ring.

One of the congratulatory notes was from Karen Gallagher:

> "Dear Kit,
> Congratulations on being presented with the
> Lifetime Achievement Award. Nobody deserves
> it more, you have had a major impact on the
> women's program at UW. The Wisconsin softball
> program certainly would not be here if it wasn't
> for people life yourself."

Gallagher was the UW women's softball coach. That the Badgers had a softball team was the result of a reckoning at the UW athletic department that occurred in March 1991, less than a year after Kit's retirement. Athletic director Pat Richter, a little more than a year on the job and faced with a large department budget deficit and scrutiny over the department's compliance with Title IX equity requirements, announced the cutting of five sports: baseball, men's and women's gymnastics, and men's and women's fencing.

Within three years, it would be announced that UW was adding two women's sports: ice hockey and fast-pitch softball.

If the most painful cut – or at least the one that brought the most outrage among fans and alumni – was men's baseball, the addition that brought the most optimism was women's softball. (Women's hockey, however, would eventually garner an amazing six NCAA titles through 2021.) The softball team debuted in 1996, but it was in June 1998, when ground was broken on a new 1,600-seat stadium, that women's athletics got a jolt of excitement and much attendant publicity.

Madison jewelers Bob and Irwin Goodman, rabid sports fans and dedicated philanthropists, donated $500,000 to launch what became known as the "Goodman Diamond."

Irwin Goodman told *The Capital Times* that the seed for the gift had begun in conversations he had with Kit while she was still with the department: "In [early] conversations with Kit Saunders-Nordeen," Irwin said, "we knew immediately this was something we really wanted to do."

Kit and the Goodmans had been close since the 1970s, and in 1982, at a WIS-Club meeting, Kit spoke of their efforts on behalf of women's athletics and awarded them a plaque honoring that support.

The Goodman Diamond groundbreaking was in June 1998. That was also the year Kit was inducted into the University of Wisconsin Athletic Hall of Fame, in a class that included a star women's basketball player, Theresa Huff, who finished her career as the school's leader in both scoring and rebounds and led the Badgers to the quarterfinals of the AIAW tournament in 1982.

In January 1998, Kit performed the ceremonial opening tip-off for the first women's basketball game played at the Kohl Center, UW's new campus arena, between the Badgers and Iowa. The building was named for U.S. Sen. Herb Kohl, whose $25 million gift made it possible.

While UW lost a tight game to the Hawkeyes, a sellout crowd of more than 16,000 packed the Kohl Center, the largest crowd to watch a women's basketball game in school, state, and Big Ten Conference history.

It was an amazing turnout. Head coach Jane Albright-Dieterle called it "a night everyone will long remember... there was a women's basketball game and we had a whole bunch of people here. The sport's come a long way... I'm 42, and I think the biggest crowd I ever played in front of was about 130."

One of Albright-Dieterle's assistant coaches was Dawn Crim, a Philadelphia native who was a standout basketball player at the University of Virginia in the late 1980s, under a legendary coach, Debbie Ryan. Crim arrived in Madison in 1996.

"I had a keen awareness of the struggle for equity in sports," Crim said, in an interview for this book. "My mom was an athlete, pre-Title IX. She often talked about how different it was when I came through from when she came through. I was always mindful of the impact of Title IX and the opportunity I had."

Crim worked as an assistant basketball coach at Penn State and then the University of Kentucky, returning to Penn State in 1995 to do athletic fundraising. A component of that job was doing color commentary for women's basketball.

"I'd travel with the team," Crim said, "meet with alumni, talk with them about Penn State athletics, and invite them to the game."

On a road trip to Madison, Crim did a radio interview with Jane Albright-Dieterle, who was in the early stages of turning around the Badgers women's basketball program.

"How have you done it?" Crim asked.

"The fans in Madison love the girls," Albright-Dieterle said. "It's a great university. I have a lot of resources. It's been great."

Not long after that, Crim got a call from the Badgers coach.

"I appreciated the interview," Albright-Dieterle said. "I know you used to coach. What do you think about Wisconsin?"

"But I'm not coaching," Crim said.

"You should be!" Albright-Dieterle responded.

Crim finally said yes, and spent five years with the team, during which time the Badgers made the NCAA tournament once and the NIT twice, winning the NIT championship in 2000.

Crim met Kit and appreciated her legacy, as well as the many women – Mayor Sue Bauman, County Executive Kathleen Falk, and Congresswoman Tammy Baldwin – in leadership roles in Madison circa 2000. Crim made it part of her recruiting pitch to parents.

"We said we were ready to receive their daughter and she was going to get a well-rounded experience," Crim said. "She would be exposed to women leaders who are doing great things and they are fans who come to the games and support the teams."

Crim – who in 2019 was named Secretary of the Wisconsin Department of Safety and Professional Services by Gov. Tony Evers – said she spoke with Nancy Johnson Nicholas about the importance of having her name – Johnson's – on the practice

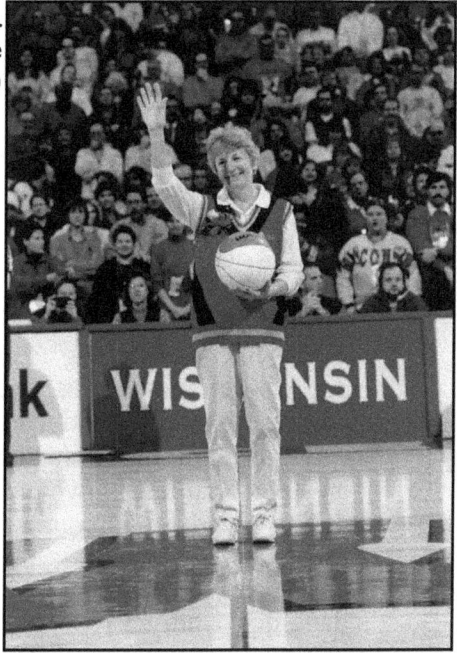

Kit at the Kohl Center. (courtesy of the Nordeen family)

pavilion adjacent to the Kohl Center. Ab and Nancy Nicholas were major UW donors.

Crim said Johnson was reluctant. "It was Ab. He played here. It has nothing to do with me."

Crim replied, "You're part of it. But more than that, I want our players to see your name."

The Nicholas-Johnson Pavilion houses three full basketball courts and is used for practices when the Kohl Center isn't available.

The month of January 1998 was – not untypically for Kit in retirement – a busy one. Not only had Kit tossed the ceremonial tip at the new Kohl Center, she did a television interview Jan. 11 at the Field House during the last women's basketball game held there. To get to the Field House on time, Kit had to duck out early of a reception for a new UW professor of restoration ecology who would be working closely with the UW Arboretum. In 1997-98, Kit was president of the Friends of the Arboretum, a 3,000-member organization which since 1962 had supported the work and mission of UW's beautiful, 1,200- acre nature preserve and teaching and research facility on Madison's near west side.

Kit loved the Arboretum. Years later, commenting on a *Madison Magazine* story that referenced Kit, a woman named Donna Thomas wrote:

> "I met Kit while working at the UW Arboretum in the 1990s, so my memories of her are of her community engagement and love of the natural world. She was serving as president of Friends of the Arboretum—tireless, energetic and always so positive. As a role model and in many subtle, kind ways, she lent important support to women, which on a personal level gave me courage and strength during several challenging times."

If nature, in retirement, was a passion of Kit's, so was travel. Buzz's daughter, Kathy Snyder, noted that Kit used her influence to get Buzz to travel outside the United States.

"She and Buzz traveled broadly in Europe," friends and neighbors John and Norma Magnuson noted. "They went to Buzz's ancestral homeland near Lake Siljan in Dalarna, Sweden, and we think Kit enjoyed it much more than Buzz did. They biked across Holland as well."

In 1999, Kit made a gift of a Wisconsin Alumni Association trip to the Galapagos Islands to Kathy Snyder, who regarded the trip with Kit as one of the best travel experiences of her life.

"It was an incredible trip," Kathy recalled. "We had the best time."

In August 2008, Kit traveled with a group of women friends for an arctic adventure in Churchill, Northern Manitoba. "To be with the polar bears along the shore of Hudson Bay," the Magnusons recalled.

The awards kept coming, too. One of the most significant arrived with a March 22, 2006 letter to Kit from Jennifer Alley, executive director of National Association of Collegiate Women Athletics Administrators.

"It is an honor to inform you that you have been
selected as one of the five individuals to receive
the NACWAA Lifetime Achievement Award...
This award recognizes individuals who have made
outstanding contributions to the promotion of
intercollegiate athletics for women [and] who have
dedicated their professional careers toward
advancing women in athletics. Because of your
tireless efforts, more girls and women participating
in sport today can truly enjoy competitive athletic
opportunities."

The award was to be presented NACWAA's annual convention in
October in Sacramento. Kit wrote back that she'd be thrilled to
attend. "I have never been to Sacramento," Kit wrote, "so if there
are any folks who will arrive early or stay later to visit any of the
national parks, which I notice are relatively nearby, I would love
to join them."

Kit was asked to fill out a question/answer form prior to
going to California about some of her career highs and lows.
While many of her answers have appeared already in this narrative, Kit responded with this when asked about a special memory:
"Knowing that we were making dreams come true for our women
athletes. Knowing what it was like to want those opportunities
and not have them."

Asked about role models, Kit replied, "It was great getting
to know some of the other women who were creating the programs at their different schools. [But] until we started conference
structures on the state, regional and national levels, there were
NO role models for us."

The awards luncheon was Oct. 8 at the Hyatt Regency in
Sacramento. Kit was delighted to spend time with Judy Sweet,
whom Kit introduced to women's athletics administration in
Madison in the late 1960s and who served as the NACWAA
president in 2000-2001.

On returning home, Kit wrote Sweet, "I guess that I have
known all along that not only was the University of Wisconsin

fortunate to have you as a student leader, but the NCAA and NACWAA are also fortunate to have benefited from your knowledge, sharing, and friendship."

Kit added: "It was great having you back for our 30th anniversary celebration."

The 30th anniversary of women's athletics at UW-Madison gaining varsity status was in 2004, but the gala celebration – and it was a gala – was held Jan. 29-30, 2005. Everyone connected with the program since its inception was invited back, and many came. One of the most moving parts of the weekend occurred when some 35 women who had participated in the club sport – pre-varsity – era were awarded their honor letter "W."

Kit told *The Capital Times*, "We have these women in their 50s and early 60s who cried over the telephone. They were so excited about becoming letter-winners."

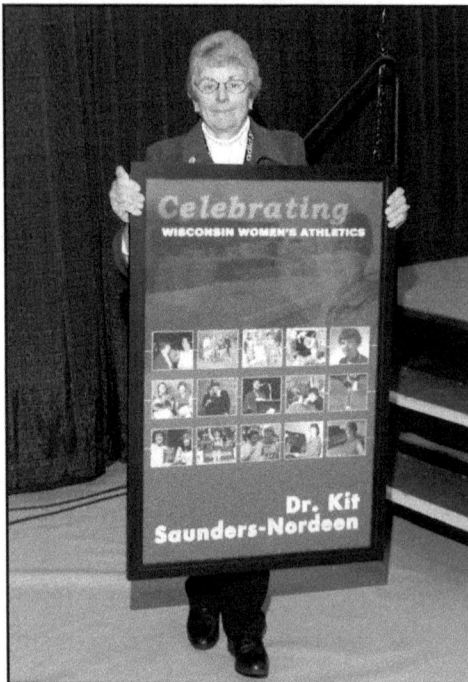

Kit celebrating three decades of UW Women's Athletics.
(courtesy of the Nordeen family)

Kit added, "I think it's going to be terrific for current athletes – and a lot of them will be coming – to meet and hear some of the stories from people who were here in the beginning."

Kit, Judy Sweet and others were interviewed for a 30th anniversary documentary.

In her interview for the video, Sweet recalled the miniscule budget for the club sport program in the late 1960s, adding:

> "To really put that into perspective, when we
> would go to competitive activities, we would
> either pay our own way or we would have fund-
> raisers. And I know everyone hears about the good
> old days where there were bake sales, but we took
> a little different approach. We didn't have a bake
> sale, we actually went out to a tree farm, cut down
> trees and sold Christmas trees on campus to the
> students so they could have a little semblance of
> the holiday spirit in their dorm rooms. That's the
> way we generated our resources."

Asked the highlight of her collegiate experience in Madison, Sweet said it was the 1968 trip to the University of Arizona she took with Kit for the national conference of Athletic and Recreation Federation of College Women.

In June 2007, Kit was presented the Madison Sports Hall of Fame's Pat O'Dea Award, named for the legendary "kangaroo kicker" from Australia who in 1898 made a 62-yard dropkick field goal for the Badgers against Northwestern. The O'Dea award is presented annually to individuals who have demonstrated outstanding support and commitment to the UW athletic department.

The ceremony for Kit was notable in that she was presented the award by Barry Alvarez, the highly successful Badgers football coach who in 2004 was named UW athletic director, replacing Pat Richter.

In introducing Kit, Alvarez listed a number of her recent awards, while adding,

"Kit has never been about awards. No, Kit is all about working behind the scenes to make things better for other people. And there's no question that she's been successful in doing just that.

Kit truly had a positive influence on athletics at the University of Wisconsin. She was a pioneer who fought many battles in support of women's athletics. She was a role model for young women athletes and administrators. And she always challenged those who worked with her to do things the right way... Kit and her husband Buzz continue their support of the Badgers in so many ways. They attend most of our home games, are active volunteers and generous donors who have endowed a scholarship in Kit's name."

In August 2007, two months after receiving the O'Dea award, Kit was on the cover of Madison's *Brava* magazine, with a lengthy profile inside that recalled her pioneering career and included a great color photo of Kit, Buzz, and their dog, Cami.

"Buzz and his family have made my life really wonderful," Kit told the writer.

They had several more good years. Then, a heartbreaking diagnosis.

Chapter 13

FULL CIRCLE

Buzz's first wife, Nora, died at 58 after a diagnosis of early-onset Alzheimer's, the insidious brain disease that slowly destroys memory and afflicts millions.

Buzz knew the signs: Getting lost while driving on familiar streets, repeating oneself in conversation.

"She'd sit right there," Buzz said of Kit, pointing at a chair in the living room of the home they shared on Yuma Drive in Madison, "and she'd cry because she knew things weren't right."

The Alzheimer's diagnosis came in 2012, when Kit was 72. She lived at home for a time. Friends and family helped. Kit resisted giving up driving, but finally relented. Norma Magnuson drove her to hair appointments. Other friends picked Kit up for Downtown Rotary – she enjoyed dressing up for the Wednesday noon luncheons.

Despite his grief – the unthinkable cruelty of Alzheimer's upending his world a second time – Buzz was indefatigable in doing his best for Kit. He attended a support group for spouses of Alzheimer's patients and held out hope she could remain with him at home. But Buzz was 84 at the time of Kit's diagnosis, and he eventually accepted the idea she would be better cared for in a treatment facility.

Buzz's son Andy, Andy's wife, Joanne, and their daughter, Natalie, helped Buzz with the paperwork for Oakwood Village University Woods, a facility with an excellent memory care component. The family helped set up Kit's room. On the morning Kit was to transition to Oakwood, Joanne and Kit took a walk through the Arboretum while Andy and Natalie brought the last of the furniture, artwork, and UW memorabilia to Kit's room. A bit of good fortune, or karma: Kit's hallway in the memory care unit was decorated in red and named "Badger Boulevard."

Once Kit was living at Oakwood Village, Buzz visited her daily, even when she could no longer recognize him. Other family and friends visited, too. Kit was loved.

Buzz established the Nora Nordeen and Kit Saunders-Nordeen Alzheimer's Disease Research Fund at the Wisconsin Alzheimer's Institute. Madison television station WISC-TV interviewed Buzz:

> "Medical people and others have told me, you've got to remember that this is not the person you married and you've got a different kind of respon-sibility now. You accepted that responsibility when you got married, and so you deal with the cards you are dealt."

The family was involved, too. Joanne accepted a position as a research coordinator for the Wisconsin Registry for Alzheimer's Prevention (WRAP), an organization Andy had been involved with since his mother Nora's death from Alzheimer's in 1986. Buzz signed to be a brain donor with the UW Brain Donor Program. He was eligible as the parent of a WRAP participant and liked knowing he was contributing to Alzheimer's research. Kit was a brain donor as well.

Buzz died on July 8, 2019, age 91. His obituary included the following paragraph:

> "Although Buzz accomplished many great things during his professional career, family always came first. Buzz could often be found riding his tractor around the trails at his hobby farm, and his family often joined him to take joy rides on the golf cart and walk through the trails. Buzz was proud of his family, and it showed through his ability to update you on the activities of each member of his extended family."

Kit died a year and a half later, Jan. 1, 2021, at 80. There was a lengthy news obituary in the *Wisconsin State Journal*.

Paula Bonner was quoted: "She's the pioneer... It takes a big team, but you've got to have somebody that starts it and moves it down the field."

And Tam Flarup: "She was the generator for all of it... She worked with everyone. She was very humble. She was very low-key, very smart. She was able to have people change their minds. She was persuasive that way."

Athletic Director Barry Alvarez, too: "She was a tireless advocate for the implementation of Title IX and deserves credit for much of the success of women's athletics at the University of Wisconsin... Her legacy will live on forever."

Kit, it will be remembered, first came to Madison in 1964 to study for a master's degree in physical education. While her opportunities to compete as an athlete had been limited in her native New Jersey, she was dismayed to find that the situation in Madison upon her arrival was even worse.

"I felt like I had stepped back five, six, even seven years when I came here," Kit told *Brava* magazine in 2007, "as far as what was available [in competitive sports] for women."

Part of Kit's evolution into a prominent proponent of intercollegiate athletics for women meant becoming an historian of its past. She would eventually earn a doctorate degree with a dissertation titled, "The Governance of College Athletics," which included a deep dive into how and why women for decades were actively encouraged not to participate in competitive sports on the campuses of America's universities. The mantra – participation good, competition bad – of Blanche Trilling, the longtime leader of women's physical education, both at Wisconsin and nationally in the first half of the 20th century, reflected broader, societal values.

In her dissertation, Kit wrote, "The physical education leaders who imposed such strict limitations on women's athletics were not hypocrites, they were women who were brought up with the same social mores as everybody else."

But it is worth noting – indeed, it's fascinating – that Kit in her research uncovered that women did play competitive sports on the UW-Madison campus prior to Blanche Trilling's arrival in 1912.

Kit unearthed "Badger" yearbooks that included photos of women participating in crew and basketball before 1910. The competitions were not against teams from other schools but rather "interclass" matches that were nonetheless quite competitive.

Kit interviewed Ruth B. Glassow, a long-time UW-Madison women's physical education department professor, who upon retiring in 1962, began work on a history of the department.

"Glassow," Kit noted, "explained that there was a great deal of excitement at Wisconsin about the women's class teams. Great numbers of students attended class games in every sport. She remembers one basketball game for which there was even an orchestra."

Kit found "Badger" yearbooks that showed women's teams receiving honor letters and wearing athletic sweaters with the year of their accomplishment. She found yearbook photos of the "ladies boating crew" dressed in shorts, which, Kit noted, "must have been really something at that time."

Yet by 1920, the anti-competition proponents had seized the day.

"Things just kind of died for 40 or 50 years," Kit said.

It was left for Kit and her colleagues to rediscover what had been lost. They did. It took years, the passage of Title IX, and ultimately a generational shift, to a time when young girls could go to an arena or turn on a TV and see dazzling acts of athleticism that they could aspire to emulate. The door was finally open.

It had always been the right thing to do.

ACKNOWLEDGMENTS

This book's genesis was a meeting between Dale "Buzz" Nordeen and me several years ago at his home in Madison. Buzz thought there was a good book to be written about his wife, Kit Saunders-Nordeen, and her role in launching women's athletics at the University of Wisconsin.

I agreed immediately, and from that day forward, this book had no greater champion than Buzz. As I got to know him, that made sense: He was a great champion of Kit. She was ill with Alzheimer's when he and I met. Buzz visited daily and established a research fund in her name, as he had done earlier with an endowment benefiting UW women's athletics.

When Buzz died in summer 2019, his daughter and sons – Kathy, Andy, and Chris – and their spouses were steadfast in their wish to see the project cross the finish line. Buzz and the Nordeen family made this book possible.

Buzz's friend Bill Richardson provided my introduction to Buzz, as well as encouragement throughout.

This book is largely based on original interviews by the author with numerous former University of Wisconsin women athletes, coaches, trainers, and administrators, as well as others in Kit's circle.

Two women deserve special mention, in part because they were interviewed on more than one occasion: Tamara Flarup, the long-time sports information director for UW women's athletics; and Paula Bonner, who took the women's athletics leadership baton from Kit and later headed the Wisconsin Alumni Association. Tam and Paula's encouragement and insights were invaluable. Tam read and commented on a draft of the manuscript; it is better for her suggestions. My friend Joe Hart, former sports editor of *The Capital Times*, also read the manuscript in draft and offered valuable feedback.

Diane Nordstrom at UW athletics provided valuable assistance tracking down photos. Terry Gawlik, now the director of athletics at the University of Idaho, invited me into her office while she was a senior associate athletic director at UW-Madison and shared a box of women's athletics historical documents. Diana Dunn kindly provided early Saunders family photos.

Of great importance, too, were the two lengthy interviews that Kit did with the UW Oral History Program. Kit's illness meant I could not interview her. Her Oral History interviews are excellent. My sincere thanks to the program and its head, Troy Reeves, for permission to quote from them in this narrative.

I also wish to thank all those who consented to an interview. They include: Peter Tegen; Cathy Branta; Jane Ludwig; Peggy Van Emburgh Kelly; Art Brown; Bonnie Morrow; Kathy Riss; Becky Sisley; Nancy Page; Bobbie Konover; Claudia Pogreba; Kathy Tritschler; Judy Sweet; D'Lynn Damron; Jerry Darda; Jay Mimier; Sue Ela; Carie Graves; Cindy Bremser; Tony Gillham; Karen Bleidel; Gail Hirn; Jackie Hayes; Debbie Ambruso; Rose Chepyator-Thomson; Karen Lunda; Pam Moore; Ann French; Mary Chrnelich Nellen; Liz Tortorello Nelson; Beth Benevente Miller; Suzy Favor Hamilton; Kathy Snyder; Joanne Nordeen; Ruthie Bartlett; Alan Fish; Dawn Crim; and John and Norma Magnuson.

The reporting in the sports pages of Madison's two daily newspapers, the *Wisconsin State Journal* and *The Capital Times*, helped me track the progress of women's athletics at UW. Despite one sports editor proclaiming he would never cover women's athletics in his paper, coverage grew.

Along with being interviewed, Kathy Riss, who knew Kit from their college days, shared some of their life-long correspondence. Thanks to Dee Grimsrud, who assisted with genealogy, as she has for a several of my projects.

For such a seismic piece of legislation, there was surprisingly little contemporary coverage of the effort to pass Title IX. The reason is hardly anyone recognized how potent those relatively few words would be.

Perhaps the best account can be found in Karen Blumenthal's 2005 book, targeted at young adults but valuable for anyone, *Let Me Play: The Story of Title IX: The Law That Changed the Future of Girls in America.* I quote it a few times in this narrative.

Also helpful was a lengthy 2007 *Cleveland Law Review* article by Bernice Resnick Sandler – she is featured in Blumenthal's book – an academic called "the godmother of Title IX" by the *New York Times*. Her essay, which I also quote, is called "Title IX: How We Got It and What a Difference It Made."

Howard Chudacoff's 2015 book, *Changing the Playbook: How Power, Profit and Politics Transformed College Sports* – also quoted – helped me track the NCAA's slow but sure usurpation of the AIAW in the early 1980s.

Finally, thanks to my wife, Jeanan Yasiri Moe. It would take another chapter to say all that she does for me and how much it means.

ABOUT THE AUTHOR

Doug Moe has been a journalist in Wisconsin for more than four decades. His numerous publications include *The World of Mike Royko,* a *Chicago Tribune* Choice Selection of the Year; *Lords of the Ring: The Triumph and Tragedy of College Boxing's Greatest Team,* runner-up for the Derleth Award for best non-fiction book of the year by a Wisconsin author; and *Tommy: My Journey of a Lifetime,* a collaboration with Tommy G. Thompson on the former governor's autobiography.

Please visit www.dougmoe.org for more information.

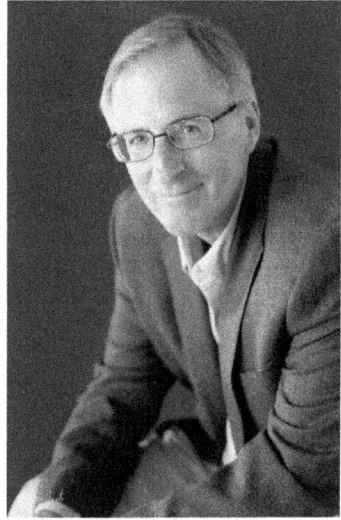

www.ingramcontent.com/pod-product-compliance
Lightning Source LLC
Chambersburg PA
CBHW072033090426
42733CB00032B/1290